SACRED

ENCOUNTERS

from Rome to Jerusalem

TAMARA PARK

IVP Books

An imprint of InterVarsity Press
Downers Grove, Illinois

InterVarsity Press
P.O. Box 1400, Downers Grove, IL 60515-1426
World Wide Web: www.ivpress.com
Email: email@ivpress.com

InterVarsity Press® is the book-publishing division of InterVarsity Christian Fellowship/USA®, a student movement active on campus at hundreds of universities, colleges and schools of nursing in the United States of America, and a member movement of the International Fellowship of Evangelical Students. For information about local and regional activities, write Public Relations Dept., InterVarsity Christian Fellowship/USA, 6400 Schroeder Rd., P.O. Box 7895, Madison, WI 53707-7895, or visit the IVCF website at <www.intervarsity.org>.

Design: Cindy Kiple
Images: Dragan Trifunovic/iStockphoto

ISBN 978-0-8308-3623-9

Printed in the United States of America ∞

Library of Congress Cataloging-in-Publication Data

Park, Tamara, 1971-
  Sacred encounters from Rome to Jerusalem / Tamara Park.
     p. cm.
  Includes bibliographical references.
  ISBN 978-0-8308-3623-9 (pbk.: alk paper)
  1. Christian pilgrims and pilgrimages. 2. Voyages and
travels—Religious aspects. 3. Europe—Description and travel. 4.
Middle East—Description and travel. 5. Helena, Saint, ca. 255-ca.
330. I. Title.
  BX2323.P35 2009
  263'.042569442—dc22

                                                                2008033845

P   25   24   23   22   21   20   19   18   17   16   15   14   13   12   11   10   9   8   7   6   5   4   3   2   1

Y   29   28   27   26   25   24   23   22   21   20   19   18   17   16   15   14   13   12   11   10   09   08

With love to the brothers,
Victor and Todd

CONTENTS

We shall not cease from exploration
And the end of all our exploring
Will be to arrive where we started
And know the place for the first time.

T. S. Eliot

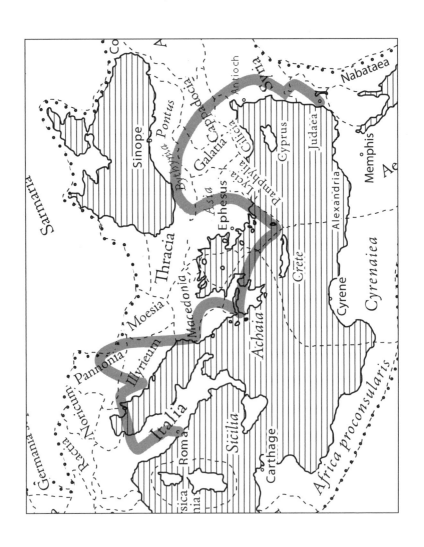

Introduction

JERUSALEM, ISRAEL

I suppose every American remembers where he or she was on Tuesday, September 11, 2001. Vivid details of that day fill spaces in one's mind like few other dates on the calendar: graduation day, wedding day, birth of son, 9/11.

I wasn't in America on September 11; I was living in the Middle East.

I had moved to Jerusalem weeks earlier to take graduate classes. That Tuesday I jogged to the King David Hotel and made it back in time for my class on modern Middle East politics. The class had quickly become a favorite of mine; my animated Israeli professor was determined to enlighten us on the complicated situation there, repeatedly describing life in the East by waving his hands and declaring, "It's anarchy, I tell you, anarchy!"

That morning—predawn in the States—my professor, Oded Yinon, laid out the fragility of the Middle East. "It's a tinderbox ready to explode." A friend and I stayed after class for over an hour mining his mind about European alliances, oil reserves and religious fanatics. After our conversation I strolled out of the classroom humming R.E.M.'s "It's the End of the World as We Know It."

After a late lunch, I meandered down to the computer lab, a converted first-century cave replete with antiquated PCs, to catch up on emails. Soon commotion engulfed us as one computer screen after another went from displaying email messages to showing images of towers being struck.

I had already learned that terrorism happens. In the two weeks prior to that Tuesday, I had heard nearby blasts of a suicide bomber and a car bomb. After 9/11 our professor added a discussion on Osama bin Laden and the CIA to the syllabus, and we carried on as usual.

During the following ten months, my days were packed with life-marker adventures, mind-expanding conversations and soul-stirring friendships. I tromped through ancient tunnels, trekked up Mount Sinai, snorkeled in the Red Sea and skinny-dipped in the Sea of Galilee. I savored whisky and cake with the Greek archbishop, coffee and chocolate with the Syrian mukhtar, and lots and lots of hot tea with shopkeepers. I volunteered with Bedouin kids through the group Rabbis for Human Rights and loved on gypsy kids through the Domari Gypsy Society.

Then my school closed down because of the increased violence of the intifada (Palestinian uprising). I moved into a Palestinian neighborhood in the Old City and took Hebrew classes in the new city. I saw firsthand how political divisions turned into personal dilemmas. Issues could no longer be abstract; they were attached to people I cared about—on both sides. I learned that increased checkpoint security had caused the stillbirth rate among Palestinian women to skyrocket. Ambulances couldn't get through fast enough. Drug use was up among Israeli teens; many teens stayed home for fear of regular bombings, and some of those teens had taken to smoking pot in their basements.

Yet I observed people in the throes of conflict face life with vast courage and creativity. I got glimpses of the risks and joys people encountered when pursuing peace with their enemies. And I experienced stunning hospitality from Jews, Christians and Muslims.

My view of God was challenged and stretched. In the middle of these complicated conflicts, these ancient cultures and my newly forming friendships, who was the Divine? Where was God in the East?

I left Jerusalem, the Holy City, changed. When I arrived back home, I could see that the States had changed as well. American flags were ubiquitous. The Patriot Act was in motion. God and country couldn't be more right.

I observed an increasing sense among Americans that our culture and our values were under attack, that the world must recollect itself into good guys and bad guys—white hats and black hats, the Coalition of the Willing and the Axis of Evil. The divisions were becoming sharper and the stakes higher.

My mind, however, was clogged with images of olive-skinned children witnessing the exchange of gunfire, and the laughter between neighbors turning silent. I wondered what would happen if we shared a meal together, we in the West and our counterparts in the Middle East; if we swapped stories about our families and told tales of our heritages. How much would we learn from each other? How much better would we understand each other?

I had new questions about God as well. Upon my arrival in the States, I began to work at my church as pastor of community. I never imagined I'd work for a church, but a dream I didn't know to dream had emerged. I started to see more than ever that in the complexities of life—with all of its intense disappointments and immense pleasures—one's understanding of the Divine matters. Yet how was I, with still so many unanswered questions about God, to lead people through their own spiritual grapplings? Was my view of God sturdy enough, global enough, true enough to relate to my friends here in the West, to my neighbors in the East, to this ever-changing, ever-nuanced world?

So an idea began to trek across my mind . . .

1

CHARLOTTE, NORTH CAROLINA (U.S.A.)

When the world feels all jittery, like it just quit smoking, and the questions of my soul start to sound like a heavy metal concert gone awry, I find I must travel. It tends to still me.

So, I have this idea. I'll sojourn East, trekking along an ancient collection of roads that stretches from Rome to Jerusalem. And, along this millennia-old path that has been trod by scoundrels, saints, soldiers and refugees, I'll ask people to describe God.

These ancient Roman roads I plan to follow cut their way through the Balkans and the Middle East. They pierce through cities that have been cracked open by conflict in the past two decades. Perhaps this swath of earth can give context to my questions about the East; and maybe the people along the way can give insights into my wonderings about the Divine.

This journey can be taken in only one manner: as a pilgrim. But I've never been a pilgrim before. And this could be problematic. First of all, I haven't even drawn up a will.

It's not that I'm opposed to having a will. I've been planning to get one since I took a bioethics class. I put it on my to-do list, just below "Go to the dentist." I'm not opposed to the dentist either. It's just I don't have dental insurance, something I've been meaning to get since I jumped off a cliff and chipped my tooth.

But, whatever. I only own one thing worth accounting for in a will anyway: my black 1998 Volkswagen Beetle.

I confess my lack of a will because it's embarrassingly unpilgrim-like not to have one. Since the Middle Ages, pilgrims have been quite particular to state what should happen to their remains and belongings if they don't survive their journey. Felix Fabri, a fastidious pilgrim of the late 1400s, made the captain of the ship he was taking to the Holy Land agree to only charge him half price if he didn't make it there alive. Felix drew up a contract and convinced the captain to sign it.

I've told my parents that I prefer to be cremated if I die on this journey. Cremation strikes me as economic, environmentally friendly and poetic. My mother hates the idea. But as I mentioned earlier, I have put none of this in writing. And as I make this confession, I realize I have not prepared for other potential disasters either.

I've made plans to travel with two friends: Krista, whom I worked with in Brussels, and Eric, whom I studied with in Jerusalem. They haven't met each other; what if they don't get along? *Potential disaster number one.*

What if I—or Eric or Krista—fall in love en route? We're single and somewhat good looking; it could happen. International relationships are a minefield of complications; Krista, Eric and I have all had our hearts shot down abroad. *Potential disaster number two.*

But most disastrous of all, what if I lose my faith, my spiritual center? Recently I've come to suspect that our view of God is the most important view we hold. It shapes how we understand ourselves, how we interact with the world and, ultimately, how we relate to the Divine—if at all. But after slogging, albeit gratefully, through six years of graduate school to get my Master of Divinity, I long to see how my theology plays out on the ground. What if God is more expansive than my American culture, more nuanced than my political positions, more global than my worldview? I need to see if the beliefs I've constructed on southern American soil will crumble on the shores of the Mediterranean. I need to find out if this image of God I've been staring at in the States will shatter when I see other people's view of God—people from different religious cultures, living in nations cut apart by conflict. I've staked my life on this relationship with God; I guess I need to see if it is durable. And the realities of our increasingly multicultural world seem too pressing and the problems too heartbreaking not to invite others into the shaping of my view of God.

That's why I've decided to ask strangers along the way how they describe God. But I know this endeavor offers a huge risk. What if I like someone else's God better than mine? What if my relationship with God can't remain the same? What if everything I think of as God must be cremated? *Ugh! Potential disaster number three.*

Oh, I really should get a will. But first I need to finish packing. Eric will be here in less than thirty minutes to ride together to the airport, and I'm still shoving T-shirts, protein bars and diarrhea tablets into my bloated backpack.

Phew. We arrive at the airport with plenty of time to savor some caffeine and try to clear up a miscommunication. Eric hasn't told his parents that he is going anywhere—let alone the likes of Serbia and Syria. And I haven't talked to Eric directly about how we'll handle finances on this trip. Neither of us is fond of confrontation.

I mention something about him possibly letting his parents know about the trip and add something vague about money. Then I leave. As he sits flanked by two huge backpacks—one streamlined and boxy with obvious breathing room (his), and the other looking like a body is threatening to pop out of it at the slightest slip of the zipper (mine), I go to purchase reading material for the flight.

When I return Eric is chatting with his mom. "I'm at the airport . . . I'm going on a trip with Tamara . . . Oh, I never mentioned her? She was one of my roommates in Jerusalem . . . We're going to Israel . . . We're starting in Italy and then traveling through the Balkans and the Middle East . . . What was that, Mom? I'm sorry; you're breaking up . . . I'll call you when we get to Rome or sometime next week. Bye."

I'm really grateful Eric agreed to come on this crazy little pilgrimage. There's no other guy I know who I would more prefer to trek this ancient, unwieldy path with. Yet in many ways Eric remains an enigma to me. Though we lived together several months in Jerusalem I feel like I only have snapshots of his world. Eric was often off studying Hebrew, Greek or Aramaic, or hanging out with his girlfriend, while I was ditching my studies and drinking coffee with some shopkeeper, rabbi or archbishop. Yet on the rare nights when we were both home, we'd savor a glass of wine and discuss the Gospel of John. Eric would patiently and brilliantly respond to all my questions about Jewish customs and Jesus' teachings. Those nights were some of my favorites in Jerusalem.

After a plateful of sushi in Detroit, two movies in air, one cup of espresso in Amsterdam and a few restless naps in between, Eric and I meet up with Krista in Rome.

Krista looks chic as always, even with her red backpack towering above her 5'9" frame and multiple camera bags dangling from her shoulders. When it comes to capturing a moment, she's got gear, and she knows how to use it.

For the past eight years Krista been an instructor of videography at a university in Minneapolis. But this month she quit her job, traveled to Russia to shoot stills of professional basketball players, and now is here to capture our pilgrimage through image. Krista and I have known each other for over ten years. We met while volunteering at a nonprofit media outlet in Brussels, Belgium, that produced video programs mainly for Asia, Africa and Europe. During the glory of our midtwenties we wrote and produced segments for kids in India; we accumulated traveling "loser-stories"; we house-sat, dog-sat and cat-sat to fund our unshakable habit to eat on a regular basis; and we laughed. Krista is one of the most humorous and talented souls I know.

Right now I lack the energy to wager how this adventure will turn out. We're all tired from the first leg of our journey, fatigued from our former lives, exhausted with utter excitement about the days ahead. I'm curious how we'll all get along—if we'll hate each other or love each other or some combination of the two—before this sacred sojourn is done. All we know for sure is that we are seeking the Transcendent on an earthy path. We are now pilgrims.

≽ ≼

As we buy our first train tickets, I think of something else. *Potential disaster number four:* What if I suck as a pilgrim?

Jerusalem is the top pilgrimage site in the world for Jews and Christians, third on the list for Muslims. Once known as the bellybutton of the world, Jerusalem is home to the Kotel (the Western Wall of the ancient temple's portico), the Holy Sepulchre (the believed site of Jesus' crucifixion and resurrection) and the Dome of the Rock (where Muhammad is understood to have been transported in a vision).

But it's not as though I worked my way up the list of Top Ten Pilgrim Sites, earning some street cred before inviting my friends into this experience. Oh, no. Only recently have I even discovered the world of pilgrimage. Somehow I missed this movement that has been the rage for a really long time.

Since the early days of human history, men and women have traveled the earth to be closer to God. They have clamored up mountains, traversed deserts, navigated wild waters and journeyed through dark forests in pursuit of the Holy. The practice of pilgrimage shows up in the most ancient religions and particularly pumps through the veins of the three great monotheistic faiths.

My own tradition, however, has experienced a clot or two when it comes to pilgrimage. The Protestant Reformation brought Scripture to the masses, but it also took away the notion of sacred travel. So here I am: a novice, a virgin pilgrim of sorts. I know it's silly to fear *potential disaster number four;* the purpose isn't to earn some Pilgrim's Progress Award but to experience the sacred and to learn from others along the way.

But I'll confess a little secret from the start: I'm wired to want to succeed, to measure my own advancement—even when it comes to spirituality. I want to learn from others, but I also like to be the one who's in the know, the one who has it all together in the important areas of life. Maybe that's what I should be most afraid of—not being honest enough with my imperfections to hear from others, not being humble enough to receive from them. Maybe that's what could potentially sabotage this pilgrimage.

Maybe . . . But I'll never know if I don't jump on this train.

Jumping on and off trains could present a problem: I don't fit through the train doors without seriously squeezing my vital organs. Besides the perhaps few too many T-shirts and protein bars shoved in my bag, I have a mini drugstore and a mobile office (including a laptop, folders full of historical research, stacks of information on hostels, and embassy contacts in case one of us needs to be cremated).

By the time I locate my notes on our first hostel, it's time for us to hurl ourselves off the train. We dust ourselves off in the dodgy side of Rome. I'm playing a little game that I haven't exactly let Krista and Eric in on; it's called "Let's stay in the cheapest accommodations in each city"—a tribute to my fabulous, frugal father. So far I'm off to a grand start.

We offload our bags at the glorious one-star and venture out. We've given ourselves one day before our official pilgrimage begins, so we decide to go where thousands of animals and humans have been slaughtered as entertainment. I don't know why we think visiting the Colosseum in the scalding heat in our jet-lagged state is the best way to inaugurate our trip, but we all find ourselves sleepwalking in that direction.

I awake sweaty and surrounded by people gathered in clumps. Each group encircles a man wearing a red pleated miniskirt, a shiny breastplate and a helmet sprouting with broom bristles. The helmet looks a wee bit rooster-esque. All the people around me seem entranced by this retro-Roman soldier; I want to be entranced too. However, I can't get close enough to hear what's being said without shoving through properly paying Colosseum customers. So the guard's stories come to me like a bad cell phone connection:

". . . then the dwarves would fight each other just before . . .

". . . they used urine for toothpaste . . .

". . . and then the lowest of classes and the women . . ."

My curiosity can't take the torture, so I locate Eric, who is contemplating paying ten euros to become an official patron. I miss the thrill of paying in Italian currency; spending millions of lira to shuffle through this old place made it seem so much more like an adventure. The unified European currency seems too pedestrian. I decide to boycott it and go find Krista.

Krista is setting up a picture of the Arch of Constantine. It sits by the Colosseum like a Volkswagen Beetle parked next to a Hummer. But both tell tales driven by politics and religion, and both are tributes to Western power that point to Jerusalem. One stack of stones tells the story of what it is like when minority peoples hold beliefs about God that the majority culture doesn't. The other mound of rocks tells a dramatically different tale.

The Colosseum was constructed largely by Jewish slaves dragged from Jerusalem after the Romans sacked their city in 70 c.e. Within a decade over 50,000 spectators packed the stadium on a regular basis to watch animals and gladiators fight to the death. Admission was free, and the seating was by class and gender.

The games were a hit; whenever the emperor sponsored them his popularity went through the roof. It was a brilliant way to handle the slave and criminal "situation," and each death apparently appeased the gods. So the games had political, economic, religious and social benefits—a true win-win, except, of course, for the thousands of animals and gladiators who died.

There's a debate about how many, if any, of the gladiators were Christians. What is clear is that neither Jews nor Christians fared well in their early days in Rome. By the time the Arch of Constantine was going up, however, human bloodshed during the games was ending. Constantine's reign in the early fourth century not only changed the activities in the Colosseum, it affected the religious atmosphere in the Roman Empire.

The Arch—etched with phrases such as "inspired by the divine," "delivered the state from the tyrant" and "just force of arms"—commemorates Constantine's victory over his coemperor, Maxentius, at the Battle of Milvian Bridge in 312. During the battle Constantine is said to have seen a vision of a cross in the sky, formed by the Greek letters *Chi* (X) and *Rho* (Π), and an inscription that read "With(in) this you win." Out of gratitude for his victory, Constantine reportedly converted to Christianity. A year later he legalized Christianity in the Edict of Milan.

Constantine became the Empire's first theocrat and Christianity's most powerful politician. He rebuilt Jerusalem as the epicenter of Christian pilgrimage, gathered bishops together to unify Christian theology and created an imperial Jesus in Roman garb. His conversion, however, didn't curtail his pesky habit of murdering people and his continuing patronage of pagan gods. Nevertheless, under Constantine Christianity was no longer carried along by the blood of the martyrs—at least in the Roman Empire. During his reign the death rate of Christians declined, but you have to wonder if some of the soul of the faith did as well.

Suddenly a thought strikes me. Perhaps the best starting point for this pilgrimage, the best place to help me recognize my own starting point as an American Protestant seeking God in a multicultural world, is smack in the middle of the Colosseum and Constantine's Arch. As I ping-pong my neck back and forth between these two edifices, I think of how politics and religion have gotten dangerously entwined through the centuries. American politicians today regularly use religious jargon to justify their actions and to suggest to voters that God is either a Republican or a Democrat.

I wonder what will happen as I move closer and closer to the land where Scripture emerged, the church began and my religion originated. Will my current view of God—cultivated as it is in a culture where Christianity holds the majority—get mauled as it enters this arena as a minority culture?

An hour later we're overwhelmed by the heat and the tourists, so we slug our bodies up a hill and discover a park. Wood benches bent by age, use and weather line the sidewalk, inviting the tired to come. A fatigued family of three is sprawled out on one; a man feeding pigeons and another reading *il Giornale* have each claimed their own. I find the closest available bench and collapse.

I'm ready for a respite, but all the more excited to simply see benches. I know, it must sound like an eccentric thrill. But the thrust of this pilgrimage is about benches, or rather the possibilities that await us on benches. Though our pilgrimage points us toward Jerusalem, in a distinct way benches are our destination en route. They are our relics.

Since the beginnings of Christian pilgrimage, relics have been objects of desire. The bones of the apostles and the belongings of the saints, said to bring healings and blessings, miracles and indulgences, have lured sojourners to experience a connection between the physical and the transcendent. Many pilgrims throughout the ages have risked their lives in order to see the remains of the faithful who went before them.

In our case, benches will be our sacred objects, connecting the here and now with the transcendent. While each of us must decide for ourselves who God is, I do not think faith is a solitary journey. Benches represent community. They are invitations for exchange. Weather-worn and common, they encourage people to sit as equals. There is no head of table or ranking of status when you sit side-by-side on a bench. It's that commonness, that free space for all, that makes it sacred to me. If all goes as planned, the strangers we meet sitting on benches will help us see God.

Krista motions me over to the bench she is photographing. Graffitied along the metal arm of the bench is the word "Ask." We simply laugh. It seems too obvious. Krista moves on, but I can't resist stretching out on it. My thoughts of intriguing encounters disintegrate into snores.

After a refreshing nap, we walk downtown as Krista shows us some of the pictures she took on her digital camera. She has a high-powered lens and a spectacular eye for detail. In Krista's viewfinder the wrinkles on an elderly woman's hand and the leg of a bench become art.

Once the sun sinks low, we find a sidewalk café by the Pantheon. Eric is giddy. Underneath that subtle upturn of lips is ecstasy. He is eyeing the Pantheon, a structure he has studied intensely. In a couple of days he is supposed to get his diploma for a master's degree in architecture from MIT. He skipped graduation to see how the edifices he's studied in the classroom look in the light of day.

Red table wine is poured, pasta is served, and gypsies with accordions belt out songs right in front of us. While we are simply paying customers, tonight we feel like royalty and feast like the gods.

≥ ≤

The disorientation I feel this morning seems to my body like a mild hangover. But as my eyes focus and my ears register the foreign phrases wafting in from the window, I realize I'm in Rome! Today is Sunday, the official start to our pilgrimage.

Krista, Eric and I embark on two morning rituals. We've decided to read a chapter from the book of Proverbs, the Bible's Wisdom literature, corresponding with the day of the month. We know that to make it through thirteen countries in forty days, we're going to be in desperate need of ancient wisdom.

We also have resolved each day to ask God for divine encounters. We have sketched out an itinerary and booked a few hostels, but there's no way we can pull off discovering the Holy en route on our own. Sacred conversations with total strangers will have to be choreographed by someone beyond us.

So, we read. We pray. And then we leave expectant.

Ancient tradition demands that we start our pilgrimage with a visit to the pope. At least that's what Felix Fabri—that super savvy pilgrim with the fifteenth-century will—had to say. The perfect pilgrimage, according to Felix, included getting permission from the pope before you proceed. To this rebel Protestant that seems over-reaching. But maybe my crazy little desire to include the pope in my pilgrimage has to do with the fact that I have few traditions stabilizing my spinning, postmodern world. I want this pilgrimage to be secured by ancient acts. So our first destination is Vatican City.

The pope has a standing date at St. Peter's Square on Sundays; hopefully a generous wave to Pope Benedict XVI will get us off to a proper start. I saw Pope John Paul II at St. Peter's when I was in high school. It was like being at a U2 concert, having that rare combination of celebrity and substance. Going to see the pope today is more for us than mere star-gazing, but our simple attempt at tradition lands us in a line stretching for blocks. We can measure our movement in millimeters. Ugh! I'm not a fan of lines, or any form of waiting.

My restless eyes finally rescue me. Across the street are a few park benches situated in an oversized median. On one bench sits an old man. And next to him is space enough for me.

Ah, this must be it: my pilgrimage's first divine encounter. I wonder what epiphanies await me. What might this old man tell me about God, about life? I dodge the perils of modern-day traffic to get to my relic, the bench. I sit down. I open my purse and pull out my notebook and my iPod with microphone attached. I begin with my brilliant opening line: *"Buon giorno!"* There goes one third of my Italian vocabulary. All I have left is *"Grazie"* and *"Arrivederci."*

The old man kindly matches my *"Buon giorno!"* with his own greeting, sounding slightly more, should I say, "Italian." I continue with "Do . . . you . . . speak . . . English?"

"Inglese? No."

I have arrived at a critical juncture. I can use up the rest of my vocabulary to thank him for the greeting and leave. Or I can catapult this conversation into oblivion. I repeat myself—*"Buon giorno!"*—and go straight to "H-o-w do you describe God—*Dio?"* I say it louder and slower. Intellectually, I know this is ridiculous, but optimism consumes me; I can't stop myself.

Across the street, Krista and Eric are smirking. But the old man is talking back. I have no idea what he is saying, but he is smiling and speaking and now I am gesturing and recording and maybe—just maybe—some significant exchange is taking place between us.

Then he rallies two words I understand. "You. Me." He gestures for me to leave with him. Oh no! This sacred bench is being scandalized by a sexual proposition. How in the world is this pilgrimage going to work? What were we thinking, expecting people strewn across Europe, the Balkans and the Middle East to share their views of God with random, American strangers?

I really should have composed a will.

2

ROME, ITALY

I like liberated old ladies. I know a couple of them. They can dole out sage advice, crack random jokes and, if need be, fart in public. It's those liberated old ladies who have lived well and loved generously that can take risks few others dare.

This pilgrimage was inspired by such a lady. Her name is Helena. She's quite dead right now, but I wonder if she's laughing in her grave about my first "sacred" bench encounter.

Helena was the mother of Constantine, the fourth-century emperor (the one with the Arch). Much of Helena's life is left to legend, but what we can piece together is that she was born around 248 C.E. in ancient Bithynia, today's Turkey. While working in a tavern she caught the attention of a Roman soldier, Constantius Chlorus. They became lovers, but as he rose through the ranks of power he moved on from her, leaving Helena a divorcée and single mother in her late thirties.

Fortunately her son did quite well for himself, making emperor and all. Helena is said to have officially embraced Christianity after Constantine's conversion in 312. So at the age of sixty-four she committed to a monotheistic religion, and almost fifteen years later, she became Christianity's first pilgrim from Rome to Jerusalem.

Helena is both a muse and a mystery to me. I envision her heading east on her historic journey looking elegant but wearing durable walking shoes. She insists on managing her luggage on her own, but is slightly scattered getting going. She's wonderfully free-spirited, still able to flirt, and yes, deeply spiritual. She is one of those women who has nothing to prove but loads to say. So to me, she's the quintessential liberated old lady.

Of course, that's simply the vision of her I've constructed. Eusebius, a church historian and contemporary of Helena's, describes the empress as handing out money to the poor, clothes to the naked and justice to the oppressed as she traversed from Rome to Jerusalem. Eusebius also notes that whenever she encountered a church along the way, she couldn't resist stopping to pray.

Helena's legend looms large once she makes it to the Holy Land. The majority of Christian pilgrim sites in Israel today are tied to her pilgrimage, as she scoped out sites attached to the story of Jesus and the early saints. Some places she visited already had a tradition of being sacred; others seem to have been declared holy after she shared a cup of tea with a hospitable local. Helena's biggest claim to fame was her discovery of the cross of Christ. Whether that was a legitimate find or not is debatable, but what is clear is that when she arrived in Jerusalem, it was considered a backwater city that had passed its prime. When she left, it was poised for a thriving pilgrimage industry.

Helena returned to Rome with a trunk full of relics, including a cross. Shortly afterward she died. In Helena's honor, Constantine built churches on many of the holy sites she visited, including the Basilica of the Holy Sepulchre.

I really don't know what compelled Helena to make the pilgrimage from Rome to Jerusalem. Eusebius portrays her as driven by religious enthusiasm, while later historians speculate that her pilgrimage was politically motivated. Perhaps she was trying to bolster her son's waning popularity. Constantine had recently made some radical religious reforms, including replacing many political officials with Christian dignitaries and suppressing pagan cult activities. He also made a few relational faux pas, such as murdering his wife, Fausta, and his son, Crispus, the year before Helena's historic journey.

I don't have the inside scoop on the empress's motives. I would like to think that in the mix of Helena's motives was a desire to see if this religion she converted to late in life was any different than the cults she grew up with—that ultimately her fourteen-hundred-mile trek from Rome to Jerusalem was a quest for truth. But what I take from Eusebius's tiny scrapbook of her life, and from all the holy sites helped along by her pilgrimage, is this: she had courage to go and capacity to savor the journey. On a trip of over a thousand miles she took time to talk to, listen to and respond to people en route. And when she got to the Holy Land, she wanted to go everywhere Jesus had been.

Helena may be my muse, but I suspect I'm a wee bit like another dead pilgrim. Remember Felix Fabri? This fifteenth-century German friar pored over writings of other pilgrims and put in great effort in his own preparation to construct a matrix of the perfect pilgrim, which included his "five pilgrim badges."

Felix's first and second badges were a gray gown and skullcap, the most apropos garb for the aspiring pilgrim. Being the overachiever that he was, Felix insisted that his seamstresses be saintly virgins. He instructed them to adorn his gown and cap with red crosses.

The third badge focused on facial hair. Like other cosmopolitan travelers, Felix grew out his beard, taking his inspiration from an ancient king and reputed god of Egypt, Osiris. Felix specified that the beard cover a serious and pale face, a reflection of the wearer's labors.

The fourth badge draws on traveler's logic. The pilgrim must have the perfect gear, which Felix identified as a lightweight knapsack and a bottle for liquids.

The last badge Felix put in his matrix would prove to be the trickiest of all: an ass and a Saracen (an archaic term for *Arab*). I don't know his thoughts on asses, but Felix's assumptions about Arabs made badge five very complicated.

Felix didn't trust Arabs. He was scared of them, maybe due to the fact that three hundred years earlier twelve thousand German pilgrims had been attacked by Bedouins during their trek to the Holy Land. This incident was one of the factors that set the Crusades in motion, as Christians rallied to protect pilgrim routes and holy sites. In that climate of fear, the Christians in power pressed hard for security and for revenge.

So why did Felix insist on an Arab and an ass? Once he made it to the Holy Land, he needed transportation and a guide. Felix likely wasn't familiar with camels, so he chose an ass. And, while he didn't trust Arabs, he thought that Jews were always out to make money off of others, and that Eastern Christians were even dodgier.

Badge five would also enable Felix to visit places with relics. In Felix's day, relics meant reward. When you saw a relic you won a certain amount of indulgences, which according to Felix's theology could absolve sins. Indulgences were like points that got you and your loved ones out of purgatory more quickly.

On the surface, I have little in common with Felix. None of the labels on my clothes read "100% Virgin Made." I go to great lengths to avoid facial hair. My backpack is bulging. And while I definitely like Arabs, I'm not a fan of the ass. So I've got nothing.

But I do share a few things in common with Felix. I too want to see the places where Jesus walked and Scripture played out in living color. And I like merit systems. If I'm really honest, a part of me wants to earn points. Like Felix, I make up rules and categories to try to control my experiences and ensure that I'm getting what I deserve. I'm not saying I like that about myself, but that's my bent.

Oh, I might as well fess up to one more thing I share with Felix: prejudice. I get enraged when I see it in others. I grieve over the insidious effects of prejudice that have played out in the streets of Baghdad, the territories in Darfur, even the neighborhoods in my home state of North Carolina. Arrogance and ignorance create a deadly elixir. But when it comes to faith, I naturally think I have a corner on the truth. I know God. I love God. If I thought a different religion was truer, I'd adopt it. Or I'd like to think I would. So will I be able to listen to Muslims without automatically thinking their God is a little more violent than mine; or that Jews' faith is slightly less complete; or that Catholics and Orthodox Christians keep trying to win God over with their good works?

I long to engage people the way Helena did, but it will take divine grace to rescue me from being like Felix.

≱ ≰

I just found out that the pope is out of town. There goes my blessed beginning to this pilgrimage. There's one more dilemma: no benches in St. Peter's Square. I was certain there would be cackles of benches, but there is not one in sight. I'll have to improvise.

A beautiful middle-aged woman sits on the pedestal of one of the columns in the Square. Her skin is sun-kissed, her hair blond and her expression serene. I walk up and introduce myself.

Her name is Maria; she's from Argentina. "Not much English," she tells me. But to me that is much better than "*No Inglese.*" As Maria begins speaking, passion and grace infuse her words. I'm captivated. This is her seventh pilgrimage to Rome—her last, she mentions with a hint of sad realism. Her family thinks she's a bit extreme, but something keeps drawing her back. She describes God as "a mystery, a force in the heart and mind. Sometimes I pray to God too much and sometimes not enough." Then with this certainty she says: "I have God. I feel God."

Maria's face begins to grow more serious but gentle. "God's timing is not our time." She shares that her older son had a baby who became sick. The family prayed and prayed. Yet the baby died. The loss has been devastating for her son and his wife. I'm sure this mother of seven has encountered many tragedies along the way, but her faith seems sturdy and flexible. She says again, "God's timing is not ours."

As Maria talks, a sense of calm and a nagging fear both rise up in me. There's something comforting about being in the presence of a person who has experienced great difficulties and still has a deep faith. Her words about God's timing, however, remind me of my utter lack of control and the likelihood that greater difficulties await me as well.

Nevertheless, Maria's weathered and tender trust is too attractive not to consider. After our conversation, we hug. In only a few minutes we've gone from being strangers to being mutual partakers in the Divine.

We are idiots. Not all the time, but certainly now. We're trying to leave Rome and we boarded the wrong train. Some CNN journalist sorts us out, but now our correct train is being delayed. Maybe there's time for one more sacred bench?

Once again there aren't proper benches, but a young woman sits on marble slab by our boarding platform. I plop down beside her and she's game to chat. Her name is Carla; she's twenty-two years old, from Colombia. She's got that hip, casual look going on and seems to have a vivacious personality. She tells me that she's studying journalism in Rome and dreams of being a writer.

"How would you describe God?" I ask.

"How much time do you have? It's complex. I love God." Interesting. That's unexpected. "He is a friend, like a boyfriend, for company," she continues. Wow! Carla has a surprisingly personal view of God.

"I don't have a good relationship with God. I am a strong woman and have my own path." What a self-aware and spiritually evolved young woman realizing her self-reliance.

"I do like Italian boys."

Oh! Carla must have thought I asked her to describe "guys" instead of "God." I'd correct her, but Carla is taking such pleasure in our conversation. She likes Italian men for their simplicity and happiness, but the tradition here is for a man to have multiple women; she doesn't like that. I finally redirect her to my real question. "I meant, how do you describe God? G-O-D? Dios? Dio?"

At first Carla struggles to talk about God. Maybe it's from trying to rally thoughts after talking about Italian men, but it seems to be more than that. She shares that she believes God is out there, but her life is not in relationship with him. And she thinks she is too young for this religion. "It's too serious for me now. It's too important . . . I am not ready for this strict life."

Carla continues to struggle to articulate her thoughts, though not because of her English; the thoughts are simply stuck in her head. Then it comes to her: "God and religion are two different things. I don't like religion—because of hypocrisy."

As I listen to Carla speak of the greed and injustice she sees in the church, I think back to the scandals I witnessed growing up. Church leaders involved in sexual affairs, tax evasions and various forms of self-promotion. While there seems to be an ever-increasing divide between God and religion in the States, it's curious to hear Carla voice these thoughts so far from home. Then Carla's tone shifts, and a stillness and a steadiness saturate her words. "I too am a hypocrite. I turn to God only when it is hard. I am the first problem. I want a happy world. But I don't make it different. The problem is ego. Everyone has an ego. We are egoist. Ego, ego, ego—thinking about ourselves."

As I hear Carla's confession, I become aware with her that something has descended upon us. Truth has come to sit with us, right in the middle of Rome's central train station. I want to confess to Carla too. I want to say, "You're right! I get so entangled with myself. I am desperate to be saved from my ego. I can critique the world around me, but I work so hard to look like I have it together. I want to have the right ideas, the right thoughts, the right words—but for my own sake, for the sake of my ego." But before I get my turn at the confessional bench, my train is called.

"Ciao Carla!" You've given me a gift. Good luck with guys. And with God. Someday may you be a liberated old lady like Helena!

3

FLORENCE, ITALY

If I had money—lots of money—one of the nonprofits I'd found would offer therapy to Italian taxi drivers. Or maybe it would offer therapy to the people who have to ride with Italian taxi drivers, specifically those people in Florence.

We are being transported through this stunning city by a full-fledged narcoleptic. Eric had tapped on the driver's window of the lone taxi parked outside the train station, claiming it as our own. Without looking up, the bearded driver had held up his hand and insisted we wait till he finished his magazine. A gigantic stack of magazines occupied the passenger's seat; fortunately he contented himself with only one. The click of the trunk was our cue to approach. We brought our bags to the back of the taxi, barely fitting them into the trunk among the piles and piles of magazines crammed there.

We are obliged to wake our driver twice during the short drive. Seriously. The vociferous honking as he dodges oncoming traffic and wanders onto sidewalks at high speeds apparently isn't enough to rouse him from his slumber.

Somehow we make it to our friends' flat alive. In lieu of psychological counseling, we opt for gelato therapy (Italian ice cream) with our friends. Kevin and Barbara are from the U.K., but we became friends while they were living in Charlotte, North Carolina. Kevin and Barbara moved to Florence in hopes of starting a church for students in the city, but in this city of the *David,* the Duomo and the Uffizi Museum—some of the finest religious art in the world—church work has proved to be a difficult gig.

We consume gobs of gelato as Kevin and Barbara give us a sense of the spiritual landscape of Italy. According to official statistics, approximately 90 percent of Italians self-identify as Roman Catholics. Only a fraction attend Mass on any given Sunday. Italy is a little over 2 percent Muslim; Christian Orthodox and evangelical Protestants linger around 1 percent. Judaism, the oldest religious minority in Italy, represents less than .01 percent of the population. In Florence, Kevin says, the statistics get reconfigured; here approximately 1 percent of the population are practicing Roman Catholics and around .01 percent are practicing Protestants.

I ask Kevin and Barbara why so few people here are active Christians. "There are several factors," Barbara responds, "but one of the main reasons is because people are quite skeptical. They're disillusioned by the Roman Catholic Church and cynical after years of corruption in business and politics."

Kevin throws in a couple of other reasons: "There's a tendency to prioritize the aesthetic over the profound, hence Italy's thriving fashion industry. People also exude an easygoing approach to life, a 'We're happy, why change?' attitude. And you can't forget about Machiavelli, Florence's most famous philosopher. He had a strong inclination toward the practical over the principled."

As Kevin and Barbara share, I find myself feeling increasingly tired and sad. In a city of so much beauty and wealth tied to religion, where is faith? I can't help but wonder if we'll have even one sacred encounter in Florence. "There's at least one more reason people aren't active in their faith," Kevin continues. "But I'll wait until tomorrow to tell you all about it."

As I collapse into bed, the sadness of our conversation curls up beside me.

Early the next morning, Kevin and I run along the waterway, savoring a simple view of the Pointe Vecchio bridge. The scent of pastries swirls in the air as the sun begins to flirt with the Arno River. While moments ago I was cursing my ambitious commitment to run, I am now grateful. One of my favorite feelings is to be in a foreign city doing something familiar. When I bring my simple routines into faraway environs I become more grounded in the world.

Upon our return Krista, Eric and I engage in our morning ritual of reading and praying for divine encounters. Last night's sadness fades like a forgotten lover; today seems stuffed with hope.

Kevin leads us to Florence's focal point. The domed cathedral of Santa Maria del Fiore, known as the *Duomo,* is glutted with tourists. Everyone has cameras around their necks and guidebooks in their hands. I can't bring myself to ask people about the sacred in this setting.

Kevin then takes us to Piazza della Signoria, the epicenter of political and cultural life in Florence for centuries. Among the sculptures that adorn the piazza is a replica of Michelangelo's *David.* The giant Hebrew king stands exposed and uncircumcised like the original. Michelangelo did a stellar job on the biceps, but how did it escape him that David was a *circumcised* Jew? Kevin guides us away from the imposing David toward a circular marker with bronze lettering embedded in the cobblestone. Here he tells us a story about why he thinks Florentines are so skeptical when it comes to Christianity.

The spot where we stand marks the glory and tragedy of one man's life. Right here crowds rallied for his cause and later cheered for his death. The time was the late fifteenth century; the man at the center of the drama was a priest named Girolamo Savonarola.

Savonarola's first visit to Florence was hardly noticed. Apparently he was, well, gangly in appearance and unimpressive in speech. But after going away to study for a few years, he returned to Florence having had an extreme makeover. His changes weren't cosmetic, however; he had become a man on a mission.

Savonarola reentered Florence mad and heartbroken over the consumerism of the people and the abuses of the church. He preached with passion, declaring the people dizzy from vain distractions, accusing priests of doling out lies for self-promotion and exposing the corruption of the age, such as the selling of indulgences. He saved his harshest comments for the Vatican and the pope, calling the Vatican a "house of prostitution" and Pope Alexander "an infidel and a heretic."

For a time people were captivated by his critique. Many Florentines were frustrated not only with the religious leaders but with their own futility. People ached for something beyond elaborate purchases, beautiful art and philosophy that made them the center of the universe. They wanted to encounter God. So Savonarola inspired people to abandon their vain distractions. People hauled their jewelry, perfumes, chessboards, playing cards, paintings of naked ladies, even their soaps, mirrors and wigs to Piazza della Signoria, dumped them into a large pile and set it aflame. Savonarola became the host of multiple "bonfires of the vanities."

Yet the flames of religious fervor seem to have consumed Savonarola's better judgment. After Lorenzo de Medici (of the wealthy and powerful Medici family) died, Savonarola took control of the city. He declared it a Christian republic in which God was the one and only true sovereign. To ensure that people were behaving as if God was mayor, a new moral order was established: no frivolity, no gambling, no flamboyant clothing. In order to enforce morality in the home, boys were taught to spy on their parents.

People got frustrated with the intrusive rules, and the pope got ticked off by Savonarola's constant critiques. So the masses conspired to end Savonarola's reign. On May 23, 1498, he and two of his coworkers were hung from a pole, surrounded by flammable objects and burned to death in the very spot where the bonfires of the vanities had been held. Savonarola was reading Scripture and writing meditations to the very end. He is said to have given his neck willingly to the noose and was in deep prayer as he was consumed by the flames.

Niccolò Machiavelli was growing up in Florence while Savonarola was creating his Christian republic, using power to enforce morality on its citizens. The writer of The Prince and promoter of power would eventually offer his own insights into my question to Kevin and Barbara: "We Italians are irreligious and corrupt above others," Machiavelli declares, "because the Church and her representatives set us the worst example."

Kevin concludes his story with Savonarola's five-hundred-year legacy. "The cynicism toward religious figures lingers like an invisible, toxic gas."

I've yet to sort out a cohesive philosophy on church and state, but I deeply resonate with Savonarola's desire to expose religious corruption and his passion to rouse people from self-destructive distractions. Growing up I attended prolife rallies and even spent a Saturday morning blockading an abortion clinic door with my dad. However, my family also introduced me to a social activism that seemed like a more organic expression of their faith. We welcomed pregnant women to live with us, cared for babies waiting for adoption, invited drug addicts to detox in our basement, and took prisoners to church and lunch with us every Sunday for years.

My parents taught me that everyone has done shameful acts and thought selfish thoughts. Each person is also valuable and created with dignity; heroine addicts, prostitutes and murderers each have a story to tell, often a story with similar themes as my own. Our family never changed any laws or held political office, but I can't help but think that we've participated—that we've contributed.

In recent years in my home country, the religious right has relied on government to legislate morality (in narrow terms) and the religious left has leaned on government to carry out justice (in broad terms). I'm left still unsure how the church is to interact with government. As Kevin leads us beyond the silver marker, I can't help but wonder how Savonarola would have described God. He had good intentions and sincere faith, but he became profoundly sidetracked, basing his hope for change on the power of force rather than the strength of love.

Maybe the task of this journey isn't just to look for God in conversations with random strangers on benches. Maybe even the ancient characters I come across as we make our way from Rome to Jerusalem can help me sort out my vision for a faith that fits a twenty-first-century world.

The click of Krista's camera connects me back to the present. We look around to interview people on benches, but there are none in the square. Kevin tells us that the English word *bench* comes from the Italian word for "bank" *(banca)*—a place for exchanging something valuable.

Is this city all about money and power? Kevin sees that he has sufficiently depressed us, so to make up for it he takes us to one of his favorite churches.

≽≼

We enter Santa Maria Novella through a garden. It feels serene until Kevin buys our admission ticket. I know the church has to pay for upkeep, and tourists add greatly to the wear and tear. I just wonder if tourism, where churches become museums, has contributed to Florence's cynical edge.

I can see why Kevin has an affinity for this place. A large painting of Jesus just inside the entrance beckons me to come close. This Jesus' long, sandy blond hair and elegant European features would normally aggravate me, but he has such a kind expression on his face. He looks like he just saw me come in and that he's really glad I'm here. His eyes are painted in that way that follows you across the room, which is often freaky. But this Jesus' gaze is so gentle and seems so genuinely pleased that I want him to keep looking at me.

While light drenches the Jesus painting, the front of the church is shrouded in darkness. There in the black rises an ornate altar, candle-lighting areas and a priest with glowing white hair. Father Alexander, a priest of thirty-nine years, invites me to sit on a wooden pew.

"We don't describe God," Father Alexander offers in response to my question. "No one knows God; it's not our idea." He glances at the altar. "The idea of God came from the Bible and the church." Oh no. The Father may have a point. Is this endeavor to ask people to describe God arrogant, misguided, perhaps even sacrilegious? He's the first religious professional I've asked. I'll have to think about this.

Father Alexander seems to notice my distress and continues. "We *can* have a spiritual experience. However, not many people are interested in faith here. Florence has a closed spirit and closed people.

"It's not easy. Florence is a rich city but with lots of poverty. When you have money you don't need spirituality. To live a Christian life takes a lot of strength. It's possible for everyone to receive strength from God. But you have to go against egoism and against hedonism." It's curious how Carla and Father Alexander have such similar insights about our ego.

While he speaks gently, I can tell his work involves struggle. I ask him a very American question: "Where do you find happiness in your work?"

Father Alexander thinks and then smiles, "When I pray. God is Father. I have a very big hope in God and I take great courage that Jesus loves me. My love for Jesus Christ and experience of the sacraments gives me joy. I pray much and I spend time in contemplation."

The gentle light of the candles frames Father Alexander's face. He exudes peace as he mentions prayer and Jesus' love. This is his career, his identity. A seriousness takes over his expression as he tells me, "I pray for poor people. I long for unity. I never want to doubt faith. I am secure that God loves me because I am a son of God. That gives me great strength." He becomes more and more animated. "We desire there to be a rebirth in the world. We need to help the poor and sick—especially in Africa and Asia." Then with a look of deep compassion he says, "Everyone has a need to be loved and to love."

My restless questions about faith and politics quiet down as I hear about Father Alexander's care for the poor and sick and his desire to be connected to Asia and Africa. What if the wealth, resources and power of the church in the West and the North served the East and the South? Perhaps that would inspire governments to follow suit. Perhaps?

Kevin has one last excursion for us. We'll hike some high hill in the city and arrive at a monastery. There we'll hear Gregorian chants sung by monks.

Exercise. Monks. Gregorian chants. *Bellissimo!*

We arrive sweaty and breathless, but once we get a glimpse of the view overlooking the city we are invigorated. The air feels more hospitable here: scented and wholesome. Gardens and graveyards surround the monastery. In front there's a whole line of benches, as if it's a small concert hall and the city is the show.

One couple sits in the audience. They look to be in their midforties, both fit, preppy and pulled together. I join them on the bench. Antoinette and Peter tell me they're from the Netherlands. They are friendly and easy-going, so I launch into my question: "How would you describe God?"

"God is there," Antoinette responds simply. "He is out there, but I don't know where." Peter follows her by saying, "God was there." Peter was educated with religion but no longer believes.

Perhaps they separate religion from spirituality. "How do you see spirituality?" I ask. Peter senses a loss of it, but Antoinette replies, "I'm a very practical person." She looks at Peter and explains to me, "We have a son, Evan. He has Down syndrome. We weren't expecting to have a son with a disability, but we've learned so much from Evan."

It's obvious that they admire and respect their son. I feel sad that God seems distant to them, but I can't help but be drawn to their honesty. Then Peter asks me about my understanding of spirituality. Oh no!

My mouth is moving but I don't know what I am saying. My answer is limp and meandering. I completely fumble around to end the conversation. Fortunately it's time for Mass to begin. I say an abrupt goodbye and escape the scene.

I descend into the dark, cold sanctuary and sit among tourists and possibly a few Mass-attending regulars. As I listen to two monks fill the space with Gregorian chants, I feel the Dark Ages of my soul. I seem to consistently be caught off-guard when someone asks me about my life. I'm accustomed to asking the questions. Why? Why did I neglect to mention that I am a Christian and believe my spirit comes alive in Jesus? Yet if I'm honest, I don't know if that's what I believe right now. What I do know is that they both seem more honest with their faith, or lack of it, than I do.

I pull out my little journal and scrawl a prayer:

God, do I hide behind questions? Do I couch my words so others won't be offended? Do I lack courage to say what I believe?

I just graduated from six years of seminary and I stammer when asked what I believe about spirituality. This is a disaster! I feel so unaware of the impulses of my soul at the moment. Please show me myself and please show me who you are more and more.

Communion is offered. Though I am not a Catholic, I'm desperate for it. Forgiveness. Steadying the soul. I chew. I hope.

The sound of ancient prayers stills me; the rhythmic chants wash over me like baptismal water. By the time the monks sing their final line, I'm reminded that if this pilgrimage is to be one of sacred encounters, I must come not with answers but with openness.

I ascend the stairs and enter the heart of the basilica. The evening sun streams in softly. A tall, thin man in a white robe walks toward me. He's one of the Gregorian-chanting monks. I conjure up courage to engage in another conversation.

"How would you describe God?" I ask Father Bernardo as we sit together on a pew.

He tells me that his English is limited, but then launches in. "For a Christian—for a monk—we have a special way of describing God which is the Face of Christ." Father Bernardo's voice is gentle and his pacing deliberate. "Christ's life is a life of love. It is a revelation that speaks better than any words. His love is so great, so unexpected. He takes a human face and human words, and connects himself to our history. He shows us on the cross the way of salvation for the human family."

Father Bernardo speaks in a way as if he were discovering what Jesus did for the first time. Then he stands up and points to the ceiling. "The geometrical lines in a Romanist church are a way of expressing the perfection of Christ." Then his gaze shifts to the crucifix: "The cross shows a different way of beauty, what Love became for us."

I've never associated beauty with the cross. But that is the majesty of the Christian faith, that horrific suffering for the sake of another becomes the most powerful act of hope.

We sit back down and Father Bernardo shares with me his journey toward being a monk. He grew up without strong ties to faith. In college he studied philosophy but struggled to understand love within that discipline. A college friend, an agnostic as well, invited him to a Christmas event. After hearing the nuns sing about a God who would make himself frail for the sake of humanity, Bernardo desired to know Jesus.

I'm captivated by his story, but I keep forgetting to call Bernardo "Father," which I imagine comes across as flirting. Oops.

For a couple of years he fought a sense that he was called to be a monk. Then in his late twenties Father Bernardo came to San Miniato al Monte monastery to join a community of older priests. The monks' role is to pray for Florence. I'm reminded of Father Alexander's commitment to prayer. In a city so cynical toward religion the clergy seem to know they are desperate for God to change people, change them in a way they alone cannot. The priests are gracious to others, reliant on God and reluctant to use the "power of the church."

The sun is parting, and so must I. Bernardo would like to give me something. He takes me to an office and hands me a lovely book about the monastery. "The monastery is like a little Jerusalem," he shares. "It serves as a Gate of Heaven." I say a long series of "ciaos" and leave this little Jerusalem.

The promise of pastries, cappuccino and one last lingering chat with Barbara compels me to rise with the morning light. Barbara is one of those kindred spirits. Though it's been over a year since we've seen each other, we spend breakfast sharing some of our most-strongly held secrets. She tells me in a gentle yet strong tone, "If you really desire simply to *be,* you'll have to become weak. You're going to have to encounter your own brokenness if you're going to be present on this pilgrimage."

Barbara's words resonate, but they also feel laced with that frightening reminder that I'm not as in control as I'd like to think I am. Her words serve as Florence's parting shot, ricocheting in my mind as I board our train to Assisi.

4

ASSISI, ITALY

As I stare out the train window at the Umbrian hills robed in gold sunlight, I'm vexed. I'm irritated with Eric.

I don't like dealing with money, especially among friends. Eric was tasked with purchasing our train tickets to Assisi. He bought them on the Internet but the pick-up system wasn't clear, so he paid for them again at the station. And we still haven't sorted out the money situation, so both rounds went on my credit card.

I know my frustrations are ridiculous. This journey will likely be a line-up of travel complications and mishaps. Yet what's really rousing me are my stingy thoughts; they feel all the more dysfunctional in light of the generosity heaped on me by Kevin and Barbara and Father Bernardo.

Such stingy thoughts seem particularly absurd when I think of the saint whose hometown we are about to visit. Francis of Assisi happens to be my favorite saint. Well before my age, Francis had cast aside parties with nobility in order to align himself with the poor and noble-hearted. He joyfully disregarded his medieval life of wealth and frivolity for one of extravagant self-sacrifice.

But I suppose his conversion from self-consumed rich boy to generous-spirited saint *did* take time. Prior to the "saint" stage of his life, Francis grew up spoiled by a wealthy father who financed his every whim.

Eventually Francis tired of his easy life and struck out for a little adventure. In those days (circa 1200), the number one adventure for young men was war. So at age twenty Francis partook in a little skirmish with a rival city. His team lost. He was taken prisoner and had to celebrate his twenty-first birthday as a captive in Collestrada. In a way this became his purgatory. He got sick and weak and aware of the emptiness of life. There he began to contemplate the eternal.

His initial response was to become a strong warrior, embracing a military career for the sake of the Neapolitan states. But after a second illness and two strange dreams, he was wooed toward the spiritual. He exchanged philandering and frivolity for prayer and solitude. And as his faith in Jesus progressed, Francis found himself increasingly identifying with the poor.

At first this didn't come natural to Francis. When he happened upon a leper, Francis instinctively pulled away in disgust. But then, shocked by his own reaction, he embraced the leper and gave him money. Francis went on to make a pilgrimage to Rome where he exchanged his clothes with a beggar and spent the day with panhandlers in the shadow of St. Peter's.

Shortly after returning to Assisi, Francis heard a voice as he was praying before an ancient crucifix in an old, forgotten chapel: "Repair my house, which as you see is falling into ruin." Francis took this statement literally and wasted no time, going to his father's shop and taking bundles of fine drapery. Then he sold the luxurious fabric along with his horse at the market and brought the money to the chapel priest.

The priest wouldn't take it, and when Francis's father, Bernardone, found out, he was furious. Bernardone had no intentions of his son becoming a man of the church. In fear of his father, Francis fled and hid in a cave for a month. He emerged from the cave emaciated and ventured back into town only to be mocked by his friends as a madman. His dad found him, dragged him home, beat and bound him, and locked him in a dark closet.

I'm curious about Francis's stint in the closet. Did he sit in that dark, small space considering how he would kill himself? Did he feel lonelier than ever? Or did Francis sense Jesus was there with him, closer than ever before?

Francis's mom, Pica, freed him when her husband left for business. She had longed from his birth for Francis to be a great religious leader. Soon after, Francis liberated himself from the expectations and obligations of his father, declared God his true Father, and took a vow of poverty.

In 1209, Francis started an order of friars. Unlike any previous order, it was free from monastic hierarchy. He refrained from being ordained as a priest; rather, his fraternity was guided by a minister-servant elected for a specific time frame. Francis and the other members of the order were called "lesser brothers." Francis had created a monastic community that was like a family—perhaps the healthy family he never experienced.

I marvel at Francis's riches-to-rags story. It is uncomfortably contrary to the American dream, and to the state of my soul right now.

St. Francis's hometown, Assisi, is a top pilgrimage site in Italy. Devoted Catholics and many non-Catholics from around the world sojourn here. Some are attracted to the persona of St. Francis; others are fascinated by the well-preserved documents and relics. People stay for days, sometimes weeks, to honor the saint and relish the peaceful ambiance of Assisi. We have three hours.

Felix wrote in his *Rules of Pilgrimage* "not to run" to the holy sites. But Felix didn't have to catch trains. In order to get our train to Ancona, so we can catch our ferry to Split, Croatia, we will have to sprint through Assisi, which for us is problematically perched atop a high hill.

Fortunately we get some assistance by a non-narcoleptic taxi driver. We arrive at our destination and split up. I enter the Basilica of San Francesco d'Assisi, which the pope built two years after Francis's death. I'm surprised by its enormity and opulence. There's a lower church and an upper church, with a labyrinth of chapels replete with paintings by Giotto and frescos by Simone Martini.

I wonder what St. Francis would think if he were to visit, looking at the art, sculptures and architecture dedicated to his life. Maybe he'd love it. He spent a great deal of effort repairing churches. Or, maybe he'd be confused by all the money and energy doled out in honor of this "lesser brother."

I have so much to learn about venerating the saints. The incense, the crypt, the candles, the icons are still foreign to my senses. In the upper church I run into Krista, who leads me to the relic room and shows me Francis's habit. I look at the ashen tunic, sewn of rough material and patched with sackcloth. Krista looks at me and says, "Could you imagine wearing something so itchy and coarse every day?"

For Francis, Krista points out, even clothes were a symbol of faith. "His habit represented his material poverty and his low social status. Daily Francis was reminded of his utter dependence on God." We both look at our own outfits and wonder what message we are communicating.

Something looks curiously out of place—an ivory horn. A placard states that Francis brought this horn back from his journey to Egypt. I didn't know that Francis had traveled to North Africa with a few companions on a pilgrimage of nonviolence. He actually expected to be martyred in Egypt. In the throes of the Crusades, Francis longed for the Saracens, or Arabs, to know the love of Jesus.

After he crossed the battle lines of the Crusaders, Francis met with the sultan Melek-el-Kamel. Francis challenged the Muslim scholars to a test: whoever walks through fire and remains unscathed has the true faith. He offered to go through the fire first, but the scholars declined. The sultan was so impressed that he allowed Francis to preach to his subjects. The sultan didn't convert, and the Crusades continued, but it is recorded that the sultan told Francis, "Pray for me that God may deign to reveal to me that law and faith which is most pleasing to him." In the midst of difficult church history, it's encouraging to encounter saints with such thorough and generous love.

Francis likely made it to Jerusalem, traveling east via Ancona, our very next stop. Oh, yikes! It's about time to go and I still need interviews.

Krista and I dash to our rendezvous place, but Eric is nowhere in sight. A collection of students are gathered by the bench—Americans on a study-abroad trip, so I don't have to attempt my faux-Italian. I pose my question to the entire group. "How do you describe God?"

Sarah jumps in first. "It's something in everything that is good." Kelly follows her with, "It's a presence that is all around." Maya tells me, "It's something different to everyone; each individual creates their own meaning of God. He's the Creator—the hand in everything." Andrew, the sole guy in this entourage of women, says, "God is something that surrounds us. It's in everything—in both good and bad."

I look around. Eric is still missing. "Any other thoughts on spirituality?" I ask.

Sarah excitedly tells me, "I felt special because we think a nun blessed us while we were in the relic room. She said something to us—we didn't know what—but the nun seemed very joyful when she did. So that made my day."

I see Eric meandering our way. I thank the students and start running toward a taxi. We round the hills, grab our packs and leap onto the train— just barely making it. As we leave the hills and head for the sea, I pull out my notebook and read back through my scribbled notes. Looking at the American students' comments, I notice they referred to God as "It," a generalized force. I imagine if I spent more time with them I'd get a clearer picture of their vision of God, yet I wonder: could their abstract force inspire such radical transformation in Francis? Could an impersonal power compel such dramatic sacrifice for the poor?

I can't help but compare those students with St. Francis, which is probably completely unfair. Maybe the better question is pointed at me: Will the God of St. Francis pull me out of my selfishness?

We lug our pack-laden bodies from the train to the ship in Ancona. By morning we'll see the coast of Croatia. But right now I'm in the moment. Krista, Eric and I sit on a bench on the deck as the sun's light dives into the black sea. We devour trail mix and drink red wine and laugh in wonder at our lives.

Finally there's space for Krista and Eric to get to know each other. We share about our family backgrounds. Krista regales us with hilarious tales of growing up with two burly brothers and two teachers for parents. She learned to hold her own early on in life. Eric tells Krista about being raised in the midst of two cultures, his mom Anglo-American and his dad Hispanic. Then he recalls the time he and his younger brother, Victor, traveled through Australia.

Krista is considering moving to Port Washington, Wisconsin, or Hyderabad, India, to do video producing. She loves seeing worthwhile stories told well. Eric recently hauled his belongings to Charlotte, North Carolina, to help me prepare for the pilgrimage. While there he landed an incredible job as a city planner, so he thinks he may stay. He has a passion for creating meaningful communal spaces in urban settings.

As Krista and Eric banter, my mind meanders back to St. Francis and his inspiring story of transformation. I wonder if such dramatic stories of change happen anymore? I refrain from lingering with the question and let myself grow sleepy. Right now I feel close to Krista and Eric, close to God and creation. My thoughts and prayers drift off to join with the words of St. Francis.

> Most high, all-powerful, all good, Lord! All praise is yours, all glory, all honor, and all blessing. To you alone, Most High, do they belong. No mortal lips are worthy to pronounce your name.
>
> All praise be yours, my Lord, through all that you have made, and first my lord Brother Sun, who brings the day; and light you give to us through him. How beautiful is he, how radiant in all his splendor! Of you, Most High, he bears the likeness.
>
> All praise be yours, my Lord, through Sister Moon and Stars; in the heavens you have made them, bright and precious and fair.
>
> All praise be yours, My Lord, through Brothers Wind and Air, and fair and stormy, all the weather's moods, by which you cherish all that you have made.
>
> All praise be yours, my Lord, through Sister Water, so useful, lowly, precious and pure.
>
> All praise be yours, my Lord, through Brother Fire, through whom you brighten up the night. How beautiful is he, how gay! Full of power and strength.
>
> All praise be yours, my Lord, through Sister Earth, our mother, who feeds us in her sovereignty and produces various fruits with colored flowers and herbs.

All praise be yours, my Lord, through those who grant pardon for love of you; through those who endure sickness and trial. Happy those who endure in peace; by you, Most High, they will be crowned.

All praise be yours, my Lord, through Sister Death, from whose embrace no mortal can escape. Woe to those who die in mortal sin! Happy those She finds doing your will! The second death can do no harm to them. Praise and bless my Lord, and give him thanks, and serve him with great humility.

Good night, Brother Sun! Good night, Sister Moon and Stars!

5

SPLIT, CROATIA

I awake as Brother Sun tiptoes up the Croatian mountains. His yellow footprints illuminate the landscape.

My first glimpse of the Balkans takes me by surprise. My impressions of this region of the world have been pieced together by the news reports I watched in the 1990s. When the Soviet Union crumbled, the Balkans broke apart. Images of bombing, gutted buildings and ethnic bloodshed blurred together in my mind.

Split bursts into view as our ferry nears the Croatian coast. The water glimmers emerald green and palm trees line the port. As we debark, a sensual breeze moves across our path. I suspect I'm going to love this city.

We breakfast along the harbor and then sit on a bench facing the Adriatic Sea. We pray for this gorgeous country that has experienced such tragedy, and we ask God for divine encounters.

Sauntering toward the Old City without a map, we cut our own path through charming cobblestone streets. The alleys are lined with elegant boutiques selling fashionable handbags and shoes. I ogle the pointy three-inch heels and the beaded bags, then pat down my bloated backpack. Eric gives me a warning glance. OK, I keep walking.

The economy looks to be thriving, but I've been told it's in flux. During the Yugoslav era, Split was an important economic center, known for its shipbuilding, food, clothing, plastics and paper industries. The transition to privatization has been tricky; many of the city's companies were thrown into a tailspin by criminal activity and corruption. These days, tourism and the service industries are on the rise.

We continue to explore the city. Eric's directional intuition is spot on. We turn a corner and happen upon a civilized mob. When I ask a woman in her early twenties about the early-morning throng, she responds, *"Bijelo Duigure."* Those around us gasp at my ignorance but are eager to enlighten me. "White Button—a rock band, like the Rolling Stones. They haven't played together for over twenty years."

Since I'm already in conversation, I might as well ask these White Button fans to describe God. Kresco, a tall and direct guy, tells me he sees no signs of any god. Then Nick says, "God is Christ. He suffered and died for our sins. We must respect that."

Nick, an energetic twenty-two-year-old, continues as he waits in line for tickets. "Life has gotten complicated; it is all about money. But that is not the life I respect. You ought to go to church, but more than that you need to be good in the soul. The church should show people how to live. It should help people organize their lives for community."

I walk away from the White Button line wondering if I would have ever considered asking Americans in a Rolling Stones concert line about God. I don't think so. In the States I don't make a habit of praying for divine encounters. Why is it so much easier to have holy expectations here—halfway around the world—than in my own backyard?

We turn another corner and suddenly we're in the midst of a bustling square in the heart of the Old City. Before us stands the well-preserved ruins of Diocletian's Palace (circa 300 C.E.). These ruins have faced the elements for centuries, as well as numerous political regimes. Their greatest test, however, may have come only in the past decade.

Split was headquarters for the Yugoslav Military Navy; it also had a large garrison of the Yugoslav People's Army, and played a vital role in the military defense strategy of the Socialist Federal Republic of Yugoslavia. So when Croatia declared independence from Yugoslavia, Split found itself in a very precarious situation. The same military that for decades had benefited the city had now become the enemy. Standoffs between Split-based Yugoslav military and the Croatian military and police forces lasted for months. On November 15, 1991, a light frigate called *Split* fired a small round of shells directly into the Old City. So Split became the only city in recorded history to be bombarded by a military vessel bearing its own name.

Thankfully, the damage was limited. I survey the square and see no signs of recent devastation. As we head toward the ruins, we decide to divide. Eric will stake out a space to sketch, Krista will capture beauty in stills, and I'll once again wander around hoping to God to find someone to chat with. I venture to the epicenter of the ruins: Diocletian's Mausoleum.

I know very little about Diocletian except that he had extravagant tastes and intense hatred for Christians. As I tour what remains of this Roman emperor's retirement palace, I assemble a greater portrait of his complex character and a sense of the poetic justice that followed this life.

Diocletian was born to a poor family in the mid 200s c.e. He climbed the military ranks and, after a short stint as an assassin, gained the title of emperor. In Diocletian's day, emperors averaged a two- to three-year reign. Whenever a war didn't go their way or an ambitious assassin came along, the sitting emperor would get stabbed, poisoned, mauled or other-wise rendered dead. Diocletian must have been a scrappy soul to beat the trend as he did. He began his reign in 284 and didn't retire to his palace until 305.

Diocletian insisted that soldiers and government officials sacrifice to the gods. When he found out that Christians weren't participating, he ordered the destruction of all churches and Scriptures in the Empire, and he threw Christian clergy in prison. In 304 he issued an edict proclaiming that all Christians must sacrifice to Roman gods or be executed.

Curiously, Diocletian promptly became seriously ill. He then did the un-imaginable; he abdicated the throne, moved to Split, built a palace and took up cabbage cultivation.

Less than a decade after Diocletian's edict, Constantine took power and issued his own edict legalizing Christianity. This ended an era of persecution and changed the plot line of the church. Diocletian's Mausoleum was eventually turned into a Byzantine cathedral. The bones of some of the Christians Diocletian brutally martyred have been buried atop his ornate tomb.

I wonder what would have happened to Christianity if Diocletian's reign lingered? What if Constantine hadn't come to power? Would Christianity have continued to spread vigorously by the blood of martyrs? Or, would it have been so beaten down and bruised that it would barely have survived?

Did Christians pray for the conversion of their emperors? Did the Christian community celebrate when Constantine converted? Did they see his reign as an answer to prayer? I'm curious how Constantine's rule differed from Diocletian's. They shared a similar approach to power. Diocletian ultimately referred to himself as the son of the Roman god Jupiter, insinuating that he reigned by the will of the gods. Later Constantine started the trend of Christian emperors ruling at the will of God. Both drew on an ideology that justified their rule by divine favor and power. I wonder how each of them would have described God.

My questions accompany me as I walk down a narrow street with ancient walls pressed in by centuries of stories. The alley is so tight I don't expect to see another soul. But before me is a horde of pilgrims surrounding the John the Baptist baptistery. This Christian heritage site was originally a temple to Jupiter built by Diocletian as one of his less than subtle attempts to align himself with the Roman god and reinforce his persona as divine ruler.

A sandy-blond-haired guy with a contagious smile—Tony—sells me a ticket but tells me I may want to come back because two tour groups wait ahead of me. I decide to chat with him instead. I ask him to describe God. Tony's eyes brighten. My curiosity is piqued.

"God is love. While some think he's a judge, he is not a judge. He is pure love."

I admit, I've developed a skepticism for happy, shiny people. But Tony expresses his belief in a God of love with such straightforward joy, I'm drawn in.

"I don't just see God as love, I experience him as love—even when I'm bad." There in front of the temple, Tony tells me his story. "I used to smoke marijuana. I was crazy about women and drinking. I'd start drinking by 7 or 8 a.m. and gulp the day away. Then my mom got sick. She wanted to go to Medjugorje."

I stop Tony there. "What's *Med u gory?*"

"It's a place of miracles in Bosnia. People pray to Mother Mary and are often healed. Anyway, my mom wanted to go and I was the only family member who could drive her. I didn't want to go, but I went."

I'm trying to keep pace with Tony, but I'm still stuck on the fact that he and his mom—Croats—traveled to Bosnia to visit a place of miracles. It doesn't fit my frame of ethnic, national and religious divides. Tony, however, seems unaffected by that anomaly.

"When we got to Medjugorje a priest from India was hosting a seminar on the Holy Spirit. When this priest spoke I experienced something new. Growing up I had only heard priests talk about philosophy and politics. I didn't care for what they had to say, and so I didn't think the church had anything for me. But this priest was experiencing God. I desired that. I realized that Jesus is alive, and here right now. As I believed that, I had an experience that felt like a shower inside. That was five years ago. I am now planning to become a priest."

I am awestruck with the reality that Tony's life has been utterly altered. For a moment I'm captured in quiet joy. I don't want to speak. Then Tony lowers his voice. He'd like to share a secret with me. I love secrets. I lean in close to hear.

"I'm a part of the charismatic movement."

A red flag begins to wave in my head, cuing a parade of childhood memories. I grew up in a charismatic church. But I halt my memories; this is Tony's story.

"The pope, before the Second Vatican Council, prayed that the Holy Spirit would come like at Pentecost. The Spirit came, giving Catholics renewal. This movement started in America with professors who believed that God's promise for the Holy Spirit wasn't just for the first Christians. The Holy Spirit came on these professors in strength, and the movement spread."

My parade of childhood memories has been frozen in midstride. But the memories can't hold their positions any longer. They resume their march. From the time I was six till the time I was eighteen, my dad worked for a multimillion dollar Christian ministry called PTL (Praise the Lord). The founders, Jim and Tammy Faye Bakker, were equal parts spiritual gurus and televangelist superstars—the Christian celebrities of their day. They built a Christian Disney World of sorts, with Christian restaurants, Christian hotels and a Christian shopping mall. There was a Christian water park (where I life-guarded), a Christian school (which I attended) and a Christian neighborhood (where I lived).

PTL believed that if the secular world was going to have all their entertainment and expressions of capitalism, the Christian world should have a shinier, cleaner version of it. They pulled it off with zest and excellence. A colorful cast of characters was always jetting in—Kentucky Fried Chicken's Colonel Sanders, 1980s tough guy Mr. T, high-octane exercise guy Richard Simmons—alongside charismatic preachers, healers, people in suits who prophesied and tax evaders.

These were by and large well-meaning people—even the tax evaders—and many, including my parents, were actively caring for prisoners, addicts and poor people, not making much money but desiring to follow a God who resided in a charismatic church.

This God was showy but generous. This God wanted people to be healed and rich and happy; all you had to do was ask. But eventually the gurus of this God went to jail, and the Christian Disney World fell into disrepair.

When I pursued a graduate degree in religion, I studied charismatic Christianity without any lingering loyalty to it. My memories became a mere specimen to me. I dissected the movement with all the "objectivity" and emotional distance academia offered me. I had moved on from the God of the charismatic church.

Yet here is Tony telling me that a charismatic God changed his life. He speaks of the American professors' experience with the Holy Spirit as something to be honored and celebrated, perhaps revered. My parade ends again as I ask Tony what it's like to be a charismatic Catholic. "I like the traditional teamed with the charismatic movement. It's very important to link the ancient with the present." Tony's nonstop smile suddenly comes to a halt. "It's very hard to be a charismatic Catholic. There is something inside of me that is drawn to the Bible and desires certain experiences with God, but the priests don't understand that here."

I wonder if Tony feels ostracized as a charismatic Catholic. Does his belief in the current-day activity of the Holy Spirit, in terms of prophecy and healing and speaking in tongues, cast Tony as a religious fanatic in the eyes of his fellow Catholics here in Split? Have the scandals of the West affected perceptions of charismatics in the Balkans? Are charismatic Catholics persecuted in Croatia?

I wonder, but I don't venture to ask. Perhaps I'm not ready to delve into my charismatic roots any further. I change the topic, asking Tony what he would want others to know about God.

"I want to love everyone. I don't want to be a priest who doesn't care about others; I want to like them. It won't be just a job. I desire people to love God and people, even if it costs my head." Tony declares his willingness to die for others without a hint of heroism. He first knew he wanted to be a priest one day when he was in church. "I saw this boy without limbs. I almost began to cry. I thought if I was a priest I would hug that little boy and love him. I'd ask God to do something special for him."

Tony and I chat about other things—the war, reconciliation—until it's time for me to enter the baptistery. My expedition through this ancient space now feels like an afterthought to a much deeper encounter.

I shuffle forward with a multitude of Italian Catholics, thinking back to Tony's words "I am willing to die for people." I touch the cold stone walls of the baptistery. Does Tony think about dying for God and for others because he's surrounded by the temple of an emperor who murdered Christians? Do the stories of the Christians who chose martyrdom echo through the walls as a reminder that Christianity miraculously continued?

The baptistery contains a striking combination of church symbols and Roman sphinxes made of marble. I place my hand on the sphinx, compelled to stroke it. Maybe Tony's thoughts about dying are more contemporary.

Maybe he's been persecuted as a charismatic Catholic, or maybe his memories of the war can't let him forget that life is fragile.

My tour is done. Tony is still out front. As he smiles and waves me over, I consider that maybe Tony's life has been so changed by God's love that of course he'd die for his faith. Then it hits me: Tony is a modern-day St. Francis. Transformations do still happen!

As I turn to leave, Tony is holding out brown prayer beads. He wants me to have them. "They're from Medjugorje." I walk away clutching in my hands what is likely Tony's most significant religious relic. These beads represent Tony's transformation story, the story of a wild teenager encountering the Holy Spirit and falling in love with a charismatic God.

Krista, Eric and I reunite and begin our "bus" leg of the pilgrimage. As we follow the Adriatic south, I finger my prayer beads. I don't know the proper order of *Our Fathers, Hail Marys* and *Glory Be's*. I stare at the cross dangling from them. *Thank you, Jesus, for being willing to die,* I whisper. *And thank you for changing Tony's life and giving those followers of yours centuries ago courage to die for you. My faith in you feels so pedestrian, but I want to love you and others more. I want that kind of courage.*

I flip the cross over and read the word *Medjugorje* stamped in tiny black print. I still can't believe Tony gave this to me. I can't believe I couldn't somehow return his kindness. He has no email and I didn't even get an address.

Medjugorje. I've got to find out where this place of miracles is. At least I can honor Tony's story by going there.

6

DUBROVNIK, CROATIA

After one glimpse of Dubrovnik's ancient city walls holding their own against the vast Adriatic Sea, I became entranced. If playwright Jean Anouilh is correct that "beauty is one of the rare things, which does not lead to doubt of God," this Balkan jewel should be rich with sacred encounters.

However, tonight I don't plan to ask a soul to describe God. I've decided rather to be captured by the city's charm. So after a sumptuous dinner of *moussaka*, Krista, Eric and I promenade along Dubrovnik's main street. Candlelight flickers from one outdoor café to another. The conversations of strangers provide background music as we ease our way to the Rector's Place.

We enter an atrium. On one side rises a stone Baroque staircase with gorgeous Corinthian capitals and a small fountain from the 1400s. For centuries this was the seat of government for the Republic of Dubrovnik and the quarters for its rector (prince). In the midst of state affairs and nobility, the little fountain in front of us was fair game for the public. Inhabitants would come here to collect water, wash their clothes, banter, laugh and argue.

But right now, this atrium is almost silent. The person directing us to our folding chairs speaks in hushed tones. We are seated only feet from the violinist.

The silence soon shatters as the piano, violin and violoncello sound out a piece from the eighteenth century. The music floats up to the black sky. The open-air acoustics are superb.

As the trio plays, beauty and peace become audible. The tranquility of this eve feels surreal. My thoughts and the music seem one—that is, until the movement changes. I look at my blue and white program: P. Wranitzky (1756-1808): *Grande Sinfonie Caractéristique pour la Paix avec la Republique, Française Op. 31 (1797)*. My scant knowledge of French gives me the title: *The Large Symphony Characteristic for Peace with the Republic.*

While Dubrovnik is a natural beauty, "Peace with the Republic" hasn't come easily. The city was established under the protection of the Byzantine Empire in the seventh century around the time when the bones of the Christian martyrs were being piled atop Diocletian's tomb. But within a few centuries the Byzantine Empire fell, and Dubrovnik had to wrestle through its identity. Because of its sturdy walls, it staved off an attack by the Saracens in the ninth century. It went on to host crusaders and then became part of the Hungarian-Croatian kingdom. In the fourteenth century it broke free, becoming known as the Republic of Ragusa and dedicating itself to the cause of liberty. It abolished slavery in 1418, opened an orphanage in 1432 and was the first republic to recognize the United States as an independent nation.

In 1991, like Split, the city was attacked by the Yugoslav People's Army during its struggle for independence. For seven months Dubrovnik was under siege. In May 1992 the Croatian Army liberated the city, but for the next three years people lived in fear that it would be attacked again.

As the music rises and falls, my emotions intensify. Why does peace require such a fight? Why is the path to liberty often so heartbreaking?

The musicians start in on Beethoven's *Trio Op. 1 Nr. 3 C minor*. I become too tired to battle my questions. We stumble back along the *Stradun* to our hostel. Sleep woos me.

I awake with an idea. This morning we won't search for strangers. Rather, we'll turn the mic on ourselves.

Krista and Eric are such grand sports. After purchasing yogurt, bread and juice from a local market, we exit the city walls where the last strip of land comes to a screeching stop before the sea. Perched on the precipice of the Adriatic are benches. As we situate ourselves I ask Krista and Eric, "How do you describe God?"

I interrupt myself when I realize this is the most romantic place I've ever been. So before I let them respond, I ask if we can talk about how singleness affects our view of God. They both stop eating and give me a stereo look of confusion, but I keep talking. I feel I must. The bench becomes my confessional booth.

"Here's what I'm thinking. There's the way I'd like to describe God and then there's the 'god of my gut,' how I assume God *really* is. I may have this compelling cognitive description of God, but when circumstances collapse and life gets unwieldy often I suspect God is different from my grand descriptions. Does that make sense? Longing for a romantic relationship and yet still being single, I've found myself asking, *Is God really good? Is the Divine good enough to take care of my heart?*

"Intellectually I believe God is good and that he pursues a loving relationship with humanity, but at times the god of my gut calls that into question. When I don't feel pursued by others—especially men—I sometimes find it hard to believe that God is so bent on seeking me out."

The stunning surroundings make my doubts about God's goodness seem ridiculous. Jean Anouilh's words seem irrefutable right now.

"Anyway . . ." My confession is over. My plan to team together our description of God and the state of our singleness wasn't the grand hit I hoped it would be. So instead of forcing it further, Krista, Eric and I spend the next hour facing the sea talking about the adventures we've experienced, the community we've collected, and the ebbs and flows of loneliness and gratitude we've encountered in our three-plus decades of singleness.

We then make plans to meet for dinner.

I pull out my map and see the markings of red buildings with crosses. This is certainly a city of monasteries, convents and cathedrals. Sacred encounters today should be a cinch.

In honor of St. Francis I trek over to the Franciscan monastery, one of

Dubrovnik's cultural, historical and artistic treasures—which explains the line. The man selling tickets tells me the attached pharmacy dates back to 1317 when the monastery was founded. "It's one of Europe's oldest pharmacies and it still operates." I ask if the monastery still operates as well. "Yes, we have seven monks and three nuns."

As I ponder the bizarre combination of a pharmacy in a monastery, he asks if I'd like to buy a ticket. "Is it possible to talk with a monk instead?" My question causes a little disruption to the line, but soon I am told no monks here speak English.

I make my way to the Dominican monastery. It too began to be built in the fourteenth century. I briefly survey the beautiful structure. Like so many ancient edifices in this town, it is a collection of Romanesque, Baroque, Gothic and Renaissance architecture. I attempt to tell a priest that I'd like to interview someone. He tells me that a monk named Christian speaks English, and walks me over to a little desk where he begins dialing a phone, which he then hands to me.

The voice on the other end is disoriented by my personal question, but he graciously obliges. He tells me God is love and that it is not possible to describe God for we are human. I thank the voice and I thank the priest who directed me to the phone. But this doesn't feel like a sacred encounter at all. I couldn't see Christian's eyes. I only spoke with him ninety seconds, through a clunky black phone. I wasn't even sitting.

I drag out my map again and see there's a synagogue in this city. My route takes me off the *Stradun*, through narrow cobblestone alleys to *Zudioska Ulica* (Jews' Street). When I arrive, I'm slightly confused. It looks like a house. I ascend a flight of stairs and see it's a museum. The line is short; I might as well see what's here.

I hand my Croatian kuna to a guy with dark hair and deep brown eyes seated at a small table with tickets and a change box. Employing my objective journalistic assessment, I note that he's quite attractive. Quite.

The museum is a fabulous find! It houses part of the synagogue established here in the fourteenth century, making it Europe's second oldest Judaic house of worship. The collection of religious objects contains an ancient Torah brought by the city's first Jewish refugees. As they were being expelled from Spain for refusing to convert to Christianity, they took great care of their Torah scrolls.

I decide to make another round of the small museum, this time reading the history mounted on placards. The story of the Jews in Dubrovnik is a tale of protean persecution. While they thrived dealing fabrics and spices, the Jews were relegated to living in a ghetto. The church stirred up local hatred toward them, and the Turkish sultan stepped in to protect them, refusing to pass anti-Jewish measures.

I'm horrified by the church's history here.

I wonder what it is like today to be a Jew living in "Catholic" Croatia. I introduce myself to the guy who sold me the ticket and ask if I can interview him. Dino tells me he is a Muslim. I'm astonished! But he relays his story like it's a typical career path. He got the job through a friend of the family. He's studying tourism management. "I greatly enjoy my job."

"So, Dino, how do you describe God?"

With a pause, he tells me my question is difficult. But he continues. "I believe in what I see. Sometimes I don't believe there is a God. I don't think about it too much." I wonder if Dino will end the conversation here, but after a moment he continues.

"I believe more in the material world, but I think there is something in every person that motivates him or her. I know not everything is about money. Sometimes I make prayer and feel better."

Dino's English is superb, but his phrase "make" prayer stops me. This seems to highlight the work of it. Dino's dark eyes strengthen. "When I see what is happening in this world, it seems Satan is on earth instead of God. I think it's good to believe, but there are religious fanatics and they aren't good. I can't understand wars between religions. Every religion says good things, but then there is all this fighting."

What did Dino see during the recent war? What was it like to be under siege for seven months? Did any classmates die? I wonder, but I don't ask.

Dino looks away for a moment, then tells me: "Sometimes I do believe. Sometimes I don't. Right now I don't believe." I wonder how the war affected Dino's assumptions about Allah, how they may have shaped the god of his gut. I'm not sure how to get at this, so instead I ask, "What makes you a good person?"

"That you're honest and that you hate liars and terrorists," Dino emphatically says. "Good is everything that is not fanatical. I wouldn't die for any ideas."

"What kind of God could you believe in?" I ask.

"God is in every person; that is the good. And Satan is in every person; that is the bad. God is good." Dino pauses, then modifies. "Probably good."

We talk about Dino's future and his work. Then he says, "I don't think it's a good idea to be forgiven. If a priest forgives you, that is not good. You should be punished." I've never heard someone say that. I ask Dino why.

"God is a judge. You should receive punishment and get what you deserve."

Just as Dino is about to say something else, the rhythm of the conversation breaks. Two men are leaving. I ask them if I can interview them. Yoseph, from Belgrade, is game to describe God. "One word: love. God gave us the Torah. He gave us the rules. We study it to understand what he wants to give us. You want to know about God?"

I begin to think but then realize he's not needing me to answer. Yoseph continues. "Study the Bible. Every person has to find the answer for his own. Then live it." With that Yoseph and his friend leave, and Dino and I chat a little more about life.

I decide to go to the Cathedral of Dubrovnik in hopes of one sacred encounter with a Catholic in this city. Upon entering, however, I'm immediately drawn into the relic room. Perhaps it's the spirit of Felix Fabri upon me. There are chalices and crosses and bones and lots of gold. And there's mention of a papal bull issued by Benedict XI in 1304, granting indulgences for a year and forty days to all those who helped with the construction of the church. Now that's what I call a medieval benefits package.

In the nave of the church I see a young woman wearing a robe. She smiles back. I introduce myself to her. Marianna is seventeen, from Slovenia; she has just arrived to become a nun. We sit on a pew and Marianna grins widely as she describes God as "my big family. He is my life, my everything in the world. He is my sister and my friends."

Marianna tells me how happy she is training to be a nun. I ask her if there are other young nuns. "No. Most are in their sixties or seventies." As I thank Marianna and go to leave she walks over to a wooden stand and gives me a small book. "Take this," she tells me. "This is about my favorite saint."

As I walk along Dubrovnik's cobblestone corridors I read the small book about Blessed Marija of Jesus Crucified Petković. I would have made an awful teenaged nun. The thought never crossed my mind. I was too free-spirited, too independent, too selfish. I also couldn't have embraced the thought of a lifelong commitment to singleness, to chastity.

I believed Marianna when she spoke of God being her "big family." She said it from her gut. I hope, in the midst of singleness and an ocean of desire, for my gut to be that certain of God's goodness.

Eric, Krista and I rendezvous at our favorite outdoor café in Dubrovnik to devour what I deem to be the best *moussaka* in the world. Within twenty-four hours, I've become an official connoisseur. After dinner we amble up a hill to an open-air bar facing the water.

The sun gives its final performance for the day and exits through the curtains of sea and sky. A CD of Ella Fitzgerald belts out tunes in the background. I look up. The night appears like a box of jewels with its sparkling planets and stars set against the velvety black sky.

I recall Anouilh's reflection that beauty does not lead to doubt of God. Nevertheless, there seem to be a thousand different stones that shatter beauty's power. I think of Dubrovnik's struggle for independence, the Jews' fight for religious freedom, Dino's firsthand experience of war, my own longings for marriage—real rocks thrown in beauty's direction. Perhaps it's those unseemly rocks that cause doubt and wreak havoc on the god of my gut.

I think of Marianna. Her description of God seemed so peaceful and visceral. I wonder what it would take for the god of my gut to be so pure, so beautiful, so connected to my head's lofty descriptions of God.

Would it take me becoming a nun?

7

MEDJUGORJE AND MOSTAR, BOSNIA AND HERZEGOVINA

"Excuse me, sir, I need a stamp." The border guard doesn't understand English or is simply uninspired to answer. My passport has changed hands three times this morning without obtaining one stamp.

Oh, I miss the days when uniformed men *insisted* on stamping your passport. In Croatia, the border guard's inkpad was dry, so my stamp is barely visible. I longed for a stamp with strong, wet ink to be displayed on my page 8. I requested it to be stamped again. I asked nicely. I was denied.

Maybe my desire for stamps is more about my long-running love affair with borders. As a little girl on family trips, I always wanted to know when we crossed into a new state. Borders were the promise of a new adventure and a sign that I was going places.

More and more, borders are how I make sense of the world. In my often boundary-less life, borders bring needed containment. They mark change and declare difference. But the guard still refuses to give me a stamp to signify my crossing into Bosnia and Herzegovina. I settle back into my seat on the bus, dejected, and pull out the brown, wooden beads from my bag, the ones Tony gave me. I've been so honored to have Tony's prayer beads, but I've been haunted by the extravagance of the gift. So, today I'm determined to find that mysterious-sounding Medjugorje.

Less than twenty minutes past the border I've spotted three churches through the window of the bus. No mosques. I keep expecting to see mosques in this Muslim-dominated nation.

As we venture deeper into the country, I'm awed by the lush green hills, rugged mountains and feisty blue rivers. Amidst a wealth of majestic natural terrain, however, Bosnia's economic deficiencies are evident. Gutted structures, pockmarked buildings and concrete homes mar our way. I spy a roofless church with a grand façade. It must have been hit by a bomb.

At the Mostar bus station, I approach a stocky, gray-haired man loitering by his taxi. I show him Tony's beads. Success! He knows the place and can take us there. But when we ask how much it will cost, a mob of taxi drivers gather. The stocky, gray-haired man says $100. We protest; there's a ruckus. The taxi drivers banter in Bosnian and come back with $90. We say no. I begin to negotiate in my mind how much I'd pay to understand Tony's story.

We leave the taxi drivers behind as they call out numbers. They then throw words at us that we can't understand, but they're not likely the traditional Bosnian prayer of blessing for strangers. We find a bank in town and *voilà!* There's a woman ready to answer questions from confused tourists. She arranges a taxi for us for half the amount and walks us out to meet our driver.

We pass some concrete and brick buildings riddled with pockmarks. "Though it's been ten years since the war, there are daily reminders of it," the woman offers. Then she tells us she is very happy we have come to her country.

Once we've settled ourselves in the compact cab, music begins to blare. The taxi driver answers his cell phone in an animated voice. He talks and talks and talks as we speed through what seems to be the middle of nowhere. He keeps talking as we wind our way up a massive mountain. When one call finishes, his phone immediately rings and we start all over again. He's forced to hold his phone in one hand and negotiate sharp curves with the other. Some drivers might slow down facing such a challenge, but oh no! Not Mr. Cell-Phone-Addict.

Reckless driving typically doesn't rattle me. I come from a distinguished line of risky drivers. But this maneuvering happens to collide with my own internal drama. I'm anxious and excited to go to Medjugorje. I sense that a story awaits us. Maybe going there will help me make sense of Tony's generosity. It seems like the best way—the only way—to pay Tony back.

We finally arrive at the mountain. I'm stunned. This place is a buzz of activity—full of tour buses, hotels and pilgrims! Our taxi driver hangs up just as he pulls over to the side of the road. "Where are we?" I bust out. He tells us that the church is a couple of blocks further, but he'll park here because the tour buses get all the prime parking. "You have an hour. I'll be right here."

I quickly sum up that Medjugorje isn't some secret chapel tucked away in the hills of Bosnia. It's a world-renowned pilgrimage site. As we jaunt toward the church we pass one souvenir shop after another—all selling prayer beads.

I enter the church. This modern edifice teems with people, but there's barely a sound. Everyone seems to know what they're doing—lighting candles, praying prayers, whispering to nuns. No one needs to stop and read that the Blessed Virgin Mary reportedly appeared to six children in this town in 1981. All the pilgrims seem to know about the messages that the Madonna has been communicating to those six ever since, like the one dated June 2, 1984:

> Dear children! Tonight I wish to tell you during the days of this novena to pray for the outpouring of the Holy Spirit on your families and on your parish. Pray, and you shall not regret it. God will give you gifts by which you will glorify Him till the end of your life on this earth. Thank you for having responded to my call.

Everyone seems to be acquainted with the Blessed Virgin Mary's mission to reeducate the world and help people recenter their lives back to God, guiding them to her Son, Jesus. And they seem aware that since Mary has made her presence known here, there have been miracles.

But I didn't even know this place existed until Tony told me. I've never prayed to Mary, and I'm uncertain how I feel about those who do. I slowly walk up and down the side aisle of the church, attempting to look reverently busy like the others. I just don't know what else to do. For some reason it feels wrong to interrupt people for an interview when they're seeking miracles. I glance down at my watch. Only twenty-five minutes more and then we have to leave. I say my own prayer for a miracle: "God, help!"

On my way outside I locate Eric. The path we take leads us behind the church to an enormous outdoor stadium. It's a sea of benches! There are more benches together than I've seen in my life! It's a bench rally, a bench extravaganza!

But all the benches are empty.

I wonder if this is where Tony heard the Indian priest speak on the Holy Spirit. Is this where Tony encountered God, and it felt like a great shower inside of him? With the sun shining and the breeze blowing and the sea of benches I can't help but think of what it must have been like for those at Pentecost. In the biblical book of Acts, followers of Jesus were holed up, half-scared to death after Jesus ascended to heaven. Like a gust of wind the Holy Spirit came; the followers of Jesus spoke in different languages. Pilgrims from around the world began to hear messages from God in their native tongues. A crowd gathered. Peter, Jesus' disciple, told them about Jesus and his resurrection from the dead. At the end of the day, three thousand people were baptized, and the first church officially began.

As I remember the Pentecost of the early church, memories of my personal Pentecost come at me like a hurricane. I recall the days when the Holy Spirit would blow through PTL. Some people would utter unrecognizable words, others would prophesy a "word from the Lord," still others would get healed of random illnesses or injuries. We would all kneel or we would all dance and God felt fierce and kind in our midst.

Eric interrupts my thoughts. "Look over here. See the small chapel. Maybe you can interview people in there." I enter the chapel as a couple, both tall and thin with gray hair, are exiting. I introduce myself to Pat and

Marie. In their thick Irish accent they tell me they're brother and sister.

When I ask, "How do you describe God?" Pat muses, "If God turned off the oxygen, we'd be finished. It's hard to describe God, for he is unseen. If we'd take God at his word, we'd be able to heal people. We've lost our faith in the belief of healing. Jesus told his apostles you'll do greater works than me."

Pat speaks passionately about healing. I realize how much I've associated miracles with "nonthinking." When I was a child my success rate on answered prayers was less than impressive, but I still believed my God was a God of miracles. I used to pray for angels to clean up my room. I'd beg God to give me a pony and a singing voice. When I got a little older I'd ask God to take away my brother's anger and give me a best friend.

I did grow up seeing miracles. Once when money was tight for our family, bags of groceries appeared on our doorstep. A few times envelopes of cash were stuffed in our mailbox. Then there were the drug addicts we knew who got clean and started helping others; that seemed miraculous.

But most of those memories somehow got stored in a little box I've labeled "My Nonthinking Years." The "requesting miracles" got filed right between "pursuing my dream to be host of *Good Morning America*" and "stupid, daredevil tricks I performed to show off for guys."

As Pat tells me he's been coming to Medjugorje since 1986, I look at my watch. Yikes! I only have ten minutes and I've yet to experience "the story." I thank Pat and Marie and then go into a slight panic.

Before I zip to the taxi, I pray for one more interview. I wait outside the chapel, hoping someone will exit soon. An elegant woman with a bright purple sari and a dot on her forehead walks out. She looks to be in her sixties. What is a Hindu doing here? Though I doubt she speaks English, I approach her.

In perfect English she tells me her name is Erin. While she's from Sri Lanka, she now lives in Minnesota. Erin plunges into conversation. "This is my eighth time here. I've come twice this year. I keep returning because Our Lady calls me."

Erin refers to Mary with a tone of reverence and endearment. I open my mouth to ask Erin how she describes God, but before I can Erin's eyes widen and she says, "I have a story to tell you."

"I fell into the Indian Ocean. I accidentally fell getting into a boat. I hit my head on the boat's rudder. I prayed, 'Jesus have mercy. Mary help me!'" She quiets—the memory of being underwater seems to drown her thoughts for a moment—then continues. "I lost consciousness. Then I saw a beautiful hand. It was Mary's hand."

Erin becomes quite animated. "I regained consciousness and reached for the hand. Yet there was no hand there. But when I stuck my hand out of the water my brother-in-law saw where I was."

With a sense of wonder Erin says, "Our Lady protected me. My brother-in-law was able to reach for me. God saved me. And he has used this miracle for me."

Erin has told the story of God rescuing her to others throughout the world. "People see my sari and think that I am from India. I have the freedom to tell my story in places Westerners aren't welcome. They hear it's a miracle and are curious about my faith."

I'm supposed to be at the taxi right now. It's blocks away. Oh no! I don't have time to even ask Erin to describe God. I snap a picture of her and thank her repeatedly.

As I run past the souvenir shops with Mary paraphernalia, I wonder what Our Lady's hand looked like to Erin. And I'm curious why it was Mary's hand—not Jesus'. I don't doubt Erin loves God and longs for others to know him, but I'm a little confused. I don't understand Mary veneration, although Mary seems to take people to Jesus. How many ways are people drawn to him? Probably many more ways than I ever envisioned.

I begin to feel a pang as I near the taxi. Perhaps my box of memories has been mislabeled through the years. Maybe I can be thoughtful *and* believe in a God of miracles. And, maybe my box for Catholics has been mislabeled as well.

I grew up hearing from some that Catholics aren't Christians. I heard they believe it's good works that get you to heaven—not God's mercy. And they pray to Mary—not Jesus. I have so much to learn about Catholicism, and I have so much to learn about myself. It has taken Tony, Pat and Erin to help me begin to rethink my nonthinking years and my own description of God.

Oh, these borders of faith keep blurring—or perhaps they're being pushed back. Maybe that's "the story" of the beads.

We make it back to Mostar unscathed. It's a gorgeous day in this unofficial capital of Herzegovina. A breeze streams from the water, and the cobblestone streets of the Old Town stir with activity. Outdoor vendors line the alley, many of them selling funky jewelry. Krista collects fabulous rings from around the world. She's in her element. I make a few purchases myself, six rings to be exact. I intend them to be gifts, but immediately one of them goes on my finger.

We passed a mosque on the way. I head back there, and a man with an olive complexion and a wide grin greets me as I step through a small archway. His name is Salaam; he'd be delighted to share with me the history of the mosque.

The Koski Mehmed-Pasha Mosque was built in 1617, I'm told. Salaam walks me over to the fountain in the courtyard also built in the Ottoman era. I look over at the mosque and ask if I can go in. "Of course," he tells me. I take off my shoes and place them in a small pile of men's shoes. When I enter, I'm alone. Deep red oriental carpets warm the floor. The white walls are adorned with a turquoise and maroon border bearing geometric designs. An ornate *minber* (raised stairs where the imam delivers his speech) fills one side.

I stand barefoot and quiet, and have all the freedom to be reverent in my own way.

After a few minutes I go back to see Salaam, who is leaning by a kiosk of prayer beads and books. I ask, "How do you describe Allah?"

He tells me that his English isn't good and that the question is very difficult. But his eyes alight as he shares. "God is everywhere—in the mosque, in the garden, in this carpet, in the water, in the sky." His eyes follow his examples. Then he says, "God was not born. He has always existed. God just says, 'Be' and it happens."

Salaam struggles for words, and then a sigh of relief spreads across his face, "God is in my heart, in my head. He's everything, in life, in night, in day."

I ask Salaam, "Is your belief in God very personal?"

"Yes," he responds. "It's just personal. I believe in God just because I believe." With obvious passion he continues. "I believe not just in a religion. It's personal for me."

I'm taken aback by Salaam's understanding of God. I didn't expect a Muslim to say God is in his heart, and head, and life. I didn't expect that a Muslim would have such a personal view of God. The way Salaam's eyes radiate and the exuberance of his voice, Salaam's love for Allah appears deep. And, his words seem to come from a place of peace. It's beautiful to see, but also confusing. I guess it just goes against my assumptions. I ask him why religion has been so difficult in his city.

Salaam's eyes dull. "People who live in Mostar can have no toleration. Well, that's how I see it. No toleration. The Balkans is the Balkans. Every fifty years there is one war. I don't know. My religion is good. Yours is different. But I don't know why there is war."

We discuss Salaam's name, which means peace. Salaam is like most people here—he wants peace. But, he says, there are always 10 percent of people who want war because of hate and another 10 percent who go to war because they can make money off it. He stops and says, "I wish I could say more about religion. I wish I could say more about war and Mostar, but my English isn't good."

Are Salaam's desire for peace and his view of Allah typical? I became friends with peace-loving Muslims while I lived in the Old City of Jerusalem. But the images that come to me on my TV and show up on my laptop are of Muslims warring—battling one another or others. My understanding of a typical Muslim continues to shift.

We keep chatting. Salaam loves his job and greatly enjoys telling people about the mosque and talking about religion. He likes interacting with tourists, most of whom are Catholics. On the surface Salaam runs a gift shop and manages a mosque, but he sees his job as an opportunity to connect with people about something deeply important to him.

Salaam hands me a small book with beautiful pictures of the mosque and explanations. He insists that I don't pay him for it. His generosity catches me off-guard. So instead of arguing with him, I decide I'll buy some prayer beads. But he refuses to let me pay for those too. He asks if I know about

Muslim prayer beads. I do not, so he pulls out his own and shows me. "Say 'Bless you God' thirty-three times as you make your way through the beads. Then you go back through them saying 'Thank you God' thirty-three times. Then you end by saying 'God is big' thirty-three times." I guess I give him a quizzical look, because he clarifies: "Oh, God is great." He tells me to take the prayer beads as a gift and remember him.

With my new beads in hand I wave goodbye to Salaam. Steps away from the mosque stands Eric, with boys and girls swarming around him like bees to a flower. Some stand on their tiptoes. All are leaning close to see what Eric is drawing.

Eric's sketches become more refined in each city. He claims he hadn't sketched much before this trip, yet his drawings are stellar. I join the kids, peering over his shoulder to see what he's captured in black ink. It's the *Stari Most*—the Old Bridge—Mostar's icon and namesake. What Eric draws, however, actually isn't the original *Stari Most*. That bridge, built in 1556, was destroyed in the recent war. The bridge had survived when the formidable Yugoslav National Army held the city under siege for three months in 1992, after Bosnia and Herzegovina declared independence. While mosques and cathedrals and a library of fifty thousand books were all blasted to smithereens, the bridge stood firm. But after the Croats and the Bosnians in the area rallied to defeat the Yugoslav Army, they turned on each other. Suddenly the victorious allies were now embattled enemies. Bosniaks (the majority Muslim) lived on the east side of Mostar in the Old Town; the Croats (the majority Catholic) resided in the west part. Apparently the army of Croats and paramilitary men engaged in mass executions, ethnic cleansing and rape of the Bosniaks in west Mostar. The Old Town was reduced to rubble and thousands died. On November 9, 1993, Mostar's famous bridge was obliterated. The bridge that had spanned the divide between Croats and Bosniaks, between Catholics and Muslims, between one side of the city and the other, became a casualty of the war.

Eric has drawn the new bridge in great detail. The single arch stone atop the Neretva River looks unmovable. I glance up to see the real edifice. The white stone sparkles in the sun. On a nearby mountain stands a cross. Did anyone claiming to be a Christian help demolish the old bridge? Did any churchgoers rape mosque attendees? How Jesus must grieve over all this blood spilled in the Balkans.

Eric finishes the sketch and Krista appears with shopping bags in tow. As we cross the single-arch stone bridge, we get an unexpected show. Two guys in red swimsuits take turns jumping off the twenty-one-meter-high structure into the chilly waters of the Neretva. School children gather, oohing and ahhing. Laughter ripples among us.

We enjoy a leisurely meal overlooking the water and then sprint back to the bus station. Our bus points northeast. I'm awed by the splendor that flanks our little way. We scoot alongside emerald rivers and the rugged Dinaric Alps. Yet every once in a while we'll pass burned-out buildings and homes only skeletons of their former lives. I'm reminded that beauty and brokenness so often reside together.

I'd like to go to sleep, but the window entertainment is too mesmerizing. I see a cow on a leash and there's a goat jumping to eat something off a tree. I pull out the brown beads that Salaam gave me. "Thank you God. Thank you God."

Salaam loves Allah. And Salaam loves others. "God is great"—bigger than borders, bigger than nations and wars, bigger than me or Salaam, or history, or all my questions. *God, please help me know you more.*

At some point we've crossed from Herzegovina to Bosnia. I haven't see any signs. The border isn't marked on my map.

8

SARAJEVO, BOSNIA

Krista, Eric and I fling our backpacks to the side and sit on a cold, stone bench outside the Holiday Inn in Sarajevo. The yellow paint and uneven lines of the hotel look like a child's chalk drawing scrawled against the blackboard sky.

The doorman eyes us, evaluating our less-than-posh luggage. The hotel was built to lodge the 1984 Winter Olympics athletes and by default became the refuge of journalists during the Bosnian War. Now it offers a room to anyone ready to pay more than $200 a night.

That minor financial requirement makes us, well, spectators of this fine establishment. We glance back at the doorman, catching his eye for a moment. We go no further. We know our station in life; we're the $10-a-night sort. Through our savvy use of the Internet we've found lodging for such a socioeconomic class as ours. And if the proprietors of Sartour Hostel are true to their word, we'll be collected from this prearranged rendezvous point any moment.

As I crane my neck to trace the lines of the iconic hotel, I can hardly believe I'm in Sarajevo. This city is one of the places I've been most looking forward to visiting. I've been increasingly fascinated with cities gripped by conflict. They serve as a stage where the extremes of human character play out. People's capacity for cruelty and self-sacrifice, for harm and generosity strut out into the spotlight. These cities tell a story of stark horror and nuanced beauty.

At the dawn and the dusk of the twentieth century, Sarajevo was ablaze with conflict. The event that triggered World War I—the assassination of Austria's Archduke Franz Ferdinand by a Serbian nationalist—took place in Sarajevo. I had seen images on CNN of the city being pummeled during the Bosnian War in the 1990s. I had heard Bono sing about Sarajevo hosting a beauty contest in the midst of sniper fire and mortar attacks. I wonder what portrait of God I will piece together from these Sarajevans; I can't wait to find out.

Within fifteen minutes a tiny red vehicle screeches to a stop in front of us. It must have gotten its design inspiration from a matchbox car. Our driver, Minza, says "Hello" and stuffs our bags in his red box on wheels. He convinces us we can fit too.

As we drive in traffic our host gives us an animated social critique. People who own sleek, expensive cars in Sarajevo, he says, are trying to establish their identity and status through a purchase, often one that puts them in debt.

We take the Kulin Ban Road along the Miljacka River, connecting us from the new city to the old. My face is smashed against the tiny window as skyscrapers, shops and restaurants come into view. The night is lit with activity.

In the 1990s, as the world watched this city get assaulted night after night, I knew little of war. The Persian Gulf War—then my most direct connection to military conflict—had ended in less than three months. But Sarajevo got stuck in siege for over three years—the longest any city had been held captive since perhaps ancient Troy.

The majority of my understanding of the conflict came to me in sound bites. "Serbs bomb Bosnians tonight." "Religious conflict and ethnic cleansing in the Balkans continues." I wonder what stories of pain and grace I will hear. But right now I listen to the subtext of an affable twenty-five-year-old who wishes he had a sports car.

A gate opens and we drive into the courtyard of our hostel, which looks like it was once a home.

Sead, Minza's brother and the owner of Sartour Hostel, segues into the role of host. One might wonder if Sead and Minza really came from the same gene pool. Minza's metabolism races through his sinewy body like a Grand Prix driver on speed. But Sead's calming presence makes me want to lounge on a hammock and eat grapes.

We get a brief introduction to Sartour logistics, and though we are ready to go to bed we settle into a hearty discussion about Sarajevo society. Sead is only twenty-eight years old, but with his round face and placid ocean eyes, he has the demeanor of a middle-aged man. His words come out with the astute tone of a professor, and his voice has the quality of a radio personality.

The conversation starts in the place I suspect it often does around this patio table: the Bosnian War. Every third person in Sarajevo died or was wounded during the war. While stateside news highlighted ethnic and religious differences, Sead is quick to say nationalism drove the aggression. He leans forward and positions himself for a lengthy discussion.

"The war was about resources, essentially land. Religion was misused by leaders as a tool to mobilize and rally people. It's hard to motivate people to die, so you have to tap into deep beliefs. But most people here hate politics. They see it as egotistic and corrupted. They didn't fight for religion but to survive, to defend their homes. Our war was simple; there were innocents and murderers.

"Lots of people in Sarajevo fought—even Serbs who were Bosnians. When fighters from Serbia came in, who were predominantly Serbian Orthodox, some Bosnian Serbs joined with their Muslim neighbors and fought in Sarajevo. There isn't a monolithic unit of religion. There's not a tribe mentality. It's very individualistic."

Sead sits back in his plastic patio chair. "Yah. This of course is subjective, how I've seen it. I'm biased sometimes, because of the way I've experienced it."

"So it didn't feel like a civil war?" I ask.

Sead sighs like an instructor frustrated with the ignorance of his freshman class. "A civil war is when members of one nation that have different populations fight each other. But here you had two neighboring nations mixing with their army units. So, civil war is where Americans fight among themselves. If you bring in others—like Canadians, Mexicans, English, Germans or Japanese—that is not civil war anymore. Civil war is America north and America south: one for slavery, one against; one for an industrialized nation, the other not so much. They fight because they have divisions. Here in Bosnia the conflict had elements of civil war, because we had local people involved. The nation was partially divided, but without help of the neighbors there would have been no war."

My mind races to the war in Iraq. A decade or so after the fact, will the war be seen as an invasion, a civil war or a catalyst for democracy in the region? Will Iraqis some day have similar conversations, lamenting how religion was used to motivate people to die when in the end the story line was more about economic and political issues?

Sead goes on to explain that the war in the Balkans was primarily about Serbian expansion, then conversation turns back to Sarajevo's religious climate. Sead sighs. "The religious community is in a big crisis. For the past five hundred years they haven't offered any programs that would encourage some sort of progress for people. One of the reasons why Communism was so popular was because the Communist Party offered people something new—no matter if it was bad or good. People want to be better off; they want actual change in their life.

"You always have spiritual people. You have 20 percent of the population that will always go to mosque or church, but 80 percent of people are just interested in a better life. Sometimes God becomes all of a sudden popular because people get in trouble."

I ask him, "Did people turn to God in the crisis of the war? How did the religious community respond to the rebuilding?"

Sead responds with another sigh. "In the war the religious communities became *so* important. Blah blah blah blah. But you know—"

Krista jumps in to complete his sentence: "It faded." We all shake our heads in agreement. A gray malaise unifies us.

As Sead speaks, I can't help but think of 9/11. A resurgence of faith swept the United States in the wake of the attacks. Synagogues, churches and mosques had record attendance. I wonder how much of the religious fervor has faded since then. Sead's articulation of Sarajevo's approach to spirituality seems eerily universal—well beyond the Balkan borders and the 9/11 tragedy. At least, it resonates with my own soul. I tend to get much closer with God in difficult times—when my heart has been dismissed by a man, or rejected by a friend, or tossed around by work. Suddenly my need for God captures my attention.

"Loyalty lies with where the money is," Sead continues. "How am I going to feed my family? People go to the religious community, and they listen to the stories, but they don't get a job. If you don't have that basis . . ." Sead gathers air. "Religious communities don't give answers. They aren't social reformists in a way that they would change society. Only political parties or some movement can offer some sort of solutions."

I sink down in my chair, feeling like a popped balloon. My soul screams a silent *No!!!!!* as Sead talks about priests driving BMWs while parishioners struggle with basic needs and how religious communities embrace their holy texts while their actions betray any sense of true spirituality.

"There is a huge difference between what people claim and what they do and think," Sead declares. "It is simple to see through it. People don't behave like spiritual people here. They don't behave like there is some other world beyond this world."

In the midst of my soul scream, I realize something: Sead's frustrations are strikingly similar to those of Jesus. Jesus railed against the religious establishment for forgetting the hurting, the poor and the outcasts in their endeavor of self-proclaimed piety. Jesus healed and fed people as well as taught them. And he called people to live out their love of God by loving others—even their enemies. He appealed for all this in the midst of first-century Roman occupation of Palestine; perhaps there could be nothing more revolutionary.

Following in the way of Jesus, the early church spread across socio-economic and ethnic boundaries. They seemed to sacrifice for others out of a love for God and a hope of heaven. Does a church like that really exist today? "Where do you see the hope for Bosnia?" I ask Sead.

"Hope is the people," Sead responds. My eyelids begin to close and my

neck does one of those tilt-back-and-jerk-forward movements. Ugh! I'm
falling asleep in the midst of Sead's fascinating patio lecture. I apologize
and try to convince Sead to continue talking, but he insists on taking us
to our room.

The accommodations upstairs are pristine. I'm impressed, but I'm quickly
losing lucidity. My body moves like a magnet toward the gravitational pull
of my bed.

My mind tries to lock in Sead's words—words that seem to have exposed
the soul of the situation. In my tired state Sead's statements that "religious
communities don't give answers . . . Hope is the people . . ." loop around
and around in my thoughts. Where is God here? Will anyone in Sarajevo
describe God as real when those who claim to believe in God choose a selfish agenda?

Living out of a backpack has its perils. Each night you encounter a small
explosion and each morning you are faced with a nuclear clean-up project.
Toiletries, granola bars and tank tops escape the confines of their airtight
surroundings and spray into shrapnel for miles around your bed.

So this morning we have another late start.

We open the chunky doors of our hostel to discover amber sunlight
sliding through the streets. The Dinaric Alps appear like city walls. As we
traipse down the hill, we are greeted by a sparkling sea of white obelisks.
Our first view of Sarajevo by day is framed by the Muslim cemetery. We
roam through the aisles of obelisks reading the dates: 1976-1995. 1961-
1992. 1972-1994. Everything around the obelisks seems hushed. The
terra-cotta roofs, the green grass and the blue sky fall muted in reverence.
I point to a marker and whisper to Krista, "He was born the same year I
was."

Four soldiers stand expressionless in camouflage uniforms and green
and brown helmets, guarding the tomb of the Unknown Soldier. I wonder
how many days they have stood upright, faces wiped clean of emotion, surrounded by these obelisks. Do any obelisks mark the grave of a cousin, or a

neighbor, or a brother? With thousands killed during the siege, they must know at least one name among the sea of white markers.

I notice an entourage of men in suits touring the cemetery. Close behind them are two guys in T-shirts—one with a notebook, the other with a camera. I approach the guy with the notepad. "Hi. Do you speak English?"

"Yes."

"What's happening here?"

"It's the anniversary of a war brigade," he tells me. "We're covering the story for the *Daily Voice*, a paper in Sarajevo." Then he asks me, "Where are you from?"

I tell him that I'm from the United States, the state of North Carolina. The guy with the camera walks up and casually drops, "North Carolina, they have the Tar Heels basketball team." And so our friendship begins.

Kenan, who carries a notepad, and Eldad, the Tar Heels fan, invite me for coffee. Few invitations could entice me more in the morning. I wave down Krista and Eric to join us. Introductions are made as the guys guide us to caffeine. The front of the tavern is populated by gray-haired men sipping espresso from white porcelain demitasse cups between smokes. Most are reading the paper. Kenan and Eldad direct us to a roomy booth in the back.

Both guys work for the *Daily Voice* as they attend university. They give us a glimpse of current happenings in Sarajevo and then ask us about our trip.

"People call Sarajevo a Little Jerusalem," Kenan mentions, "because we have a church, a mosque and Jews."

"Is God or spirituality something you guys think about?" My question feels a little abrupt, so I modify it. "Or, what are your thoughts on that?" Sead began most of his sentences with a sigh, but Kenan starts his with a winsome laugh. "God. Yah, I believe in God. But I'm not a man who every day is going to mosque. I believe in God, but it's personal."

I shift my direction to Eldad. "Well, uh, I'm an atheist. I don't believe in God. I don't know what to say." As the waiter doles out our coffees, I remark, "Uh huh." Eldad continues, "I did believe in God in the first part of my life." He takes a sip of his espresso. "In the beginning of the war I stopped. I couldn't believe God would allow such bad things to happen to good people."

The weight of Eldad's response presses my lips shut. We all, almost in unison, sip our coffee. I had barely heard the music playing in the background. Now the Bosnian tunes take up our air space.

In a few moments, Kenan scoops up the shattered conversation with another laugh. "Have you found anything interesting about God here?" We share briefly about our arrival the night before, and how we were surprised to learn that the war was less about religion and more about land. "How old were you during the war?" I ask.

Kenan calculates quickly. "Thirteen years, but I remember everything."

Krista, pointing to Eldad, "And were you around the same age?"

Eldad turned twenty-four two days ago. We all erupt in "Happy birthday!" Krista, still addressing Eldad, asks, "Are you from here— from Sarajevo?"

"During the war, I lived in a certain part of Sarajevo. The Serbs took it in 1992. It was a critical situation, so many people tried to escape. It felt like forever. I remember it well." Eldad has dark, distinct features, black hair and the shadow of a beard. When he speaks he exudes gentleness and a quiet compassion. Nothing about Eldad conveys the manner of a victim. He seems strong and confident. But then there are his eyes. They seem to know too much for their twenty-four years. I wonder what his eyes saw in over three years of siege.

"How much do you think about the war?" I inquire. "Or do you try to forget it?"

Kenan replies, matter-of-factly, "I don't want to forget. Life is going on. We are just people. We are Serbians and Croatians and Bosnians. They are just people and we have to live together. That is how I function."

"OK." Eldad says this as if he is conceding. "We remember. But I don't judge people by their names or by their religions, only by action. Not all Serbs are bad guys and not all Muslims are good guys."

"That's a very generous perspective," I remark.

"Do you study with Serbs?" Eric asks. "Yes. I have friends who are Serbs,"

Kenan tells us. "I have friends from Croatia. I even have friends from East
Sarajevo. We talk about jokes together and everything."

Eldad jumps in, "It's quite normal. The politicians are the ones fighting."
He has to leave to take more pictures for the story he's covering.

Our conversation flows into a discussion about American movies, and
God edges back into our banter. So I ask, "Do you think Sarajevo is a very
religious city?"

"Yes," Kenan quickly responds. "People have a strong faith, in any religion. Why that is, I don't know. Perhaps war?" He looks down at his empty
white demitasse cup. "Actually Sarajevo in the past was a religious city.
When the Communists came here in 1945 they forbid religion, but in Sarajevo the religion stayed. People are always going to mosque and church and
the Jewish—how do you say it?"

"Synagogue," Krista says.

"Why do you think that is?" I ask.

"In Sarajevo you have a special spirit—different from Belgrade or Zagreb.
It has special people; I can't say why. We are in the middle of everything."

"How would you describe that special spirit?" I wonder.

"I don't have an English word for it. When I don't have an active language, I lose words." He pauses painfully. "People are . . ."

I feel so bad I can't help him out. All I can think to do is ask, "Would you
like to say it in Bosnian and we'll have it translated?"

Kenan's face relaxes and he passionately expresses something. I have no
idea what. "Thank you," I tell him. I don't know how we'll get his words
translated, but I'd like to think an interpretation of the "spirit of Sarajevo" is
a couple of college guys taking time out of their morning to have coffee with
three American strangers.

Eldad returns, but they both need to go back to work. We ask how we
can get the bill, but Eldad scoots out to pay it at the bar. We attempt to argue
as he digs in his jeans pockets for a few *marks*, but he refuses with a smile.
An increasingly familiar feeling comes over me—the tug of immense gratitude and sheer discomfort that started when Maria in Rome shared about
how her grandchild died and yet her faith continued. Her time, her honesty,

her hope were gifts that left me enriched and indebted. The tug intensified when Father Bernardo in Florence offered me his story and a book. When Tony in Split gave me his beads and Salaam in Mostar gave me still more, the tug almost ripped me apart.

Day after day on this journey I'm forced to receive extravagant generosity. I'm grateful, but each time my hands reach out to take what a stranger freely gives, I'm afraid I'll drop it. My hands seem too small, too sweaty, too shaky to receive others' generosity. Or maybe my soul knows that with each accumulation of kindness, my sense of balance is thrown off, my equilibrium slips. Oh, how I live for equity! I work so hard not to be ripped off or to owe anyone. I just want everything to be equal. Perhaps this is a part of my American view of God—my "earn what you get and get what you earn" spirituality.

Eldad returns from paying the bill. "Do you guys have email?" We begin the ritual of exchanging addresses. Perhaps I can send Eldad a Tar Heels T-shirt?

So, Sarajevo is a little Jerusalem. Then that hundred meters where the Catholic cathedral, mosque, synagogue and Orthodox church huddle together must be our next destination.

Eric leads us first to the Cathedral of Jesus' Heart. Though only 6 percent of Sarajevo's population is Croat, this Catholic cathedral is often used as a symbol of the city. Its Romanesque towers appear on Sarajevo's city flag and coat of arms.

The church stands large and quiet and empty. I'm relieved. I need time for the conversations of last night and this morning to take more space in me. Eldad's remark pierces through my thoughts. "I couldn't believe God would allow such bad things to happen to good people." I hear his cry for compassion, concern for justice and expectation of a good God. His concern has haunted people through the centuries, many who haven't endured the sights of war that Eldad has.

I look up and see the crucifix with Jesus hanging on in excruciating pain.

I remember my brother and the pact I made to pray for him. Many medieval pilgrimages were embarked on for the sake of another; Eric and I had decided that we would make our pilgrimage on behalf of our brothers. While Felix Fabri and other pilgrims set out to collect indulgences for others, we simply want to ask God's favor on our brothers in as many cities as we remember. I thank God for my brother. I pray for Eric's brother, Victor, as well. I ask God to heal Sarajevo from the wounds of conflict. *God, thank you again for letting me come here.*

Eric unfolds his little map. "Let's go to the old synagogue," he declares.

Before the Holocaust, fifteen synagogues graced Sarajevo and Jews made up nearly 20 percent of the population. But only one synagogue still opens its doors to serve Sarajevo's Jewish community of seven hundred.

Unfortunately, it's not this sixteenth-century synagogue. This ancient edifice with a mezuzah on its door has been turned into a Jewish museum. And on Saturday, Shabbat, its doors refuse to relinquish their proper rest.

I notice a middle-aged woman sitting on a bench close by. She wears a long, taupe dress with a fashionable scarf tied at the collar. Her dark auburn hair is whisked up and her nose dives down her tanned face. She is elegant. Perhaps she is Jewish. I introduce myself, and she tells me her name is Zijada. "That's a lovely name," I remark. "What does it mean?" Zijada smiles and says, "Someone in the heavens." I ask if she'd mind describing God for me.

Zijada's smile widens. "Allah loves us like a mother loves a child. A child makes mistakes; a child has to be corrected. A mother has to discipline a child. A mother has to say, 'It's not good.' In the same way, sometimes Allah makes distance. When I am not so good, he has to discipline me, correct me.

"Some people don't understand our God. They make so many mistakes and Allah punishes them. In the end, it's good for us. While it's so difficult, we can learn. We can learn to love each other." Zijada pauses, her eyes squint at the sun and then she continues, "But I believe in the spirit world after this life. We have to make the best in this world but hope for the world to come."

I thank Zijada and ask Krista and Eric if I can take a moment to journal. I flip the page in the yellow 4" by 7" thin notebook I've used to record conversations since arriving in Sarajevo last night; it's almost half finished. I now rely on it to help me sort out my five-minute interaction with a Muslim woman seated by the Jewish museum.

Zijada had such a lovely spirit. She was kind, and I could see that her faith ran deep and was very personal. I saw a similar passion and intimate love for Allah in Salaam. This is beautiful to encounter but confusing.

I recently had a conversation with a friend about whether Allah is the same as the God I know as a Christian. If a Muslim converts to Christianity, do they get a new God or come into a fuller understanding of the same God? I vied for a new God—a personal Father, one full of grace. However, I saw in Zijada and Salaam a deep, personal love for Allah. They seem to have a sense of the true God working in their lives.

I pray that is so. They revealed a grace and kindness of God that enriched me.

I close my journal, and we're off to our next stop: the old Serbian Orthodox church. Before the war Sarajevo's population was 33 percent Eastern Orthodox Serbs. Today they make up only about 5 percent of Sarajevo. When Yugoslav Army soldiers—mainly Serbs—fired mortars into Sarajevo, 80 percent of Eastern Orthodox Serbs joined the army or left the city. The rest stayed and fought alongside the Bosniaks. I wonder where the Serbs of this Orthodox community were during the siege.

We enter a tall iron door surrounded by an imposing brown stone wall on both sides. This looks like a gate to a medieval fortress. The only noise puncturing the silence wafts from the right corner. We navigate the uneven cobblestone to an office area. Oh, it's a museum. A young woman with long, glistening hair hands me a brochure which reads "Old Serbian-Orthodox Church Sarajevo-Yugoslavia." The "Yugoslavia" is crossed out with a black marker, but you can still read it—perhaps a subtle reminder that this old church has been present through many changes of state. Nations come and go, but it's still here.

I ask if I can speak with a priest. She can't locate any clergy at the moment, but she's willing to describe God. Her name is Jelena. "God's child; someone who is serving the liturgy. It's a relationship with God. My luck is so naive when I think about it." I'm not sure if Jelena understood my question, but then she goes on. "God is everywhere. He's not just in heaven. If you look for him anywhere, he can be found. Not all the people see that. But I feel God. It's important to feel, to understand. I felt God in Jerusalem."

"You've been to Jerusalem?" I ask. Anyone who has been to Jerusalem is a neighbor to me.

"Yes, I was there. When you read the Gospels, for us naive people, it is hard to understand. But when you see the tomb of Christ and the place of Mary, you feel the power and everything. Only then you feel powerful and strong." Jelena becomes almost giddy. "When I went to the church of the Holy Sepulchre I felt so strong. There was a freedom. I don't know why, but I just felt God in my soul."

"When were you in Jerusalem?" I ask.

"This year during the Orthodox Christmas. I kissed the icon of Maria of Jesus Christ in Jerusalem. It's so beautiful! When I kissed it, my life changed."

I'm amazed by Jelena's enthusiasm. "What was it about kissing the icon that meant so much?"

"It's the power. It's not just pictures on the wall. It's something different. I think that icon is very powerful and a miracle. It gives you a feeling. When I . . ." I find Jelena's description of the icon difficult to follow. I think she said she is longing for children and Mary gave her hope and God gave her the feeling from the icon because he sees people's struggle. Maybe that is what Jelena was saying, but perhaps not. I still don't fully understand the use of icons and the practice of praying to Mary.

Jelena walks me through the museum. She wishes the people of Sarajevo would try to understand each other. She feels the pressure of being a minority; Serbian Orthodox priests don't wear their robes on the street out of fear of encountering a problem.

As we go to leave I ask Jelena what her name means. "Sunshine. It means sunshine. But it comes from Helena, Constantine's mother. Do you know of her?"

I give Jelena a hug goodbye. "Yes. Yes I do."

The sun and breeze flirt with each other as I sit on a bench around Sarajevo's famous fountain. Situated between languid elderly gentlemen and precocious pigeons, I try to piece together a picture of God from my recent conversations—a mosaic of images of the Divine set against a backdrop of suffering.

I envision God in the midst of a makeshift hospital caring for the sick but also instructing people how they can help others. I see God beckoning people to share their resources, encouraging them to give generously to others now, for a world of heavenly riches awaits them in the afterlife.

In the mosaic God also shows up as a parent—in one image, a loving mother disciplining her daughter for her daughter's sake; in another image, a good father protecting his son from danger.

I picture a young man standing in the midst of the war zone, calling out to God: "Where are you? Why have you forsaken me?"

I wonder what my description of God—my own mosaic pieces—would look like if my hometown had been under siege during my formative years. I can't imagine growing up in the horrors of war, yet I've experienced my own loss and felt my own fear. Those times have pockmarked my own belief in the goodness of God.

When I think of God in the throes of a suffering world, my mind flips to images of Jesus weeping when his best friend Lazarus died, or being rejected by his hometown, or betrayed by one of his closest followers. And, yes, there's the sobering scene of Jesus on the cross—knowing intimately the piercing pain of injustice. My picture, at the moment, is a God fully acquainted with suffering and deeply engaged in the work of redeeming it. I wonder if I, like Jelena, will feel closest to God when we reach our ultimate destination—the tomb of Christ—or if my description of God will have changed by the time I get there?

I survey my surroundings. Two little boys chase birds. Their laughter mingles with the banter of old men. Eric sketches nearby. Krista photographs soldiers on a bench. There's so much simple grandeur in this place of suffering. I'm amazed I get to be here. I'm awed by my life. So often on this pilgrimage I've caught myself feeling as though I have ten thousand senses. I am deeply grateful. As I pen a little prayer asking God to bring healing to Bosnia, a guy with spiked hair, blue eyes and a delightful smirk plops down beside me. "Hi. My name is Hido."

"Hello, Hido," I respond. "I'm Tamara." Hido tells me he was shot twice in the leg from a sniper and lost his parents in 1993. I ask him to describe God.

Hido says, "God is one. The people are second. During the war God helped us so much. Losing your parents is like losing your fingers. How can you eat?" Hido tries to look at the positive around him, he says, and then he lifts up his pant leg to show me the scar from the sniper.

Eric and Krista join us as Hido continues to share. He is only twenty-three years old, but right now he lives like a single father to his sister, twenty-one years old, and his brother, nineteen years old. He speaks of them like a middle-aged mother talking about sending off her children to college. He's worried that they'll do drugs or drink too much or get in with the wrong crowd. He's very strict with them, holding them to a tight curfew: "I know no good things happen after 11 p.m."

Hido feels pressure to get money for their clothes, the electricity, the water. He also has to pay 35 euros for the medicine for his leg. He breathes in deeply and says, "I want to give my brother and sister money to get Fantas to drink with their friends."

Our bus doesn't leave for a couple of hours, but we need to sort out how we're getting to the bus station in East Sarajevo. "I'll take you there!" Hido declares. He guides us on and off a tram and then a bus. The charm of the Old City fades with each wheel's rotation. I peer out the window at gray block apartment buildings as Hido tells me "God is everywhere." He says it like he just saw an eagle fly by the bus window. "Allah, Jesus, an elephant, if you are in India."

Our bus pulls into a parking lot. "When does your bus leave?" Hido asks. We have almost two hours. He wants to take us to his neighborhood on the edge of East Sarajevo.

East Sarajevo may be one of the most controversial of spaces on the Bosnian map. It's officially part of the Republika Srpska. For many Bosniaks and Croats this territory was formed by genocide, but to Serbs this is their rightful home.

In order to get to Hido's flat we must walk through some Serbian neighborhoods. Hido begins to look nervous and tells us that we need to know that Americans aren't regarded so well in this area. We pass a brick apartment building, nondescript except for that "FU USA" spray-painted on the side. The word *Palestinians* is painted on the building across the way. Hido tells us that many Serb Bosnians identify with the Palestinians.

We arrive at Hido's flat, not far from the graffitied buildings. He excuses himself to go get pictures and a book about a peace tour he went on. "My place isn't too clean. Please wait here."

As we walk to the bus station Hido says again, "Losing your parents is like losing your fingers. How can you eat?" While I'm certain he has said that countless times before, he seems to need to say it again. Once at the bus station he insists on waiting with us until the very end. Attached to the bus station is a bar; Hido opens the door for us and greets the bartender with a wide smile. But we know he is out of his element as a Bosnian in a Serbian neighborhood. Loud techno music pumps through the air; we must strain our voices to be audible.

Hido enthusiastically pulls out his paperback book with pictures of him on a peace tour to Assisi, Austria and Auschwitz. He flips to the page with the photograph of him holding the Bosnian flag alongside diplomats and dignitaries. I look up from the book to see the real Hido. He's bursting with pride. I can't help but think I'm having a beer with Forrest Gump. Before me is a guy who has experienced such tragedy and extravagant opportunities, all because of a war that happened when he was a preteen. And now that war defines his whole identity. I can't imagine it.

A screech and then a voice interrupts the techno music and Hido's show-

and-tell. "You can get on your bus now," Hido tells us. We collect our bags, pay our bill and say our goodbyes like dear friends. We load our bags below the bus and each hug Hido. We will likely never see him again. We must continue the adventure of our lives and go to Belgrade, the capital of the country that took so much from Hido.

On our final round of hugs, Krista hands Hido a handful of ten-dollar bills. We collected it from each other between hugs. We give Hido money in exchange for his time, but we hug him one last time as friends.

As our bus pulls away, Hido stands alone in front of the bus station smoking a cigarette. A yellow glow surrounds him in the blackness. He drops his cigarette and steps on it, then points to his heart and spreads out his arms as wide as he can. We wave one last goodbye.

The outline of the city blurs and once again I picture God. This God is full of compassion and moved by the suffering of Sarajevo. This God makes a sign for heartfelt love and stretches out his arms as wide as he can.

BELGRADE, SERBIA

The gray sky spits rain like a crotchety old man. My enthusiasm for being in the Balkans has suddenly evaporated. With my damp hair and drab thoughts I enter a Protestant church—the first I've stepped into since our pilgrimage began.

Eric, Krista and I slide into a booth. The atmosphere of this Lutheran church seems awkward. Perhaps we've become more familiar with high-ceilinged cathedrals and incense-laden chapels. Or maybe it's because this little Lutheran church—the Evangelical Lutheran Church of the Augsburg Confession—has had such a tough life.

After World War II the church was confiscated by the government and converted into a bar, then a disco and then a gaming parlor. The property was finally returned to its small aging congregation in 2003, but they've yet to raise funds for a new altar or organ.

We wouldn't be in this battered little house of worship if my friend Luka weren't preaching. Krista and I met Luka over a decade ago in Brussels. He was studying theology nearby and we went to the same church. Luka tended to have fascinating friends who would take us to Amsterdam or Luxembourg City. Now here he stands beside an abandoned bar while teaching on Jesus' Sermon on the Mount.

The text Luka has chosen is one of my favorite swaths of Scripture, one that inspired Gandhi and Martin Luther King Jr. to lead nonviolent revolutions. Today, however, I find myself soaked with melancholy. Maybe I miss Croatia and Bosnia. Maybe it's just the weather.

After the final "Amen," the church-cum-casino-cum-bar-cum-church becomes a fellowship hall. I might as well interview someone. I meet a tall, thin guy who must be around my age, one of the lone participants under sixty. He tells me God is love. "You must find a way to realize this love. You don't deserve it. But you enlarge it by sharing it with others." Ladislav pauses for a moment and then adds, "You get reflections of God through others."

Yah, yah, yah. How do you talk of a God of love with such ease and seeming sincerity when you Serbs bombed beautiful Dubrovnik? When you funded the purchase of a gun to go in the hands of a sniper that wounded Hido's leg? When you murdered his parents?

I don't say this; I'm just thinking it loudly in my head. Wow. I wasn't expecting to have such distrust of Serbs. I ask, "You have seen such hatred in your country. Where do you see the God of love?"

"Hatred has existed," Ladislav responds. "But God is someone you can rely on." Before I can ask him to share more, he looks at his watch and says he must leave.

Shortly afterward we stroll back to Luka's flat. Cold rain slides down my forehead and into my eyes. Luka, with his short drenched hair, now looks like he's wearing a swim cap. I ask him how this stage of life is going. He replies, "It's been good to be married to Angela. She suits me well."

I haven't seen Luka since he's gotten married, and I just now met Angela. She's Hungarian, thin and simply beautiful. Her dark brown hair flows beyond her shoulders, her face has defined features. She walks ahead of us, chatting with Krista and Eric. Luka tells me about her work at the Center for Tolerance and Inter-religious Relations in Serbia. "She also writes articles and lectures on religion and worldview," Luka says proudly, adding, "She's brilliant." I don't doubt him one bit. I look forward to mining her mind.

When we make it to Luka and Angela's flat, Krista, Eric and I devolve into a vegetative state. Our sleep on the bus from Sarajevo to Belgrade, let's just say, didn't provide the world's greatest REM cycles. The air conditioner blasted like a Siberian snowstorm. That wasn't too tragic for me; I was cozy enough with the Lands' End blanket and feather pillow I had rescued from my pack before it was loaded below the bus. But Krista had to fend with only a lightweight jacket, and Eric had nothing to keep him warm. Around 2 a.m. I woke up and saw Eric desperately draping his shoulders with the tiny cloth cover used for headrests. I finished tucking my blanket around my feet and drifted back to sleep. For some reason, today Eric looks like a zombie.

After hours of lounging, we collect ourselves from the couch and go to a restaurant on the river. The clouds that have been furious all day are now subdued. It's the cobalt blue of the Danube that currently vies for my attention. When I'm not looking at the river and the city lights diving into it, I'm asking Luka and Angela what it is like to live as Protestants in Belgrade, which is over 90 percent Orthodox. (Less than .25 percent of Belgrade is Protestant.) Being in the minority, ethnically or even religiously, is so foreign from my experience in the States. The conversation, however, quickly moves to the text in Matthew. "What do you think Jesus was getting at when he said, 'Do not judge, or you will be judged?'" I ask. "What were you hoping your parishioners would take from these teachings?"

Oh how these conversations stimulate me! The Sermon on the Mount captures for me Jesus' foundational teachings on justice, peace and a revolutionary way of relating to others. It's one of Eric's favorite passages too; he studied it extensively while in Jerusalem. I'm so curious how Jesus' message of peacemaking—not judging—and loving your enemy hits Serbian ears. "Eric," I ask, "how do you see Jesus drawing on his Jewish roots in the passage?"

Luka stops me and says that I am tireless with my questions. I'm taken aback. I stare at the water. The sun has completely set. Darkness is all that remains.

Have all my questions caused me to come across as critical? I love asking people questions, discovering who they are, finding out their passions and their history. I take such joy from learning from others. Asking questions feels like the only gift I have. But apparently it's a very irritating gift at the moment.

After we pay our bill, I decide to play a horrible little game. I will not initiate a conversation on the walk back; I won't speak unless I'm spoken to. So there is nothing. Silence becomes my only dialogue partner. The others banter, but I journey in solitary confinement.

I don't have a verbal vocabulary for anger, so my legs have to scream. I begin to walk fast. I tear myself away from the isolation of the crowd. I become like a toddler hiding in the corner, feeling safe and secure with her back to the world, even though everyone can see her.

When we arrive back at the flat, I excuse myself to go to bed. And then I cry. Slow, fiery tears slide from my eyes to my ears as I lay flat on my back. I let myself be. I don't rally. I don't shut down. I cry, quietly but free.

My gift of engaging people has left me desperately alone. I was just trying to connect in the only way I seem to know how. I pursue people with questions, but I feel as though no one is pursuing me. Luka's comment wouldn't typically have hit me hard, but I'm tired. And I've been thinking how Krista and Eric have such defined and potent talents. Now my meager gift has been wounded—OK, it's been blasted to smithereens.

Morning comes with more gray clouds. I share about my teary night with Krista. She sits down on my bed beside me and listens compassionately. I gather my leather journal and little black velvet Bible and go outside.

I station myself on a bench in front of Luka and Angela's apartment building. I do not flip to the book of Proverbs like I've done every other day on this trek. Instead, I turn to the Psalms. When I am tired or sad or happy and desire the familiarity of home, I go to Psalm 119.

"I run in the path of your commands, / for you have set my heart free." I realize I long to run. It's visceral. The thought sends my soul dashing and out of breath while my body simply sits here, trapped in sedimentation. I haven't run since Florence. And while the desire of my body to run stirs in me, even more so is the longing for my heart to run free.

What does that look like? My heart feels free each time I sense God has

orchestrated a divine encounter. It's free when I see beauty—when I gaze
at a vast mountain range, happen upon a smile from a stranger, or sense
God's nearness as the sun kisses my cheeks or laughter travels to my belly.
My heart is free when I learn some gorgeous truth, have a meaningful conversation or explore a foreign land. Oh, and it's liberated each time I can
see a story and tell it, and every moment I feel close to others, and love and
acceptance are not in doubt.

As I pray, a memory comes to me from a time I stayed in a convent in
Virginia. I had a dream that felt more real than the day. I was at the beach. It
was early morning and the gentle scent of grilled fish wafted on the breeze.
I noticed that Jesus was grilling breakfast. I wasn't surprised, just pleasantly
aware. His large olive-skinned hands offered me a plate of fish and motioned
for me to sit. He sat on a rock; I chose to sit on the sand right at his feet, sliding myself closer so that my knee touched his calf. He was my rabbi—and he
let me ask question after question and patiently taught me.

I don't think I've ever felt so alive and perhaps so free as I did in that
dream. The memory of it comforts me. While this morning Jesus doesn't
feel as close as he did in the dream, I still pray.

*Rabbi Jesus, please free me from the fatigue of trying to be strong, from the
sadness and ache of longing for others to pursue my heart. Please help me
give generously and receive graciously. Oh yes, and help me just be myself.
Thank you.*

Luka and Angela have taken the day off to properly show us Belgrade. As
we leave their flat, I make a silent vow: I will try my best not to be tireless
with my questions.

Our first stop is the Kalemegdan Fortress. Perched on the point where
the Danube swallows up the Sava River, the fortress stares down would-be
invaders. Yet like the little Lutheran church, it's had its lineup of conquerors
and comeback stories. After gallivanting through its Roman cisterns and
gazing at its towers, we meander to the Chapel of St. Petka. All good for-

tresses with Byzantine pedigree have chapels where one can request God's favor before battle and confess one's sins after war.

As I enter this little chapel I feel wet, wetter than the Roman cistern. Not one drop of water has touched me, but bottles and bottles of holy water make me feel like I'm swimming in St. Petka's pool of sacred solutions.

I speak with the assistant minister, Father Vladamo, who excitedly tells me that the blessed water of St. Petka comes from a miraculous spring. "If you drink the water or wash with it, you will be healed. And if you put small amounts of the water in your own water at home, it will purify it."

Father Vladamo escorts me to a wall. "All the bodies of the saints produce miracles," he explains as he runs his finger down the wall. "Marrow from the bones of saints were placed in these walls, like the walls of many chapels. People rub against them and are healed." Father Vladamo explains the marrow and miracles to me as if he is explaining gravity or the orbit of the planets. I ask him to describe God.

"I am not a priest, I am just studying theology," he says meekly before going on to recite the seven councils of the church and explain that God is Creator and Jesus was conceived by the Holy Spirit and born of the Virgin Mary. Jesus died and was resurrected and one day he will return.

It's funny: I got a more succinct, tightly organized articulation of Christian orthodoxy from a nonpriest fixated with the miraculous folklore of Serbian saints, half a world away from home, than from any class I took in seminary.

We progress downtown along *Marsala Tito* (Marshal Tito Road). I can't resist asking Luka to help me understand recent Balkan history. With the precision of a seasoned professor, Luka shares how Serbia for centuries has enjoyed being one of the dominant nations on the Balkan Peninsula. "The desire for a 'Greater Serbia' that played out in the past decade has historic roots. With the constant redrawing of borders, Serbs now reside in areas that fall outside of the mother-country. This has created a significant problem." Marshal Tito seemed to hold Serbia in check under his dictatorial control of Yugoslavia, but "after Tito died, Yugoslavia was left with a parliament led by rotating presidents from the different constituent republics. The presidents tended to filter resources to their own republics during the time of their service.

"During the late eighties the Yugoslav federation was also experiencing financial woes. Debt was abundant, salaries were decreasing, and people were becoming disgruntled. Different views of government and old disagreements reemerged. Then when Slobodan Milosević took power, he made his nationalistic intentions overt.

"Slovenia was the first republic to pull away in 1991. They had protested the treatment of Albanians in Kosovo and had different economic aspirations from the rest of the country. When they declared independence, Milosević set the army on them. The war lasted only ten days. The much larger republic of Croatia then declared independence, and Milosević focused his attention on them with full force."

Luka grew up in Croatia. He turns to me soberly. "As you know, there was great damage, and it spread from there to Bosnia." I wonder how it is for Luka to live in Serbia. Does he struggle with not judging his neighbors and loving his native country's enemy? I refrain from asking; I suspect I've already asked enough questions for the day.

Discussion of war ceases as we enter the gardens of St. Mark's Serbian Orthodox Church.

While this neo-Byzantine structure houses the remains of Stefan Dušan, perhaps Serbia's greatest leader, as well as one of the most treasured collections of eighteenth- and nineteenth-century Serbian icons, right now I just want to see grass. I'm itching for green space. I scan the interior of this edifice with the interest of a typical teenage boy. And then I walk out, leaving Krista to appreciate the icon collection and Eric to sketch the columns that stretch to the seemingly endless ceiling.

Luka and Angela lounge on a bench outside. While I imagine we've worn them out, I can't resist asking Angela to join me as I chase an older gentleman donning a long black gown and a cascading salt and pepper beard. The priest is strolling toward the church from the other side of the gardens. Angela agrees to come with me. I run toward him, trying not to look like I'm running. I'm totally out of breath as I arrive right in front of him.

"Uh . . . uh . . . Excuse me, Priest, my name is Tamara." I attempt to pronounce my name the way Russians say it. The priest grins and so I continue. "May I interview you?" He responds, I learn as Angela translates, by saying he doesn't speak English. Fortunately, as Luka had suggested, Angela is brilliant. She seamlessly translates the priest's Serbian words to my English-only ears, bypassing her Hungarian native tongue.

Father Bosko is from Zadar, Croatia. He came to Serbia thirteen years ago, which means he must have left during Croatia's War of Independence. I wonder, did any in his congregation take up arms against their neighbors? How did Father Bosko and other Serbian Orthodox priests react? How many people in his congregation chose to follow their ethnic identity over their faith identity? To my silent questions he offers only that he "saw horrible things in the war."

Through the voice of Angela, Father Bosko tells me, "God is everything. God is around us. He is everything we see. He's the sky, the world, the ground. We are all a part of him. Every creature that exists here; they all have a part of God's creation in them." His words are strikingly similar to Salaam's description of Allah. They seem pantheistic, but perhaps this is just an Eastern way of expressing the unity of God's creation. I just don't know. But then Father Bosko takes his description of God in another direction. "My faith consists on the basis of natural laws, the laws in which God created. It is the most perfect law, this nature God has created.

"As the Scripture says, God has created the world and has given man to rule over it. So everything that was created God gave man to take use of it. But unfortunately we have abused it; we have not used it wisely.

"All men are the same in this world," Father Bosko continues. "They all have their own gods. We have Christ. We have the Holy Trinity—Father, Son and Holy Spirit. In this I have a strong faith. There isn't one nation which doesn't have its own faith. Just like the ancient Slavs had their own gods, everyone has their own gods. Each has their own fears of things and their own rituals. But not all have been able to hear about Christ. There are still nations in this world where people live in prehistoric times. I'm not judging them. They still have their own salvation or enlightenment."

"How will their salvation come?" I ask.

"God is all merciful. We who are mortal men in this world often say that God punished me for something. But I as a minister and witness ask what kind of God is one that punishes man? God doesn't punish people; it is the devil.

"If we sin, we have to repent and to pray to God through the Eucharist and through confession and we try to change our ways. We all live under sin, but it doesn't mean that we can't change our ways and be better."

As Father Bosko speaks I realize something: I haven't been factoring in the presence of evil and the reality of sin as I've collected my descriptions of God. We don't live in the world we were intended to, and because of this we don't see God accurately. Our betrayals of God certainly affect the way we understand God. They provide static in our perception of Divine love. And the presence of evil, with all the pain that comes with it, creates so many wrong notions about God. The god of our gut must get tied up in knots of confusion and false assumptions because of sin and evil.

Yet Father Bosko says God is merciful and makes a way out. What a gift to consider. I prepare to thank Father Bosko, but he continues. "I would like, as a minister who serves God and his nation, that we overcome all of our human disagreements and that we become as happy and good as possible. But we're not able to do that without God. For God is all loving." He pauses and looks at me gently with kind eyes that seem like they've worked hard to see. "We're able to be different, and we are different, of course. That is a fact. But in God, there shouldn't be any differences because he is the truth, life and the way to our salvation. Hallelujah! Thank God!"

Father Bosko wishes me a good trip and tells me to love Jesus Christ. "There is only one Christ. He is our salvation for all. And when you see the tomb of Christ, pray for me, a sinner."

I thank him for sharing; it was a gift to speak with him. I begin to walk away when he says, "Just to talk about God and Christ is something eternal. It is like a prayer meeting almost. Our love is being expressed to God. And if we are thinking about God we don't have time to think about evil. If we think something bad toward our neighbor or toward our enemy, then we must remember God—ask him, 'Son of God, have mercy on me.'"

Father Bosko suddenly looks in the direction he had been walking and seems to remember that he was en route. I say to him, "It's obvious your love for God is very deep." He quickly says, "Thank God!" and briskly walks away.

The sun shines more vibrantly than I've seen it in Belgrade. I walk back to the tram stop in silence; this afternoon's quiet is filled with deep contentment. I admit, I don't understand how Father Bosko's portrait of God fits together. His response defies my convenient categories of faith and orthodoxy. However, I sensed in him a generous spirit. He seems to hold tightly to the evasive paradox of not judging others while desiring all to know his God through Jesus.

Wow. I wasn't expecting to learn such grace and humility from a Serb.

In the evening I check my email. I have a note with the subject line "heloooooooooooooo." It's from Hido.

> Dear tamara how are you? I am one boy my name is Hido i dont know do you arived in belgrade. I hope you and my friends arived good. I am just person with clean heart and Bosnian spirit. you and krista good. sarajevo have spirit but i dont feel him inside in my body . . .

Hido has attached pictures of Sarajevo in snow, in summer, bombed out. There's a cartoon character that perhaps was Sarajevo's mascot for the Winter Olympics, or maybe the image of a fox wearing a turtleneck just makes Hido smile and he wanted to share it.

Well, it makes me smile. "Dear Hido . . . Good night, old friend."

In the morning I slip on a sundress that feels like a nightgown and return to the bench in front of Luka and Angela's flat. The sky and the gray communist buildings conspire once again to make me feel drab and mildly depressed. Weather and architecture wield such power.

Since my morning rhythms have been off-beat here, I open my little Bible to Matthew 7, the chapter that Luka spoke from. "So in everything, do to others what you would have them do to you, for this sums up the Law and the Prophets."

The Golden Rule. As my eyes traverse across those familiar words, I realize that my struggle to love others—to respect others—seems to be in the spotlight here. I've noticed I have a general aloofness to Serbs. I guess my heart aligned with the Croats—seeing the beauty of their land, hearing of their struggles with war, talking with Tony and Dino. Then my heart was broken and pieced together again in Bosnia, learning of atrocities and encountering generosity from Salaam, Kenan, Eldad and Hido.

I haven't given Serbia a real chance. I haven't expected its collective story to be filled with both pain and beauty—like my own. Jesus' way of acting toward others doesn't come naturally for me. I look around at this gray neighborhood one last time before I go in, confessing my inability to treat Serbia as I would want to be treated. I ask God to help me love and receive love with greater intention today.

I pray for Serbia. I have completely failed to do so since I've arrived.

God, help Serbia experience healing and hope and dignity draped in humility. And thank you, God, for Luka, Angela and Father Bosko. Amen.

Luka and Angela take us downtown again. The city teems with new construction, but occasionally we pass bombed-out buildings and graffitied bridges, sprayed with patriotic symbols and slogans. I'm reminded of Belgrade's difficult past.

In the 1980s Slobodan Milosević began to voice the plight of the minority Serbs living in the Albanian-dominated region of Kosovo. Milosević's fight for his fellow Serbs in Kosovo is considered to have swept him into the presidency. Tensions burned between Albanians and Serbs for the next ten years. Kosovars voted overwhelmingly to become independent from Serbia; Milosević responded with a stiff "No." In 1999, NATO voiced its own opinion in seventy-eight days of air raids.

Initially, Luka and Angela explain, the bombing was targeted to hit defense, media and government buildings. But civilian streets, markets and bridges eventually became targets as well. NATO even bombed the city on Easter Day, the holiest of Serbian Orthodox holidays, fueling Milosević's rhetoric that he was waging a religious war against the forces of Islam (Albania's majority population) and its anti-Christian advocates in NATO.

I hadn't considered how it must have been to live in Belgrade when bombs were falling from the sky. People must have felt afraid and violated.

We exit our tram and sally through the revitalized downtown. Belgrade has a vibrant cultural scene with a famous ballet troupe, an expansive opera house and a growing film industry. But with such a harsh history, I'm most curious about Angela's work with the Center for Tolerance and Interreligious Relations in Serbia. Angela gladly tells me about her work. "We desire to raise awareness of different religious groups in Serbia and promote more interaction between them. This is quite new for Serbia. We're trying to bring about some legislation that would allow equal rights for all religious communities. We are drawing government officials as well as leaders of nonprofits and religious communities into that process."

"Do people see a need for religious cooperation?"

Angela's defined facial features grow more serious. "A lot do not see a need for tolerance or don't want to find out about others. But I think that is the legacy of the wars. There's been a lot of propaganda, false information or lack of information. For example, many people don't even know that Protestants exist in this country and have been here for three to four hundred years.

"During the war, although there was no fighting here, there was a lot of pressure on religious minorities. Many Croats, who were mostly Catholics, left the country. There continues to be pressure; each year there are fifty to eighty violent attacks motivated by religious intolerance. They range from attacking ministers to breaking windows of churches to hate mail and so on."

"What do you see as the biggest challenge at this point?" I ask.

Angela reiterates, "People not realizing the problem. They don't even see a need for tolerance or for people to express their differences."

It begins to sink in that most Serbs don't see the river of blood spilled in the last decade as something needing attention. I'm shocked and confused. "Angela," I ask, "Do people equate tolerance with Western ideals?"

Angela nods. "We have to be very wise about that. Some organizations have been coming in calling for human rights and tolerance, but bringing in their own societal values that have nothing to do with this culture. We want to pursue our work in a relevant way."

"Is there something you believe the West could learn from this process that Serbia is going through?"

Angela laughs in a diplomatic but telling way. "Lots! But I'm not going to go into that. One very important thing is that the West cannot just export its own models. It often exports applications as opposed to the principles that lie behind those applications. That's a problem. Take economics, for example. What is a free-market democracy? If you look at the basic principles, it doesn't necessarily look like American or western European economies. You have to look at the cultural and local values and then try to bring the principle into that economic sector. It's ultimately about respecting human life no matter what the circumstance. But it's a very complex issue."

I ask Angela how her faith factors into her work. She sees it as a very natural connection. "First of all it comes from principles that the Bible teaches, such as 'Love your neighbor as yourself.' To live that out in a postwar situation may sound radical. But it wouldn't look very radical in a normal situation. I think we should be doing much more of this."

I'm so encouraged by Angela's work with the Center. I know my personal struggles to live out the Golden Rule. How much harder it must be for nations facing down other nations, both with histories of ethnic cleansing and fears for survival. In Belgrade the Golden Rule feels far from a childhood mantra or Sunday school lesson. This work of peacemaking in the way of Jesus seems to call for a daily dedication to honoring each other's dignity and generously living out the law of love.

≽ ≼

After a loop around a museum and a hearty meal, Angela must go to work. Luka walks us through the art district and then to another church. The church is empty, but a kind-looking woman sits on a bench outside. With Luka as my voice, I introduce myself, tell her a little about my pilgrimage and ask her if she would describe God.

She had been staring at Luka up until this point but now she looks at me like I'm crazy. I reframe the question but once again she declines. Luka asks, "Do strangers actually answer your question?"

I shout back in my mind, *Strangers have shared their dreams with me. They've given me gifts and taken me around their city. And they've changed my view of God through their responses. Do strangers answer my question?* How can I expect Luka to know this? All he's seen is this one woman. So I calmly return Luka's question with my own, "Can we get some coffee?" The wind has awoken and the sky threatens to bawl again. Luka spots a tavern, but when we go to order our cappuccinos, Luka says we must leave. The picture proudly framed by the bar is that of Radovan Karadžić, president of the Bosnian Serbs during the early 1990s. Karadžić is still wanted by the Hague Tribunal for heinous war crimes, but he's been given safe haven by Serb nationalists.

I greatly respect Luka for walking out but I'm taken aback by my animosity toward the bar owner and the Serbs harboring this war criminal. We acquire our cups of caffeine at a coffee house devoid of nationalistic paraphernalia, then happen across a religious bookstore. Luka sees my interest and suggests we go inside. I purchase a long strand of brown prayer beads. As I finger the wooden beads, I look at the cross. *Jesus, I can't love people on my own. I can't.*

Luka has one final site to show us: St. Sava Orthodox Church. This church, the world's largest Orthodox church with over ten million congregants, is still under construction, so we hike through red dirt to locate an entrance. The glorious, mammoth structure seems fitting for the Serbian Orthodox Church, which traces its heritage back to Andrew, Jesus' disciple. But like the Serbian people, the Serbian Orthodox Church has had a complicated and difficult past. It established itself and spread beyond the borders of Serbia well before the Great Schism in 1054, when the Greeks and the Latins (the Roman Catholic Church) parted ways. This schism created a quandary, for the Serbian Orthodox Church contained both Latin and Greek speakers. In the early thirteenth century, St. Sava, whose bones are said to have been burned right here, wrote a letter to his friend Irenaeus.

> At first we were confused. The East thought that we were West while the West considered us to be the East. Some of us misunderstood our place in this clash of currents, so they cried that we belong to neither side, and others that we belong exclusively to one side or the other. But I tell you . . . we are doomed by fate to be the East in the West, and the West in the East, to acknowledge only heavenly Jerusalem beyond us and here on earth—no-one.

Through the centuries not only has the church struggled with its identity, it has gotten entangled with the Serbian state. Ultimately, the church has had to choose between Jesus' teaching to treat others as one would like to be treated and the state's not-so-golden rule.

In the clamor of bulldozers, Father Bosko's words whisper back to me, "When you see the tomb of Christ, pray for me, a sinner."

I'll pray for you, and me both.

10

TIRANA, ALBANIA

"American?" The JAT ticket agent, with her perfectly pressed skirt, inquires as she hands me back my passport. "You're going to Albania?"

The Serbian airline worker phrases her question in that way that conveys, "Albania? How did your travel agent make that mistake? Certainly you mean to be zipping off to Greece; there you can gaze at ancient acropolises and guys who live up to the reputation of Greek gods. Have you ever heard someone refer to a handsome gentleman as an Albanian god? Maybe you mean to be flying to Albany? Yes? Albany, New York? Or Aruba? I hear Aruba is quite lovely during this time of year."

"Yes," I reply. "This is our first time visiting Albania." The JAT ticket agent smirks.

I settle into a window seat. I'm a window-seat flyer. Rarely can I refuse an invitation to see ground level from 16,000 feet above. I've always gravitated to the big picture, but I wonder these days if some of my distance from the dirt comes from my desire to avoid the muck of life. I'm still slightly shaken by how passive-aggressive I can be. In all my intrigue with cities in conflict, I'm discovering that I fear traveling close to the ground of my own personal battles.

The pilot announces that we'll be taking off in five minutes. If our little ATR 72 plane does its very best we'll touch down in Tirana in one hour and ten minutes, 10:45 p.m. local time.

While we're terribly pressed for time on our pilgrimage, we had not planned to fly over any space of it. I wanted to plod along the roads like Helena and push across the seas like Felix. But when we looked at this leg of the journey, we confronted two realities. One, Albania has yet to connect itself with the rest of the Balkan soil via railroad. For a significant chunk of the twentieth century, Albania lived in isolation—perhaps more accurately, in utter denial that the rest of the world existed. Its dictator Enver Hoxha was paranoid about foreign invasion, which led to such extreme actions as banning the general populace from access to cars. Perhaps Mussolini's tour through Albania in order to invade Greece had a little to do with it.

At any rate, even after Hoxha's death in 1985, Albania still doesn't participate in the Balkan rail system. I was told, however, that we could rig together a transport plan of Serbian trains, multicountry buses and Albanian taxis to get to Tirana. We *could* do that, but then we'd encounter our second obstacle: Kosovo. I wanted to go through Kosovo, but my Peace Corps friend and my diplomat friend and my U.S. State Department recommended we not.

So here I sit, looking out on an opaque night as our little ATR 72 points its nose up in the air. Half an hour passes and we're cruising smoothly over Kosovo. I peer out and see only fog. I feel so far away from understanding this volatile region.

The little I know of Kosovar history reads like the journal of an abused woman poised for revenge. Powerful nations have come and swept her off her feet with promises of love or offers of sheer survival. Then, just when she thought she was safe, they've unleashed their rage.

The latest abusive lover was Milosevic. He changed the house rules by limiting Kosovo's independence and giving the minority Serbs the key positions of power. Bitterness set in and Kosovo fought back, in its own passive-aggressive way. The Kosovo Liberation Army launched guerrilla tactics against the Serbian police, starting a devastating domestic fight as Serbia brought in the big guns and the Albanian Kosovars responded with their sheer wills. Over ten thousand Albanians and three thousand Serbs are said to have died in the conflict. Beyond the killing, roughly a million ethnic Albanians were kicked out onto streets far from their homes, and an estimated twenty thousand Albanian women were raped by Serb police or paramilitary soldiers—an estimate that may be low, given that in a shame-based society such as Kosovo, women hesitate to report rapes due to fear of being ostracized.

While Kosovo's fighting ended with NATO's intervention in 1999, unrest broke out in 2004. A few minor events exploded into large-scale riots. Kosovar Albanians set fire to Serbian homes, Serbian Orthodox churches and UN facilities. Currently the situation is quiet, but no one considers the Albanians and the Serbs a functional and happily married couple.

Kosovo's troubles continue to affect its neighbors. Tens of thousands of refugees were forced to flee their homes and trek south into Albania. I'm curious what these Kosovars have found coming across the border. My impressions of Albania have been limited to three sources: (1) Kat, whom Eric and I lived with in Jerusalem and who now works with the Peace Corps in Albania, (2) Greg, whom Krista and I met while living in Brussels and who is a U.S. diplomat in Tirana, and (3) NPR, whose stories on Albania have been scarce these days.

Kat has sent me excellent first-person reports; among her stories is her encounter with a group of burley construction workers who spent their break not smoking or having a beer or even eating homemade baked goods. She found them dancing. When Kat emailed me about the dancing construction workers, I knew I must get myself to Albania as soon as I could.

Greg has dispatched more practical information: snippets on current political happenings, stats on religion and the most prized bit of info—the promise of airport transport and a place to stay.

The "fasten seatbelt" light comes on, so soon enough I'll be able to collect my own impressions. Our little ATR 72 makes it across the airstrip without even huffing and puffing. I follow the Albanians out the back of the plane, down the tail stand and into the airport. Within minutes of my backpack's first ride on an Albanian luggage carousel, Greg appears. I haven't seen him since he let a friend and me crash in his flat one night in Tel Aviv about ten years ago. I thank Greg for picking us up and prepare to launch into a game of Twenty Questions. Even though it's past eleven, I can't help myself. Greg had mentioned before we came that his diplomatic calendar would be packed, so this may be the only time I'll have to cull his insights.

Before I can ask my first question, however, I realize Greg has a driver. Greg explains almost apologetically, "The State Department prefers that I don't drive on my own, especially on this road. No need to fret, but occasionally there are bandits." While I suspect I should have more somber thoughts, my gut reaction is, *Wow! I've never seen a real live bandit. I wonder if we'll meet one.*

"What's crime like in Albania?" becomes Question One, and quickly moves into a discussion of Albanian economics and the 1990s pyramid scandal. "The free market was finally opening up in Albania, but people weren't financially savvy and there weren't proper controls in place," Greg explains. "Several companies formed in 1996 promising quick and large returns on investment. Within less than a year, two-thirds of the Albanian population and almost half of the country's GNP got caught up in pyramid schemes."

As Greg gives us context on Albanian economics, our driver grips the wheel. The streetlights are scant and the potholes are many. Krista and Eric calmly gaze out the window. As I soak in Greg's words, my eyes actively scan the area for bandits. Before I can ask Question Two, Greg offers to give us a night tour of Tirana. My remaining questions come from just staring out the window. "What's that maroon building adorned with gold?"

"The Parliament building," responds Greg.

"Why are the bridges lit with blue lights? What's a Ferris wheel doing on Main Street? Is this Albania's attempt at the *Champs-Élysées?* And what's that brick pyramid with all those satellites on top of it?" I finally give Greg white space to answer. "Oh, that's Enver Hoxha's mausoleum, or at least intended mausoleum. He didn't make a lot of friends as dictator so when he died people threw his body in a nondescript place rather than immortalizing him as he envisioned."

Greg, the consummate diplomat, obliges my curiosity about Hoxha. "When Tito was rising to power in the 1940s, Hoxha was also beginning his career as a Communist dictator. Hoxha eventually broke ties with Russia when he perceived they no longer lived up to Stalin's ideals. He then aligned himself with China; however that relationship ended in the late 1970s when China began engaging the United States. Hoxha was horrified that any self-respecting Communist would meet with Nixon. This left Albania as one of the most isolated countries in the world."

"So, what is Hoxha's mausoleum used for now?"

"A concert hall," Greg says nonchalantly. Of course. Within minutes we're at a guardhouse and then entering a gated community that suddenly feels like Middle America. This neighborhood of expatriates is referred to as the Ridge. As we pull into a driveway, Greg hands our driver a fistful of Albanian lek. I want to offer to pay, but I'm lek-less. I'm also feeling low on funds, and we have six more countries to move through. That feeling of awkward gratitude emerges again. I barely know Greg, yet he's lost sleep and money over our visit.

We drag our packs into a spacious living room. Greg takes us through the formal dining room and into a large kitchen, where he pours us each a glass of wine. As we situate ourselves on the living room couch, I can't believe how much this house reminds me of the United States.

Maybe I've used up my twenty questions, but I've gotten my second wind and Greg still has a pulse and vocal chords to answer. He's yet to shut me and my questions down, so I continue. "What's Albania's relationship with religion?"

"From 1967 to 1991, Albania was the only official atheist state in the world. Hoxha declared religion illegal. Practice of any religion—Christian, Islam or otherwise—was punishable by imprisonment, hard labor in work camps and in some cases death. Ironically, despite the anti-Western, antireligious propaganda fed to them for so many years, Albanians have no problem accepting people of all faiths. They also managed to escape the mindless intolerance of Yugoslavia's ethnoreligious wars raging around them in the 1990s.

"There's a saying here, 'Albania is 70 percent Muslim, 20 percent Orthodox Christian, 10 percent Roman Catholic and 100 percent atheist.'"

I wonder how I'll get a sacred encounter if that's the case. But I'm so curious how people describe God when they've grown up in a world of isolation and a culture of atheism. I wonder what my own description of God would be if that was my personal story line. I voice my concerns that we may not get any interviews, and Greg says he'll try to connect us with people at his own church.

With that I pose a question about Albanian blood feuds and begin my serial yawning phase. Greg's words drift out slower and slower; Krista and Eric are basically snoring in their seats. I finally concede; our game of Twenty Questions has become a race for our beds.

When I convince myself I can't sleep any longer, I move to the shower. I stand under the flow of hot streams of clear water. I look at my feet standing on pristine ceramic. I whisper to the heavens, *Thank you. Thank you.* After slipping on clothes I stumble downstairs in my surreal state of contentment. I consume corn flakes and grab the directions Greg left for me to meet Kat at a nearby coffee shop.

Holding my little paper in front of me, I step out the door and face Albania in the light. I'm surrounded by two-story homes, each with a landscaped yard, a paved driveway and a garage. I head down the hill through this Middle-America suburban neighborhood, not fully persuaded I'm in Albania. Grassy mountains frame the background; tall green trees shade the homes, and blue and white signs show a stick-figure dad playing ball with a stick-figure boy, and a car and house pictured alongside them.

Pleasantville abruptly ends when I exit the guardhouse. The sun that had lit the mountains and shone its favor on the trees becomes usurped by ornery clouds that sneeze rain at me. My feet that had meandered past manicured lawns now patter past trash-filled ditches. I no longer see the blue and white signs of stick-figure families playing, but rather large billboards of grinning politicians. After getting sufficiently soaked, I locate the Flamingo Café.

I see Kat and spontaneously laugh. Laughter always seems to be Kat's sidekick. Over cappuccino Kat orients me to vital facts about Albanian culture, facts a little different from what Greg shared. Albanians, Kat suggests, are known for their candor, perhaps thanks to years of living under a dictator who had basically given the finger to the rest of world. For instance, Albanians feel compelled to notify people if they think they're fat. Kat has a stout friend in the Peace Corps who has experienced this firsthand; a bus stopped in front of him and opened its front doors just so someone could tell him not to eat so much pasta. Even the mayor of his town told him he was fat.

All this talk of fatness has made me both paranoid and hungry. Krista and Eric meet up with us, and we walk to a restaurant downtown. I try to suck in my stomach each time I pass someone. I try.

The sun has conquered the rain gods for now. I finally get to see *true* Tirana drenched in light. The city blares color. Whole buildings are covered with yellow or blue, but it seems that every other apartment building has geometric shapes painted with a rainbow of shades. "Kat, the city seems so different from the rest of the Balkans. Why does Tirana look like Fruit Stripes Gum?" Kat's features get very intense, something that happens whenever she's ready to explain something that makes her amused. "The mayor essentially ran on the platform 'What Tirana needs most is bright paint.'"

"Well," I respond with shock and awe, "there's a politician who actually keeps his word."

Tirana has become famous for its color; all this bright paint has brought a new spirit to the city. But while people don't have to look at the old gray Communist-style buildings, they still have to contend with the old pipes and dodgy electrical outlets. As we pass little grocery stores, paper supply shops and a butcher, Kat describes Albania as a study in contradictions. "People tend to focus on the appearance of things, rather than reality. Take, for instance, computers propped up in people's offices. The computers don't work—everyone knows they don't work—but at least this office has computers. What is perceived as real *is* real."

We pass one pizza or pasta place after another until we arrive at Kat's choice, Elka Pizzeria. Apparently Albanians have an affinity for Italian culture. Maybe it's a nod to Mussolini's visit. As we eat I notice there aren't many women around. "Men are primarily the ones who socialize," Kat explains. "Women will sometimes be out with other women, but rarely will you see a woman and man out together."

"Why is that?" I ask.

"Some of it has to do with Albanian dating practices. Albanians don't really date; they go straight to engagement. If a guy asks a woman to go for coffee, it means he's seriously interested. If they go out twice, they're looking at marriage. It's similar to the Middle East. If a girl is seen out with a guy, she can be perceived as loose. And when a girl's behavior is called into question, the entire family's reputation can be ruined."

I'm confused. "I've seen several women out shopping who look like they're off to a disco."

"Oh yah," Kat responds. "In this new democracy people are still sorting out images of beauty and what outward appearance represents. They can dress provocatively but still have conservative ideals. Mothers let their daughters walk around scantily dressed as an advertisement to marriage. But women wouldn't dare be seen out with a man unless they were engaged. If people know you have a boyfriend, it can ruin your reputation. So there is lots of lying."

My thoughts take flight back to the States and our own contradictions—like how we are carefree with spending money during the day, but then our debt haunts our sleep. It seems like so much of capitalism, well, capitalizes on our desires to impress others.

"Who's got lek?" Kat's question and the arrival of our bill jar me from my musings.

"Here. I've got plenty of lek," I say nonchalantly.

As Kat's Tirana tour continues I see at least three fake McDonald's restaurants. One is spelled *MacDonald's,* but the other two don't even bother to change the spelling. We pass a guy sitting on a stool; beside him are a bathroom scale and a jar for coins.

"There's an entrepreneur at work," Kat tells us. "People have begun all sorts of little businesses as they try to sort out a free-market economy."

"So people here will pay to stand on a bathroom scale in public?" I ask.

"Yep."

"Even when a bus driver or ordinary Albanian on the street will tell them whether they're fat or not *for free?*"

"Yep."

We visit Enver Hoxha's pyramid again. I see a sign advertising a jazz concert tonight. A concert in a real live dictator's would-be mausoleum; that should be almost as exciting as dancing construction workers.

We finally turn to our search for divine encounters as we approach a Catholic church. The façade is modern and enormous, but I step inside and find it vacant. I resort to calling out, "Anyone here?" Not a soul can be found.

Kat then takes us to the mosque. A crowd of men congregate in front. Kat mentions that it may not be apropos for me as a woman to go into the mosque. However, I walk slowly up the stairs and ask cheerfully if anyone speaks English. I get only aghast looks. I sprint down the stairs to Kat, Krista and Eric, who stand on the sidewalk keenly aware of their proper place in Albanian society.

Kat gives some context to Albanians' approach to religion. "They're survivalists. Since so many powers have tromped through, they have tended to go with whatever religion is tied to the power structure. Ultimately nationalism trumps religion.

"Christianity was the dominant religion for centuries, and then Islam came through here. The first people to convert were the rich landowners, mainly because of tax benefits. Then more and more people converted to Islam. There were pockets that didn't convert, but 'turning Turk' remains an expression in the culture for people who sell out. An Albanian proverb captures the mentality: 'The Albanian's faith is like a gold bar.' It can be exchanged."

It begins to drizzle again and we lose any momentum to locate an Orthodox church. Anyway, Kat needs to get back to her Peace Corps base in Elbasan. As we stroll to the bus station, we pass a mural spray-painted on a wall. In red paint, outlined in black, an Orthodox basilica flows into a mosque, which merges into a cathedral. The words *paqe* (peace), *tolerance* and *mirekuptim* (good understanding) are painted in block letters below it. Despite Albania's struggles, they appear to have staved off the religious disputes that have plagued other parts of the Balkans. Beside the mural is another black and white one. "*Te gjithe te ndryshem. Te gjithe te barabarte.*" It roughly translates, "Change together. Equal together." As the country moves toward democracy, Kat tells us, it desires more consensual leadership.

At the bus station we wave goodbye to Kat. We have one more opportunity for divine encounters; Greg was able to contact the pastor of his Protestant church. Apparently there are one or two people we can chat with there.

We turn off a main road to a street lined with leafy green trees and large apartment buildings painted as colorful as a New England fall. Pastor Barry Ogden, an American in his late thirties, greets us at the gate of the church. As we walk through the collection of unpretentious buildings, Barry tells us how he came here to help start a church in the early 1990s. He ventured here amid the missionary rush into Albania, when the recently collapsed Soviet Union opened up to religion. Barry doesn't linger on his story, however. "I've lined up a few people for you to interview. They are here waiting for you."

Barry guides me to a windowless room upstairs with a couch and a couple of chairs. After an interview drought today, three people back to back feels like a flood. The first person is a twenty-something woman named Valbona. Her dramatic brown eyes, arched eyebrows and dark, long hair give her the look of a Greek goddess.

"I haven't been to church in a month. When I don't go to church I just go down. So God has felt far away. I start to think God is not providing for me, but I know God is my Father. Whenever I go to church and talk with people I get encouraged."

In a startling American accent Valbona continues, "This morning I was thinking God is so great. Because I was telling God I don't want it to rain because I hate umbrellas. I don't like them. And it didn't rain. God does a lot of small miracles for me and I sometimes feel too much spoiled. Now I need to know him deeper. I just need self-discipline to spend time with him."

"How did you come to know Jesus?" I ask.

Valbona makes herself comfortable in the couch and launches in. "When I was a child I went to Sunday school in the Orthodox church and heard about God. Then I went far away from him, but in high school I came back. At that time I loved the Backstreet Boys. And they got a Grammy Award. When Brian—who is my favorite—said, 'We first of all thank God,' I was like 'Wow!' God. That must be something. And I started making hearts and writing JC for Jesus Christ. And my friends would tease me, 'Who is JC?'

"When I finished high school I wanted to enter university. But university here is such a big deal. There's a lot of family pressure. If you don't go to university your life is over. So I just wanted it. Every night I'd pray to Jesus. I had this idea I couldn't talk with God the Father. So I'd tell Jesus, 'Please let me go to university. And if you do this favor for me, I will serve you.' I prayed that without knowing anything of the gospel. I prayed for three months. Then the miracle happened. God did great, great things. So, when I came to Tirana to go to school I decided to go to the Orthodox church to express my thanks to him.

"Then I had this idea that I had to read the Bible. I thought it would be interesting to read. Soon after that someone from this college group, Campus Crusade, asked if I wanted any religious or school materials. I chose a Bible. I got involved with that group and here I am five years later."

"How would you have described God five years ago?"

"Some external force," responds Valbona. "Something beyond my comprehension. That was the Father. But Jesus, I saw him as a friend, making hearts and stuff. Jesus came himself to me. There wasn't a certain time, but faith just came bit by bit."

"What's difficult about your faith right now?" I ask.

"I don't have a lot of faith when persecution comes. At first I didn't tell my mom about the importance of my faith. She knew I went to church with religious people. Now she knows it's serious but I don't give up. I have a lot of persecution," Valbona pauses, "but I don't mind. It's OK, because I know it's persecution for the name of Jesus."

"What is your hope for others in Albania?"

"Wow!" Valbona exclaims, as she did when she spoke of the Backstreet Boys thanking God. "I hope we Christians can move the nation. In the southwest, in my town, people are becoming too modern. It's about getting things for yourself. They believe there's no God, or who cares about God? You just get things for yourself. Then they follow all these superstitious practices mixed with the Orthodox religion."

I imagine Valbona and I could chat for hours, but I remember two others are waiting. "Thank you, Valbona. It seems like God has a distinct call on your life." A gentleman and woman enter as Valbona leaves.

I share with them a little about our pilgrimage and how I'm asking people along this ancient path to describe God. Beta, a salty-haired sixty-something, tells me about the *Via Egnatia*. "This road originates in Rome and goes to Brindisi, Italy, and through Elbasan, Albania, and on to Jerusalem. It was used by the Roman Army to occupy the Balkans. It has two directions: one leads to Constantinople and the second to Jerusalem. It's very important."

As Beta tells me this, I'm freaking out. How did I miss this? I did research. Really. I looked for maps. I read about Helena's travels, but a conclusive map of her journey doesn't exist. So, we've had to make up some of the route. Albania seemed like an appropriate place to venture, since perhaps Paul and Timothy, Paul's protégé, ventured through here, as did Titus, recipient of one of Paul's New Testament letters. Missionaries came to Albania in the first century to preach the gospel; the area was Christianized by 80 c.e. But our tour of Albania was also inspired by the fact that Kat and Greg were here, and supposedly so were dancing construction workers. It takes a random stranger in Albania to tell us we're on the right track. In the midst of my ignorance being exposed, I voice a quick prayer of thanks.

"Beta, how do you describe God?"

"It's a very good question. Love, joy, peace, hope and salvation."

I turn to address Anila, who must be around my age. Religion has only been legal in Albania since she's been an adult. She looks like a model, with tall, thin, distinct features.

"God is everything for me," she beams. "Everything good, not the bad emotions."

"How did you see God before you came to know him?"

"I knew for sure that God existed, but he was in heaven and was far from where I was."

"How do you know God differently now?"

"He is with me twenty-four hours a day. In everything I do, he is with me. He is no longer far away."

"Is there something you would like your friends who don't know God to understand about your faith?"

"God is a gift—not only for me but for all people. There's enough to be shared."

Since Valbona had experienced persecution from her extended family, I ask them, "Have you experienced persecution from others?" Anila responds. "I come from a Muslim background. There have been cases I've faced judgment, especially with one person in our family. But I live far from home, so they don't have the chance to see how often I go to church and how often I share and speak about God."

I look at Beta. "Same. Same," he responds.

I'm curious how they both came to know Jesus. "It's a long story," Anila begins. "God used many people to tell me about him. It's been those people's deeds and actions that showed me God. There was a period of time when I faced Muslims, Jehovah's Witnesses and Christians. The actions of the Christians are what drew me to know more about God."

A cell phone rings. It's not mine, but it does serve as an ending bell. "Thanks. This has been a rich gift. My picture of God has gotten larger through talking with you."

I thank Barry for arranging the interviews. The midweek service is just about to begin, so Krista, Eric and I scoot off. Krista returns to the house for some rest, but Eric and I cannot resist the lure of a jazz concert in Enver Hoxha's ex-mausoleum.

Within three notes, I realize that tonight's concert won't be an ode to Dave Brubeck but more like a Balkan tribute to John Tesh. I know people who find the slow-motion-stroll-through-the-woods-with-whistling-birds-and-joyful-crickets genre of music quite winsome. But I can't take it. So

I try to reflect on today's interviews. I would have never guessed that the Backstreet Boys' Grammy appearance would be someone's catalyst to faith, but there seems to be so many unexpected ways God provokes people to get to know him.

I'm struck by Anila's story of faith as well. After observing friends from different faith backgrounds she was drawn to Christianity. But it sounds like she was on a quest, a quest to discover God. If I grew up in atheism, I wonder if I would search for God. Or, being born into a religious family, would I willingly leave the comforts of what I knew and even risk my family's approval to search for truth? If I take our pilgrimage seriously, I guess that is what I'm doing: risking my own description of God for a larger one, possibly even a different one.

Ba-ler-ing! Ba-ler-ing! The alarm clock's eruptions feel extra harsh today as I lay in the best bed so far on the journey. Greg has already left for work, so I can't tell him thanks or goodbye. Krista announces some good news. "Greg offered to post anything we'd like to get rid of at this stage of the journey."

We do a collective "Woohoo!" "Let's get rid of all our warm clothes," I suggest. "It's bound to be steamy as we head toward the Middle East." Krista and I pillage our bags, pulling out anything remotely warm. Eric, however, is content with his belongings. Perhaps he's not willing to let go of warm clothing after the bus headrest cover incident.

With lighter bags we're off to see Kat in Elbasan. As I gaze through my little bus window I see cement domes and spears appear to sprout from the ground. I grab Krista's attention to make sure my mind isn't playing tricks on me. "Yah, those look like spears stuck in the dirt," Krista confirms. A remake of "Electric Avenue" plays on the bus's radio. I don't ask Krista if I'm really hearing that. A stray cow crosses the road. A small stand selling cherries is situated on a harsh curve. Ah, Albania.

The road gets so curvy and hilly I can no longer keep my eyes open. We finally level out and I'm told we are in Elbasan. Kat greets us at the station and verbalizes my favorite question: "Do you want to get something to eat?"

We inhale pitas, and I ask Kat about the bunkers and spears. "Hoxha had thousands of bunkers built. He said the West was planning to invade Albania. The spears were placed throughout the country to impale Western soldiers if they parachuted from planes. Albanians have an interesting relationship with the West. They're obsessed with comparing Albania to America. They constantly ask which is better. They love America, but were once afraid of U.S. plans to invade their country. They were convinced that Americans thought about Albanians as much as they fixated—and still fixate—on the West."

Well, enough about Albania. We finish our pitas while catching Kat up on the latest summer blockbusters playing in the States.

Before we leave for Macedonia, Kat suggests that I interview someone back at the Peace Corps. Kat's supervisor, Diana, is a middle-aged Albanian woman; she serves as the community development manager. With her dark hair and instant smile, Diana reminds me of my mom, who shares the same name. I ask her to describe God.

"From my family background I am Muslim. But I started to learn about the Bible and the Holy Qur'an. I was reading both, and I kept asking myself, *How do I feel?* I did this without influence from my family or others around me. I wanted to make a personal decision. I began asking which god makes me feel better. When is my soul most comfortable? For me, God is the inside world. It's love, a love you carry inside you."

Albanians seem to have expended such effort and risked persecution to discover God. I ask Diana, "You went through a significant process of exploring both Islam and Christianity. Have you decided on one?"

"I've decided on Islam," replies Diana. Wow. I wasn't expecting that. I ask if she knows others who have explored religions the way she did.

"Everyone should have one mighty power to believe in. The Albanian community is different from other European countries. For fifty years, during socialism, we weren't allowed to practice any religion, but now we've started to analyze again. Socially we are more strict, but people are accustomed to deciding religion for themselves. A lot of religious groups are coming and trying to make young people choose. Islamic groups are pushing the people to decide a certain belief." Diana takes us both back to my first question. "I go to the mosque very, very rarely. Often I ask myself what I am. But I believe in God. I can't say that the beauty of a butterfly or the colorful flowers just happened. It's the creation of the Mighty Power. I believe in God, but not a specific god."

I thank Diana for her time. "We need hours and hours to talk," she says as we part. I agree. Diana seems like such a thoughtful soul; it would be wonderful to talk with her more. Admittedly, though, Diana's story leaves me confused. When Anila said she looked at Islam, Christianity and Jehovah's Witnesses and decided on Christianity, I thought, *of course*. Diana has obviously put thought and energy into her spiritual search and has felt comfort with Islam. What's going on?

If I'm honest, I expect an authentic search for truth to end with Jesus. I'm expecting it for my own pilgrimage. But what will my God look like once I reach Jerusalem?

Kat must get back to work, so she walks us to a busy intersection. "This is where you can get a *Furgon*—a transport van, like the ones we'd take in Israel. Someone from the Peace Corps told me it will take you to Macedonia." Within minutes a beat-up van comes to a stop, so we climb on in, wave goodbye to Kat and hope for the best.

In Jerusalem we'd take a van with about ten other people to the airport in Tel Aviv. It's a lot cheaper than a taxi. This *Furgon* should be fairly straightforward. We smile at our driver and the two other people in the van, and we're off. As we pull out it finally sinks in that all my thorough plans for this pilgrimage terminate when we reach the Macedonia border. Our contacts there have fallen through. All we have is Kat's suggestion; fortunately it's right on course with the *Via Egnatia* and Helena's sojourn. I hold a scrap of paper with Kat's itinerary for us: "Cross border. Go to Ohrid."

"Oh, that's too bad." Krista grabs her camera, but not fast enough. "I just missed a great shot of a fruit stand." Five minutes later, Krista and the rest of us are staring at the same fruit stand. Two guys with blue work clothes scramble in and we're off again. Five minutes later, there's the fruit stand. We circle for a good forty minutes until each seat in the van is occupied and paid for.

I have a window seat, so my nose and eyes are pressed against glass rather than the flesh of strangers. "Krista, there's a donkey . . . and an old woman shepherd . . . and there's another donkey standing over a little donkey lying on the ground." I shout out the sights to Krista like a radio announcer calling a baseball game. She can't hear me above Luther Vandross wailing through the van's radio.

Our *Furgon* stops and lets off the two guys wearing the blue work clothes. Soon it picks up another person on the side of road. Within an hour there's almost a full change of passengers. Then it hits me. Does this *Furgon* really go to Macedonia? How will we know? No one else has luggage, and no one else speaks English.

If we do get to a Macedonian border tonight, how will we get to Ohrid? Where will we stay? "How much cash do you guys have?" Krista and Eric rummage to find their money. "Lek? Dollars? Euros?" Krista replies. "Any kind of currency? And do you remember if Kat told us how much our *Furgon* should cost?" In the midst of our collective panic, a voice floats to us from the back of the *Furgon*. It's coming from a teenage boy we picked up from the side of the road minutes ago.

"American?" asks the teenager wearing a wrinkled white T-shirt.

"Yes."

"Cool. I can help you."

11

OHRID, THE REPUBLIC
OF MACEDONIA

Our Albanian teen angel instructs us where to get off, and fortunately we have enough lek left to pay for the *Furgon*. We now stand in line to cross the Macedonian border. I hold my little sheet of directions, though I have the entire contents memorized: "Cross border. Go to Ohrid."

Backpack laden, we slouch in between a car and a bus. Though we must look ridiculous, the passport policeman doesn't speak enough English to ask us what we are doing or to blatantly mock us in our mother tongue. He simply grins and marks our passports with a bright blue entry stamp. Yes! Now there's a passport stamp that shouts, "Welcome! We're thrilled you're here! You've traveled a far way, so never mind the fact that you are straggling into our nation looking like refugees and smelling like vagabonds!"

I mark "Cross border" off our list. Next, "Go to Ohrid." How? Before I can get anxious a husky gentleman approaches us. In a gruff voice he inquires, "You have Albanian lek?" "Yes!" we exclaim. We hand him a wad of bills, and he gives us one crisp twenty Euro. What a delightful man. He may be our first Macedonian guardian angel. Or perhaps he's a full-fledged Balkan mafia guy? Before I can ponder that question we're accosted by another man. This gentleman is lanky and his words come out like rapid gunfire. "Doyouwantaride?"

"Yes!" we bellow. "Will you take us to Ohrid?" I plead, losing all negotiating power.

"Yes.Of course.Ohridisabeautifulplace."

Within minutes from obtaining our bright blue passport stamp, we are liberated from our lek and are heading to a town verifiably on the *Via Egnatia*. The sun's magic wand douses the Macedonian hills with a golden glow. The air even smells purified by the yellow light. Now that it looks like we will successfully move through our itinerary, I celebrate by falling asleep.

"We'rehere," our taxi driver declares. "What? What?" I mumble from that realm of quasi-consciousness.

"Whereareyoustaying?" His question is logical, but I'm not prepared for such sanity. Our taxi driver is gregarious, and he doesn't even condemn my lack of preparation. He drives us around until we stumble on rooms for rent located in a lovely elderly couple's house. Upon introduction we are invited to call them Mama and Papa. Once we fling our bags down we, along with our taxi driver, are shuffled out to their back garden. They have a bamboo-walled patio with a long table and a small outdoor kitchen. Papa motions for us to sit as Mama places shot glasses in front of us. Then Papa begins pouring. "*Rakija*"he says. "Very good!"

Our taxi driver leads us in "Cheers!" and it's official: we have housing in Ohrid. Krista, Eric and I raise our glasses to our lips and go for it. The clear libation smells like a vineyard on fire, alluring and assaulting my five million olfactory cells. I've never swallowed a torch, but I wonder if fire-eaters may compare drinking this grape brandy to their vocation.

I can count on two hands how many times I've had hard liquor, and from the look on Krista's face, I imagine she can count on two fingers. Our taxi driver, however, obviously takes pride in his national drink. Though a common language doesn't exist at the table, our conversation brims with laughter, natural stretches of silence and shared appreciation for the lovely serendipity of the moment. Papa gets up to prepare our second round of libations: espresso. One of my favorite fragrances begins to revive my scorched senses. The aroma travels through me like a healing salve.

As we sip our potent espresso from dainty demitasse cups, my focus drifts. I stare at Papa and Mama's backyard. There may be nothing that captures the essence of a nation's people so well as their yards, and Papa and Mama's yard is quintessential Macedonian landscaping. Weathered tools hang aloof on one side of the fence; a jungle of vines, flowers and plants potted in cartons socialize on the other side. A garden and a clothesline join the party.

Our taxi driver must get home; we say farewell like family. Papa then offers to introduce us to his city. He takes us to the ancient theater that likely hosted the culturally astute in the days of Alexander the Great. The city has a lively past. In 353 B.C.E. King Philip II, one of Macedonia's great military leaders and Alexander's father, came tromping into Ohrid. When the Romans rumbled through a couple of hundred years later, the theater went from putting on melodramatic plays by Euripides to presenting live-action gladiator fights. Men here wore ladies' wigs in one lifetime and were chased by lions in the next. What great lengths humanity goes to for the sake of amusement.

I wonder if Helena visited this theater as she passed through Ohrid? I don't know what kind of entertainment the town had to offer her, since her son had just banned all forms of violence for show. As I survey the stone stage a breeze splashes me with the scent of fresh water, which brings me back to the present. Lake Ohrid spreads its shimmer across the backdrop of the theater like a permanent prop. The lake is considered to be one of the world's oldest, yet it smells as young as the day. I breathe deeply.

Papa insists that we don't linger too long; he wants to show us more before the sun vanishes. Within minutes we face an encore of ruins and startling beauty. "This was where St. Clement of Ohrid had his monastery," Papa announces.

Ohrid's favorite son lived in the ninth century and is credited with creating the Cyrillic alphabet. St. Clement had a great passion for the Slavs to become literate and know God. This compelled him to found one of the first Slavic universities; over 3,500 students were educated here and then set out as far as Russia to teach Slavic literacy.

Marble columns mark the Roman basilica where St. Clement of Ohrid was first buried. Apparently his remains were removed when the basilica was converted into a mosque by the Ottomans. The mosque didn't stay for long, however, and recently—in 2002—the church was rebuilt. The expansive new basilica rises up past the ruins; its terracotta roof alongside its bell tower stretches to the sun. Lake Ohrid and forested mountains guard it from behind.

We rattle the doors, but the church has closed for the day. Tomorrow we will return. I can't wait to find out how people describe God in this city that has been graced with splendor and scholarly saints.

With just a splash of sunshine left, Papa gives us directions to downtown. The lake's edge serves as a magnet for fine restaurants, pita stands, pizza kiosks and meandering people, either starving or stuffed. We haven't eaten since Albania, but Krista's not in an eating mood. She ducks into an Internet café as Eric and I decide to splurge on Ohrid's famous trout. This ancient lake boasts of an exquisite trout that can't be found anywhere else in the world.

We enter a barely lit restaurant shared by only two other patrons. My savvy intuition tells me these are not the signs of an award-winning restaurant, but the maitre d' and waitresses seem so happy to see us that we can't leave. Eric dives into his trout platter and I sip my trout soup, and we discuss the magic of our day. We were in Albania only hours ago, not knowing what awaited us across the border. Now our conversation gently floats across candlelight in an enchanting town.

It's been so long since I've been on a date. And this is not a date. It just has the perfect props of one: gorgeous city caressed by water, set in the midst of a tale of adventure, recounted over candlelight. I wonder if props matter. Do inhabitants of Barbados, Paris or San Diego fall in love faster or more often than, let's say, people in Cleveland, Ohio?

As we saunter out of the restaurant we're greeted by a brisk lake breeze. The fragrance keeps the memory of our meal alive, but the air sends my skin into shivers. "Wow, it's chilly!" We collect Krista, and I lock arms with her on the way home. I'm a huge proponent of sharing body heat, and I guess tonight I want to know I don't walk alone.

≽ ≼

There are benefits of sleeping in dark, cavernous places, one of which is that you are oblivious to the sun's alarm clock. When I stammer outside the world is wide awake and—oh my gosh!—it's incredibly cold. Papa had mentioned last night that a bizarre cold front was coming through. And with our brilliant timing, Krista and I have no warm clothes left in our packs.

Espresso perfumes the air. Mama and Papa lounge at the patio table. My entire senses ready themselves for a potent cup of espresso, but Mama sets out the shot glasses again. So, we toast the morning with homemade *rakija,* and only after we diligently scour clean our esophaguses with brandy are we allowed to drink espresso.

Papa asks if we would like breakfast. "Sure. Something simple sounds . . ." Before I can complete my sentence Papa hops on his bike and Mama morphs into lightning-speed motion. Sooner than our espresso can take full effect, our hosts signal for us to eat. The feast begins.

"Would you pass the sausage?" Eric asks. Though I'm not a big fan of the pig, this sausage wins me over with its smoky aroma. "Is that plum jam?" Krista inquires. Papa eyes Mama and declares, "Homemade." The bread is homemade too, and it's the kind with the tough crust and the soft innards that casts a spell on anyone who partakes. Even after a whole loaf, you're convinced you need just one more piece. Papa serves eggs from the skillet, and Mama offers us her special chili sauce and green peppers. We eat, and eat, and eat.

When our stomachs bulge like our backpacks, we waddle to the water's edge downtown and topple onto a bench. In our gluttonous stupor we pray. It's been days and countries ago since we prayed together.

Father, Son and Spirit, thank you for the generosity of Papa and Mama. Please show them your kindness. And thanks so much for leading us here. What a gorgeous country. Thank you for Macedonia's beauty and rich history. Yesterday could have been a disaster, but you orchestrated amazing surprises. What a gift, God. You've protected and provided for us with such extravagance—even when we've failed to ask for your guidance. Please give us divine encounters today; lead us to the people you'd like us to talk with. Thank you. Amen.

A combination of the lovely breeze, a deep sense of contentment and a bad case of food-induced coma convinces me to loiter a little longer. I make conversation so Krista and Eric won't feel compelled to get up. "It seems the country has had a fairly smooth segue into democracy. I've heard Macedonia's been a model nation in the region."

"Yah," Eric offers. "It's remarkable how it staved off war when so much of the Balkans was engulfed." Then he and Krista get up. So much for that plan.

We stroll along the boardwalk beside multicolored fishing boats bobbing in the wind. They look like children's toys that have drifted to one side of a vast tub of aqua-green water. Grassy hills serve as the rim, ensuring that the water doesn't spill over.

Within six or so strides an older man taps Krista's shoulder. "Hello, Miss, would you and your friends like a boat ride?"

"Not right now," Krista quickly responds.

The gentleman bursts out with, "I have a God-given talent to guess people's ages and names!"

In midstride, we all turn around. We're not ready for a boat ride, but we've got time for a man who starts conversations by guessing your name and age—especially when there's no admission charge or stuffed animals involved. We forgo his guessing game and introduce ourselves.

Christopher wears a blue and gold captain's hat, the kind you might buy your son at Sea World. An oversized black bomber jacket hangs on his tiny frame, and his blue shirt is buttoned to the top. Blue pants gather at his waist with a thin leather belt. Everything on him is weathered and two sizes too large. Even his face looks threadbare, but he has the nervous energy of a teenage boy. We tell him about our pilgrimage and how we've asked strangers to describe God along the way.

With energetic pitch and broken English Christopher says, "I know I have the spirit of the God in me. God gives me visions and power to know about other people—"

A man walks by and Christopher—in midsentence—calls out to him. "The United States. From Texas." Christopher points to Eric and carries on. "George Bush state." Then Christopher turns to us. "I am kidding, just making relaxing." I try to reel in the conversation. "So, Christopher, you were saying . . ."

"I see many things. Before my mom died, I was already crying. I somehow knew she was going to die soon. It was like seeing the final curtain go down." Christopher mimes a curtain going down. "Believe me, I knew.

"I already gave my heart to the Jesus. Do you know how I did it? I went to the God-world." Christopher points his hand to the heavens. "It was a special feeling. I never felt like that until I gave my heart. I felt the Spirit. I feel that I have the Holy Spirit in me from the God and all the power of our Creator."

"When did you feel God's Spirit?" I ask.

"It was fifteen or twenty years ago. It was American Christian missionaries. Some Americans your age."

"How did that happen?"

"We met each other like I met you. Actually, it was right here. It's a very strange thing. Believe me—this is impossible—all the people who are missionaries, who spread God's Word, whenever they come to this city, I am the first person they meet. I'm not speaking lies. They tell me, 'Christopher, you are the first person we've met. See, we go close to each other. We are like magnetism.'"

Christopher starts walking in front of us to demonstrate. "They didn't go to thousands of people—excuse me, I'm going through thousands of people. I'm going left, right, left, right." He weaves as if he is in a crowd. "But I don't feel the real people who belong to each other. And then I come to the people I belong with, people who have the Spirit of the God, the followers of the God, we always meet each other. Do you understand me?"

We all nod, but he starts walking back and forth in front of us again like we are the stage. "When you go through a thousand people—left, right, left, right—and then you go to the right people."

"This morning we prayed that we would meet the people God would want us to meet," I relay, grateful that our paths have crossed with this curious character.

"Yes, but many things are upside down. This is a material world. It is not spiritual. We don't follow the steps of Jesus, of the God. We go in the opposite way. But God is coming soon. I am feeling something. Again we can survive the fleeting? The footing?"

Eric interprets. "The flood?"

"Yes, the flood. Water will come like the days of Uncle Nohel."

"Noah?" Eric clarifies.

"Uncle, Noah, yes." Christopher continues, "Do you know what will happen? Everything will turn around, like the days of Uncle Noah. Then we can go the real way of the God."

I'm slightly confused by Christopher's apocalyptic prophecies, but I can't get my words out fast enough to ask for explanation.

"But again and again we are persistent. We do stupid things. I don't think we deserve to live on God's earth, on his homeland. This is a kind of paradise. Which planet can you find such a beautiful, nice world? Not on Neptune or Pluto, or Mars. Not a paradise there. The God chose for us to live in real paradise. Other planets, there's no paradise.

"But for people here the number one thing is money. Money talks. It's money not justice. If you are a believer, a Christian, you don't have money. You are nobody. If you work with prostitution, drugs and crime—it's a crime-world I call it. Not just here, but all over, even U.S., even Australia, even Europe."

I finally shove in my words. "What is your hope for the city?"

"My hope is that there will come more bad times. It will be worse; the life will be more difficult, more complicated. There will be more killing, more wars, and the world will get more hungry and thirsty."

I think, *Oh my gosh. How disconcerting!* But I don't get to say it because a guy walks up. He's been sitting near us and decides it's time to join our conversation. Christopher says, "Americans."

"Nice people. I could overhear," declares the guy.

"These people are more patient." Christopher says, "They want talking, discussing. That is different. Still we not have journalism. No journalism is a part of the devil."

Christopher's segue in the conversation seems a little surprising, but our newest conversation partner takes things in a totally different direction, talking about how some people don't like these people or those people. "What?" Christopher is as confused as the rest of us. "Who don't you like?"

Then Christopher decides he's talking about ethnic disputes. "Stupid. Primitive. Old fashion." Christopher fires off. "In the United States people from 178 nations live there, from all around the world. They build a democracy, but we can't build a democracy. How can we build one when we have so much crime? Always have to give money for no good. There are all sorts of problems."

"Everyone doesn't want to do work," says the brawny guy.

"Easy money," Christopher chimes in. "Everyone wants easy money."

"Everyone stealing."

"People say they can't get along. He's Albanian and he's Macedonian or Turkish. That is primitive. But we are good friends." Christopher points to the stout guy. "I don't care; he's my brother."

I finally realize that the guy who walked up must be Albanian. In the midst of all the ethnic disruption in Yugoslavia, Macedonia survived fairly unscathed throughout the 1990s. Yet, when the Kosovo War broke out in 1999, around 350,000 ethnic Albanian refugees fled to Macedonia. This seriously destabilized the country for a time. While the refugees left shortly after the war, Albanian radicals stirred up support for independence in Albanian-populated areas. A short conflict broke out in the spring of 2001. The war ended with NATO's intervention, and the Ohrid Agreement was drawn up, saying that Macedonia will give greater recognition to the Albanian minority and the Albanian separatists will withdraw their demands.

Christopher lays his hand on the shoulder of his new brother. "There's killing. It's crazy. People don't trust each other."

"They don't like each other, but why? They are the same," says the Albanian. Conversation between the two gentlemen begins to sound like an old married couple finishing each other's sentences.

"They are human, from Adam, from one God. You are Macedonian, I am Albanian. We both have blood. Same blood. Everybody same, but nobody thinks that way. We have to be close to each other, not distance."

"This was true before, not now. When Tito died everyone went crazy."

"Yes." Christopher now looks at us, "You know, there comes a democracy from America and from Europe, but not here. It doesn't work here. People are selling drugs: heroine and cocaine. And, there is crime. They show the rifle like Colombia; they shoot like Colombia. These Balkans are like Colombia. And now you can be attacked, you can be beat and people don't care. In Tito times, they immediately catch you. Excuse me," Christopher motions to Krista like he's going to take her camera case. "If I steal your bag—"

"Oh, they'd catch you," the Albanian man jumps in. "In one hour they are going to catch you."

"Believe me, I know, it was very good. In Tito times they said it was not democracy. But people were protected."

"In that time all the people were safe," the Albanian concurs.

"You can leave the bag here and in two hours you can find it. But now it disappears."

"Back then you go to Albania, and you leave your watch somewhere. You come back in one month you are going to find it. They don't catch anyone now."

"If you steal in Albania," Christopher stops midstream and asks his new friend, "What hand do you steal with in Albania? Your right hand? So, they'd cut off your right hand. In Yugoslavia, I know one guy who stole a camera and he went to jail for four years. You think Europe has such big power. But Tito was a dictator. He could make assassinations—like Kennedy assassination. He could kill immediately with his dictatorship. He was taking care of people."

The Albanian nods with Christopher, "He was a nice guy."

Calling a dictator "nice" seems so far from my realm of understanding and my experience growing up in America. I don't know what to do with that idea. Krista and Eric's looks of bewilderment reassure me that I'm not alone in my thoughts, but our perplexed expressions seem not to phase our two new friends.

"Tito had all these nationalities—like the United States—living together," Christopher declares. "There were people from different nations and religions: Islam, Christian and Catholic. Now people are reporting, asking, 'Do you like the time of Yugoslavia or now, with Europe and democracy?' Ninety-three percent of the people say the old Yugoslavia."

"Tito, he put his wife in jail and he put his son in jail because they did something wrong," the Albanian adds proudly.

"That was the way of justice." Christopher pauses and shakes his head. "Now, no justice."

"Now anarchy."

"Yes, anarchy." Then Christopher addresses us, "Excuse me, it may work in America. But you can't make the system in some distant country work. It doesn't work here. People get more wild, more crime. If I sold drugs in Tito times, it was twenty years in jail. Now, they say, 'Good boy.' People are shocked by this democracy. Back then we were educated. And, we were . . . what's the word?"

"Honest," the Albanian says without a pause.

"Yes, honest."

"Did people have religious freedom?" I ask.

"In Tito times we had religious freedom," Christopher assures us. "We could go in church or mosque, like we can today. But people are more religious today. Do you know why? Because there are more poor people. Poor people hope in the religion, like saving. It's the peace they find. Believe me, people don't know where they can go."

"Where are you from?" the Albanian man suddenly inquires.

"America," I say. Then I tell him about our pilgrimage. I realize I've yet to ask Christopher to describe God. I pose the question and Christopher says, "I already told you about the God."

"You said you felt the Spirit of God within you. Has it been difficult for others to understand your personal experience of faith?" The talk about faith seems to bore the Albanian guy. He leaves. But Christopher invites us to sit on some nearby stone benches.

"Some believe God can't be human, that's the Islamic view. But I still believe that God can go with someone through his Spirit. How can I say it? I think he can be transforming with his Spirit. I can't be God, but he can be in us. I am Christian. The Albanians don't believe in that. But you can't change their minds—never—because they have different points of view."

"Is it difficult to be a Christian here?"

"It is not hard. You can know about God. But what I know is that these are miserable times. Now people are fighting, they are not looking too much to their religion. They are looking at their suffering and they don't care. Sometime people are asking, 'Why now am I starving? Why the God doesn't give me some money?' People don't believe in an empty peace, they believe in reality.

"Easy money, prostitution, greed. People want to build a house. Every child wants a home. Do you know how difficult it is to create a house? It cost lots of money. You would have to work all your life. People believe in money. Money walks and talks. People change the God with money. Money is now their god.

"Ninety-nine percent of people don't care about religion. But I could never leave the God. Money for me is nothing. I can make money anytime. I pray to the God to be healthy, to keep my strong spirit and be hard working. Before we all help each other, especially Tito. Believe me, he had such a big spirit, a big love. Now democracy. What democracy? To take your things, and no one help you. Excuse me, this is an American, an Australian, a Canadian democracy. I see it on the television on these crime investigations show every night."

A couple in their twenties walks by. Christopher quickly excuses himself and approaches them about a boat ride. They're interested and we agree that we shouldn't miss Captain Christopher's great excursion ourselves.

We load into a green and white dinghy that is slightly larger than a bathtub. The exterior is aged and the wood seats are weathered. It would have the character of a hardy fishing boat, except for the fact that a Flintstones bed sheet is strung above it to provide shade. It's *so* Christopher. I wouldn't want to traverse one of the oldest lakes in the world in any other way.

Our little boat motor spits and sputters, perhaps in boat-language saying, "Excuse me, Christopher, but I'd rather not work today. I want easy money." Christopher grins determinedly and jerks on the starter again. We're off. Translucent aqua water splashes around as the wind laps across us. The fragrance of this old lake is subtle yet has an aroma of its own. It smells like turquoise. No, rather, it smells like aged wine. Or perhaps it's like the scent of my mother's cheeks? No, that's not quite it.

Christopher dives back into his predictions about Uncle Noah and the apocalypse. The couple looks increasingly frightened. I glance up at Fred Flintstone traveling in his Stone-Age automobile and then down at the ancient fresh water. A deluge of questions washes over me. Is the church so weak and susceptible to the corruption of power that we must rely on Uncle Noah and another colossal flood to get us out of this mess? Will there always be priests like Savonarola in Florence who rally people to give up vanities for the sake of God, and then coerce sons to spy on their parents in the name of morality? Are our priests destined to be no better than our politicians?

Will men like Sead in Sarajevo always wish for religious institutions to serve in practical ways during war and bring new ideas to crumbling societies, but only see clergy driving BMWs and passing out platitudes? Were Jesus' teachings too difficult—too impossible—for his followers to take seriously?

Will people in Belgrade always have to choose between national loyalty and allegiance to God's law of love? Will the pull toward political, economic and societal compromise never let up? Is the church such a dim beacon of freedom in the unwieldy waters of democracy that people like Christopher long for the days of a dictator? Is the apocalypse our only hope?

Christopher interrupts my grappling to offer me his black bomber jacket. I realize my teeth are chattering from the cold. As I slip on his coat, I ask him, "How did you learn English?"

"I learned it from watching John Wayne movies." Christopher starts talking with an impressive John Wayne accent. "A man's got to do what a man's got to do."

After a proper tribute to John Wayne, Christopher turns off the motor and we float alongside a jagged cliff. Atop it stands the famous Church of St. John at Kaneo. Christopher eases the dinghy beside the water's edge. "You can take the stone steps up to the church," Christopher instructs us. We climb out of our miniature ark and pay Christopher for the ride. I give him a hug, take a few steps and turn back. Christopher stands on his little boat waving. As I wave back I notice his eyes. Set into his weathered face are two lakes of aqua. *Thank you, God, for letting us meet this old soul*, I whisper.

The Church of St. John the Theologian at Kaneo rises up from a clearing, perched far above the lake. It sparkles like a cut gem, with its cruciform shape catching every angle of the sun. I stand in front of this medieval architectural jewel for minutes, soaking in its beauty and the warm sun. It's not the impressive icons or the sage looking priests that capture my focus as I enter. No, it's the smell of the place, the aroma of centuries upon centuries of elderly women wearing their finest perfumes as they light candles and whisper prayers for loved ones. It's the fragrance of generations upon generations of priests who have administered the Eucharist and sprinkled holy water on babies and married the young and eulogized the old. It's the odor of incense and liturgical books and an oversized Bible. These ancient fumes surround me: the scent of the sacred.

I stare at the fresco of Christ Pantocrator (Almighty) on the ceiling. The frieze shows him so serene, only stained by the whiffs of the holy and the wear of time. Yet Jesus' life had been touched and tainted by the pedestrian smells of the sick pulling at him, of the ill-repute anointing him with perfume and tears, of the hungry begging for bread and of his friends drifting away when he longed for their companionship. I inhale. I exhale. I do not ask a priest or a parishioner or a visitor to describe God while I breathe in this glorious cloud of aroma. I look up again at the fresco of Christ Almighty. I inhale. I exhale. I leave.

The pureness—the plainness—of the open air catches in my lungs, like a baby choking on its first breaths. Krista and Eric are outside soaking up the sun. We decide to split up for the afternoon. Krista leaves to capture the day with her camera, and Eric heads off to sketch. I drift into a few more ancient churches.

During a chat with a local in one of the chapels I find out that before the
Turkish Empire came through there were apparently 365 churches in the area.
Ohrid is considered the Second Jerusalem, so it's a fitting place to visit as our
last stop in the Balkans. Yet the mention of Jerusalem once again orients me
to our pilgrim path. I can't wait to return to the Holy City. Yet after hearing
Christopher say his hope for the world lies in a massive flood, I wonder if we'll
find even one church on our journey that is bringing hope to people *right now*.

On my circuit through Ohrid I discover a marvelous shop selling homemade paper and artwork. The owner tells me more about Ohrid's favorite
son. Beyond St. Clement's work on the Cyrillic alphabet and his efforts to help
the Slavs read, in his spare time he became the first writer among Macedonian
Slavs and the first Slavic composer and music teacher. He also had a hospital
where hypnosis and teas from healing plants were used to treat the ill.

Something within me takes a deep sigh when I hear how St. Clement's
faith inspired him to help the Slavs experience wholeness through education, health, beauty and devotion to Jesus. When I think of a church that
can navigate the waters of a democracy or dictator, it's one that brings hope
spiritually, physically, emotionally and intellectually.

That was the vision of the early church. Emerging in an atmosphere of
dictators, Christians courageously cared for others in society. They were
known for their generosity to the widows and the orphans. Often when a
new church was started, a teacher and a doctor would come along. A culture
of learning, devotion and service was encouraged. My question persists:
does that kind of church exist today?

In honor of St. Clement I purchase a portrait of St. Luke on hand-
painted paper with Cyrillic text. The Gospel of Luke is one of my favorites. His account spotlights Jesus' compassion for the underdog. Women,
children and foreigners take on surprising roles. Great reversals, toppled
assumptions and countercultural visions progress through the pages of
Luke. I stare at the words of Jesus painted in Cyrillic. Though I cannot
make out their meaning, I take comfort in St. Clement creating an alphabet so that millions throughout the Balkans can understand them.

I meet up with Krista and Eric and notice that they are carrying bags from the same paper shop. Krista purchased a page from the book of John; Eric had, like me, bought a hand-painted page of Luke.

We stroll through Ohrid's outdoor market, where a guy cajoles us into having dinner with him at an expensive restaurant. The guy is charming, then sleazy. By the time the bill arrives he has flirted with—and offended—both Krista and me. Then he sticks us with the entire bill.

I'm so mad. I hate getting ripped off. The feeling of fury, however, dissipates in the night's fresh air, and the closer we get to Mama and Papa's abode, the more grateful I am for their generosity and the kindness we've experienced from so many on our journey.

I awake before Krista and Eric and retreat to the patio. In the solitude of the morning I turn to the reading for the day, Proverbs 11. The first verse stops me short. "The LORD abhors dishonest scales, / but accurate weights are his delight."

Perhaps because I've had to deal with comparatively little injustice in my life, I haven't described God as just. Yet God desires justice more than Christopher, or Sead, or Eldad, or myself. So what would it look like for the church to be an advocate for the marginalized, for the war-weary, for the threadbare in the Balkans?

Krista, Eric, Mama and Papa collect on the patio. We are served one last espresso before we must leave. Today we travel to Greece; the cradle of Western civilization beckons. But right now I savor my coffee, lingering over each sip. We say our farewells to Mama and Papa. As our bus turns us southeast, away from Croatia, Bosnia, Serbia and Albania, my mind journeys back to Tony, who describes God as pure love and desires to be a compassionate priest in Split. I recall Salaam, who describes God as everywhere, longs for the cycle of wars to stop in Mostar, and welcomes Catholic tourists, Orthodox neighbors and fellow Muslim worshipers to his mosque. I give thanks for Father Bosko in Belgrade, who understands God as all-merciful and instructs people to remember God whenever they are thinking something bad toward their neighbor or enemy. My mind meanders to Anila, living in Tirana, who says God is her everything—even if it means risking relationships with her family to live that out.

As the last visions of the Balkans blur past me and my questions about the church and politics collide within me, I can't resist having hope and gratitude for this region of the world. There are people in the Balkans who call God love when they know the reality of hatred—hatred because of their nationality, religion, last name. There are people who say God is everywhere when they have seen their neighborhoods ripped apart by war and their land soaked by blood every second generation. There are people who have risked greatly for their faith, even when they've grown up in the throes of atheism.

I don't feel ready to describe God right now, but I pull out my little brown beads from my coin purse, the beads Tony gave me. My fingers move from one bead to another, stopping at the cross.

How will I repay all this kindness?

12

METEORA AND DELPHI, GREECE

I did not fall in love with Greece in my twenties. There are many reasons for that, some of which entail a crowded train, a toga party gone awry, a painful bushwhacking experience and some misguided Australians. The other reasons I care not to think about.

One day I was in a friend-of-a-friend's flat in Athens, flipping through a book to see other places in Greece. I found Athens to be congested with low-quality air and high-strung tourists. I turned to a page heralding a place called Meteora. The name sounded magical. On the glossy page were rock formations flowering from the ground reaching to the heavens. Atop the rocks were monasteries.

Here I am, over a decade later, no longer separated by the glossy page and the touch-up techniques of travel marketers. It's love at first sight.

These sandstone pillars, located in the Plain of Thessaly in central Greece, have been sculpted by water and wind for thousands if not millions of years. The voluminous sun gushes over the rugged, half-naked rocks. Light spills down all around us. We sit in the shadow of one of the pillars outside our hostel sipping homemade house white wine and recounting our favorite moments in the Balkans. The night silently appears amidst our nattering about tomorrow's trek through monasteries. I venture into sleep wondering how I could have so misjudged Greece. I feel myself falling fast in love as I fall sound asleep.

≳≲

I awake giddy. I tiptoe out of the room in my expectant state. Last night we had seen a path alongside our hostel that ascended to the Holy Trinity Monastery. My emotions are too active—my body too full of cravings—not to climb a mountain. I'm too anxious to wait for the others to awake; I set off on my own to hike.

My hike turns into a gallop. I'm surprised by my energy as the path becomes increasingly vertical. *Meteora* means "suspended in air" or "in the heavens." There's a good reason for this: the pillars seem to shoot from the ground to the sky like fireworks.

The rocks are majestic, but they're not the sole reason for Meteora's name and acclaim. Centuries ago monks came here seeking solitude and safety, a retreat from the masses. Hermits scaled these rocks, clamored into caves and settled into fissures to pray alone. Between the ninth and eleventh centuries C.E. a semicommunity formed and the Church of Theotokos (Church of the God-Bearer) was built. Every Sunday hermits took the harrowing challenge of rock climbing without modern equipment to meet together for mass. When a fourteenth-century Serbian emperor named Symeon Uros stepped down to become a monk, he used his inheritance to endow one of the first monasteries here; building projects exploded, so that at one time twenty-four monasteries (including a couple of convents) adorned the pillars. These monasteries bloomed high on the rocks, and the place officially got its name: "Meteora." Ironically, these "suspended in air" havens for monks and nuns have landed the area on the UNESCO Cultural Heritage site, drawing thousands of tourists annually.

After centuries of looters, invaders and wars, only six monasteries remain. I make it to the base of the Holy Trinity monastery but realize I must immediately turn around to make it back for breakfast. As I dash down the mountain I'm halted for a moment and look up. I envision monks and nuns scaling these rugged stones in order to worship God and be with each other. I wonder how they would describe their God: their rock, their high tower, their immovable feast? The mere motion of my body ascending in nature, surrounded by beauty in silent conversation with the Creator, has been a sacred act itself. I careen down the path in anticipation of what I'll hear from nuns and monks today.

After breakfast Eric, Krista and myself trek back up the same path to the entrance to Holy Trinity. We must climb 140 steps to reach the monastery doors. The first ascetics had created primitive scaffolding—secure beams wedged in holes of the rock—to mount the cliff. Later, rope ladders were used. It wasn't until the twentieth century that all these stairs appeared.

Fortunately I'm hiking in a skirt, which happens to be an entrance requirement for the ladies. For the nonskirt-wearers in our midst, the monastery provides wraps. I must restrain myself from running in the monastery; I'm so curious who I'm going to meet and what they have to say about God. This morning I have a heightened sense of living in story. However, the charming person who takes my ticket tells me the one monk around who speaks English is on break. Everyone else I lay eyes on looks as foreign and nonmonkish as myself. Suddenly the monastery becomes just another run-of-the-mill fourteenth-century holy site with several famous frescoes. I descend the 140 stairs disappointed.

By the time the fifteenth-century Roussanou Monastery comes into view, my hope for a sacred encounter has resurged. Though the complex was intended for men, it is now a nunnery. I pay two euros to enter a space reverberating with angelic music. Before I can ask about the CD being played, I look around the corner and spot a lone nun, staring at sheet music as she sings.

I don't mean to interrupt her, but she stops. I introduce myself and discover her name is Theodora. "It means 'gift from God,'" she says demurely. I ask if I can interview her. She obliges, though she tells me apologetically, "I only have a few minutes. I must get back to my singing."

I pull out a new aqua notebook and ask Theodora to describe God. "God is love, very patient. He is one who knows our hearts, knows what we want before we know it. I am his daughter. He is above all, above parents, above relationships. I try to have a relationship with God, then life runs smoothly."

Theodora pauses and a look captures her visage, a look like she's just been handed her newborn baby. She shares, "Your description of God is a treasure in your heart. You're almost afraid to speak about it because you're afraid it will be taken from you. Yet you want to share it because it is so beautiful." With that Theodora returns to singing and I walk around contemplating what she said. She spoke as one who has kept a magnificent secret she finally got to share. I open up my notebook and stare at her words: *God is love, very patient. He is one who knows our hearts, knows what we want before we know it.*

Perhaps Theodora's depth of joy in her relationship with God has come from years of practicing silence. Silence is such a rare commodity in my world. I cram my ears full of music, news, conversations with friends and, ruefully so, sometimes reality television. I continue to stuff my increasingly cluttered head with emails, projects, books and ideas. Even in my prayers I tend to chatter on, rather than listening for the whisper of the Divine. I imagine all these intriguing sounds and stimuli have distracted joy from tunneling deep within me.

One of the first times I went to a convent felt like coming to a screeching stop at the edge of the cliff. The silence jarred me and the sense of order socked me in the gut. I was in the throes of an addiction to work, but I was finally realizing that work's power to secure my spinning identity was no longer strong enough. I was considering further education. Should I go to film school, pursue a master's degree in journalism or go to seminary? My boss recommended I pursue journalism, but for some reason I was drawn to seminary. Was that God whispering into the little ear of my soul? I went to the convent to find out.

I got to know myself more in the silent halls and in the meals shared without words. I saw my selfishness and desire for affirmation, but I also discovered more of my free spirit, my capacity to laugh at myself, my deep desire to simply follow along the path God wanted to lay out for me.

And in the midst of my quiet, I found God to be more talkative. His voice was loving and patient, as Theodora described. I felt a grounding that God knows my desires even better than I know them myself. After that stay I decided to go to seminary, and I learned silence could be a friend.

After talking with Theodora I realize I want my friendship with silence to deepen. I'm quite excited about this, so I decide to hike to the next monastery in quiet. As I do, I find myself skipping down the mountain. I haven't been a professional skipper since about age eight, but I must say I still have skills! I'm so content that my legs can't hold back my exuberance. I love being in places of beauty out among nature and surrounded by a community of saints. In the absence of words my wobbly legs utter "Thank you. Thank you. Thank you."

As my Chaco sandals clippy clap toward the Church of the Transfiguration, I remember the biblical scholar Walter Brueggemann's description of God: "wild, dangerous, unfettered and free." Here in Meteora God feels more wild and unfettered than ever. That sense of freedom overtakes me until I see that the Church of Transfiguration is hemmed in by a bank of tour buses. People with matching hats and tour books are packed into a nonstop loop from bus to monastery to bus. I'm caught off-guard.

This monastery is the largest and most frequented holy site in the area. Thanks to Symeon Uros's endowment, the place is expansive. A stash of some of the finest religious relics, manuscripts, icons and paintings in the country reside on this particular pillar.

Even still, I wasn't expecting to see so many tourists today. Yes, this is an epicenter for Greek Orthodoxy; yes, it's on the UNESCO Heritage site. Yet I was hoping magical Meteora would be somehow reserved for Krista, Eric and myself. I try to move past my disillusionment and approach a couple of guys standing in line, but they don't speak English.

I just don't have the energy for tourists right now. I eat my lunch and then wander around this complex aimlessly. I spot Eric in the dark chapel admiring a wall hanging. We decide we will light a candle and say a prayer for our brothers. I close my eyes. No longer in a sea of tourists, I now find myself in a sequestered forest with only tiny rays of candlelight dispelling the darkness. God listens to my whispers for my brother.

I know so little about the Greek Orthodox Church. Their experience of corporate worship has seemed so foreign and isolated to me. They come alone. They pray alone. They stand the entire service. They've always struck me as being so individualistic. Yet they evoke tangible practices to remember friends and loved ones and the community of the saints who have gone before. Maybe they too are with friends in the dark forest?

I linger in the prayer-drenched woods for a few moments more. We only have time for one more monastery before it closes and we collapse.

As we make our way to the Varlaam Monastery, once again tour buses are ubiquitous. I am grateful to have chatted with Theodora and prayed for my brother, but I'm a little frustrated. I've only gotten one interview at this significant Greek Orthodox holy site. I just don't have the heart or the energy to approach tourists.

I enter the Chapel of All Saints and see a dark-haired, dark-eyed guy around my age. Perhaps he's a little younger. He looks Greek—the Greek-god-type Greek. He also looks to be a priest. I introduce myself. He tells me his name: "Vallis. I am a student priest. You can call me Bill."

When I ask Bill to describe God, he explains, "In Orthodox theology, God appears as a person who cares about us and has a lot of ways to love us. But the most important way to his love is his crucifixion. Jesus died out of love. The Jews are not responsible for his death; our bad life caused God to do this. Out of his love he took on the human nature to do a new beginning for the human nature."

Bill stops and looks across the chapel. With an energized tone he motions for me to walk with him. "The book of theology is written in art." He shows me the frescos of the Last Judgment. A portion is gray and gory. The scene reminds me of what I'd like to rip out of my faith, what I'd like to tear from the pages of the Holy Book. I avoid thinking about hell; the very idea that anyone will be banished there horrifies me.

Bill starts explaining the scene. "See the people who appear to be ethers?" Bill asks. "Those represent people outside of the light of God's love. In hell, we don't understand who is who." Bill goes on to tell me, "Outside the light of God's love people's individual humanity is lost, what makes them who they are blurs." Then he brightens. "In the situation of paradise there is more light with white that symbolize purity. In heaven we understand who is who. We have personalities and become most human and defined."

Bill leads me to another scene. A man awaits judgment. Before him is a scale. On one side are reams and reams of paper. Each paper symbolizes the man's bad deeds. On the other side is a meager loaf of bread. The small loaf represents the good deeds this man did to others. The curious thing is, the reams and reams of paper would naturally outweigh the little loaf, but the scales are reversed.

"This is God's mercy," Bill shares. "It's different than human judgment. The cross is the center of God's mercy; it's where the fullness of his love is shown. If you have sins and change your life, God forgives you."

As Bill, in a straightforward manner, lays out the paradoxes of justice and mercy and mentions the mystery of how God flips human notions of judgment, I sketch furiously. The scale with its reams of paper and the little loaf that defies gravity are rendered in stick figure fashion. I suspect I'll have a hard time thinking about the Last Judgment without envisioning this fresco and hearing Bill's explanation for years to come.

I thank Bill for his time and insights. He says goodbye and then nonchalantly mentions, "We're different from the Protestants; we don't believe we're saved by our good works." My gentle thoughts turn to visceral defensiveness. Oh my gosh, Bill! Really, that's not what Protestants believe. Our Reformation was about being saved by faith. Do you know about Martin Luther and his ninety-five theses? More than a couple of those were about us not being saved by good works. In fact, some Protestants believe the Orthodox and the Catholics tip the scale in the works-salvation direction.

I thank Bill again and fast-walk outside the chapel. There I sit on a makeshift bench and stare at my drawing. So many paradoxes reside in my little sketch. These scales defy human justice. Somehow Jesus, out of love, took on humanity's judgment for all our wrong deeds. But why are there even scales? Why not just mercy? Still, there they are. Somehow our little loaf of bread *matters*. Our kindness, our sense of community, our love for others must matter, a lot.

I suspect a large piece of our little loaf of bread is connected to how we regard each other, the prejudices we release and the humility we embrace. I'm so surprised by Bill's comments that we Protestants believe we're saved by good works. And I suspect he'd be just as amazed by my own assumptions about Orthodox and Catholics. I wonder how much of the true staples of life I miss out on because of my preconceived notions or sheer pride.

As I look at the sketch I realize there's that issue I like to avoid: hell. Is the very thought of hell heartbreaking to God? If he went to all that effort to create humans and then didn't even spare his Son to rescue people's humanity, isn't it awful for God to think of his creation living outside his love? Or would it be worse to force people to live with God for an eternity when they rejected him in their lifetimes?

Neither the fresco nor Bill even hinted at my questions regarding hell. As much as I desire answers and resolution, one of my favorite aspects of Greek Orthodoxy is the embrace of mystery. The Orthodox let paradoxes exist; tensions lay exposed without disturbance or apologies or cynicism. I imagine my angst with hell must come across as something like, "If I were God I'd be a little more generous, slightly more loving and definitely more merciful—I'd do a little better than our current God has done." I wonder if the Orthodox comfort with mystery rises out of a deep trust in the character of God.

Oh, those Orthodox. I can learn so much from them.

I find Krista and Eric, and we descend from the holy sites suspended in air. Thoughts of heaven and hell tumble around in my mind. We settle into contented silence.

We hiked almost eight hours today. In our fabulously fatigued state we sit outside our hostel in quiet watching the sun fall into a canopy of stars.

We decide that on our way to Athens we will swing by Delphi, the holy site for the most important oracle in the Greek world. To get us there our hostel host arranges for a taxi driver. Pete shows up wearing a sparkling smile with a silver-capped tooth and a gold necklace prominently displayed amidst his ample chest hair. He takes to Krista immediately, so she gets to sit shotgun.

The route winds up and around the Grecian mountains. Pete drives fast, and he likes to look at Krista. I can't make out most of what he is saying, but every couple of sentences he leans over to her and says, "You know what I mean? You know what I mean?"

I am dizzy, nauseated and possibly dehydrated from hours and hours of hiking yesterday. I try with all my might not to throw up on Eric. In the midst of clutching my stomach with one hand and gripping my seatbelt with the other, Pete pulls off the road and screeches to an abrupt stop. "I must pray to St. Christopher for protection. These roads can be dangerous. You know what I mean?" We all nod yes and go with him to light a candle and pray a prayer.

Shortly thereafter we arrive safely in Delphi. Before we amble through this major worship site for the god Apollo, we stop at the bus station.

Oh no! The last bus to Athens leaves in less than one hour. We scuttle to the archaeological site, but by the time we have our entrance ticket in hand, we're down to thirty minutes. We have the equivalent time it takes to watch a *Seinfeld* rerun to tour the site of the oracle that provided sacred wisdom to a large portion of the Western world for centuries. We have a full half an hour to live up to the oracle's etched commission: "Know thyself."

"Come on guys!" I declare in my dizzy, dehydrated state. Then I break out in a sprint. Where's the oracle? Where's Apollo's temple? How am I going to know myself better? I pass stone foundations and Doric columns left and right, not knowing what I'm seeing.

I circle back, having actually seen nothing. Then I notice Eric leisurely strolling toward something. He calmly points to a stone foundation and asks, "Have you seen Apollo's temple?" I run toward ruins I have passed twice. I had completely missed what has been heralded as the center of the earth; here in Apollo's temple the oracle gave advice about how to avoid imminent disaster and be cleansed of impiety. The eternal flame burned here, and Apollo was worshiped as a god of reason and logic.

A couple in their sixties join Eric and me on the temple foundation. Although we have only about five minutes left, I decide to ask them to describe God.

Eva and Harant are from Salzburg, Austria. Eva tells me, "We're typical Austrians. I don't believe in a personal God. God is everywhere—one part of nature. I am still Catholic but I don't participate. I think the church is interesting because of the arts."

Harant responds directly by saying, "Art and culture are my religion."

I thank them. It's time to go, and I find myself running once again through a holy site. I imagine Felix would be quite dismayed. But we make it to the station just in time to jump on the bus.

As I settle into my seat, I start to laugh aloud. How ridiculous was I just now, running around obsessed with the ruins of an ancient oracle? Oh, the crazy little props I pursue to know myself. The image of the Last Judgment and Bill's explanation of it fills my mind. It's in the light of God's love we know ourselves, that we become our true selves. What a freeing mystery.

13

ATHENS, GREECE

I can't help but look up, again and again. The Acropolis, lit against the black of night, is spellbinding. Tomorrow we will step into the age-old current of pilgrims and tourists flowing to its heights. Tonight, however, we follow the tradition of those Greek philosophers, the Epicureans. We will seek happiness and avoid pain by feasting and making merry.

We choose an outdoor café where the music is played like a drunken sailor stumbling around. As food is served the festive music enraptures our tiny little portion of the Plaka. A table full of slightly tipsy and abundantly jubilant Greek women begins to sing. Their revelry is contagious.

I sit back, sipping Retsina and realizing that I'm in the cradle of Western civilization. This is the soil in which democracy was planted. These are the sounds of a society that birthed Socrates and Plato, Aristotle and Alexander the Great. Rome paved roads and codified laws, but Athens provided the thoughts, language and culture that unified the West.

I scoot my chair back from the table, gather my knees to my chest and wrap my arms around them as I let a magical world keep me awake until midnight.

Being in the cradle of Western civilization calls for a toast to start the morning—a toast with Starbucks coffee. When we spy the black-and-white mermaid in her sea of green, we momentarily forget about Athens and our agenda for the day. The Greek siren proves irresistible.

When our lingering over venti helpings of caffeine turns into loitering, we rally and pray for divine encounters. I wonder if any of the millions before us who've made their procession to the top of the Acropolis were in a rush. We don't have a set schedule today, but I feel compelled to scamper up the Herculean set of steps that lead to the Parthenon. My capacity to scamper is thwarted, however, by the dense reality of tourists on all sides. I am forced into their slow march up the stairway officially called the *Propylea*.

As I tramp and sweat with these crowds, I'm curious what the ancient pagans felt as they marched up to their holiest of sites. Were they captured by reverence or religious sentimentality during their festival processions? Were some distracted by the crowd? Did any try to engage the moment then slip into boredom, like me?

Though the Acropolis was one of the finest feats of Greek architecture and culture, its legacy is a tribute to ancient Greek religious life. In the fifth century B.C.E. the Delphi Oracle declared that the Acropolis in Athens was to be devoted to the gods. Four times a year people would enter the city gates, cross the Agora (marketplace) below and snake their way up to the Parthenon's east front. A statue of Athena—the great deity of their city—greeted the faithful upon their arrival. Athena stood elegant and strong, wearing a long flowing dress and a warrior's helmet. What did the masses feel as they gazed at her marble figure? Would they describe her by her titles—goddess of wisdom and war, the arts and industry, justice and skill—or with their own words? Did her reputation as "Virgin Athena" inspire or frustrate the single women in the processions? Did the thought make the men swoon or feel like they should restrain desires?

One legend says that Athena's father was Zeus, king of the gods, and her mother was Metis, the goddess of wisdom. Their relationship was slightly dysfunctional; when Metis became pregnant Zeus was afraid that his wife would bear a son mightier than himself, so he ate her—well, he swallowed her, at least. Metis seemed unbothered by being eaten, for she went about making a robe and a helmet for her daughter. The hammering of the helmet caused immense headaches for Zeus. He had someone split his head open, and out came Athena fully grown and dressed in the robe and helmet her mom had made for her.

Would the Greeks, gazing on this statue of Athena, have contemplated her miraculous birth? Or would they have recalled the story of how she outdid her uncle Poseidon in the contest to be the patron of the city? Legend has it that both Athena and Poseidon claimed the city, and decided to let the citizens settle their dispute. Each gave the city a gift, and the Athenians mounted the Acropolis in a procession to determine which benefactor would be their patron. Poseidon kicked things off. With his trident he struck the side of the cliff, and a spring burst forth. The people were amazed at his mastery, but when they tasted the water it was as salty as Poseidon's sea. Athena then gave the city an olive tree. It provided food, oil and wood. Her gift was embraced, and the city was named Athens.

I wonder what it would be like for modern cities to choose their own deity. My hometown's god would definitely be Money. Charlotte, North Carolina, is second only to New York City in banking in the United States, with almost $2 trillion tied to banking resources. In our city Money anxiously keeps people up at night and inspires daydreams. Our loyalties run deep—perhaps deeper than the Athenians', who were known less for their fidelity to Athena and more for their attraction to the latest ideas and the trendiest gods.

Krista, Eric and I meander about Nike's temple and then the Parthenon. For two millennia the Parthenon remained virtually the same, despite being converted into a church and then a mosque. Eventually it housed a harem. Things went to ruin in the seventeenth century when the Ottomans used it as an ammunition dump and the Venetians attacked it, causing an explosion. The Parthenon required extensive cosmetic surgery after that.

As fascinated as I am with this place, I can only stare at columns and façades for so long, especially when the scaffolding is conspicuous and tourists are omnipresent. I approach a young lady who looks to be traveling with her family, and she appears to be as bored with the sight of tourists as I am.

Emily is from Atlanta. She's been traveling throughout Europe with her mom, dad and brother. They've visited the major cities, including Rome. I tell her about my pilgrimage and she's up for describing God. As we walk over to a bench, she mentions she is eighteen years old and Jewish.

"God is very complex," Emily begins. "I believe in God; I talk to him and I ask him questions, like how some things happen. But I think that God is over us, watching us, protecting us, especially when things are going wrong for the wrong reasons. Certain things are supposed to happen—they're predetermined. I believe God makes sure things go in the right direction."

"So you see God as a guiding force?" I ask.

"Yes, I believe God will help you if you deserve to be shown the right path. God doesn't show you the *one* path, but he shows you the light at the end of the path."

Since Emily had visited Rome and other cities with large cathedrals and diverse beliefs, I'm curious if that experience has changed her in any way. "It's just sort of made me understand how it affects other people's lives. I used to not be religious at all. Now—"

Emily is cut off in midsentence. A woman working for the Acropolis asks us what we are doing and what my iPod is. I can't interview anyone here, she tells me, so I thank Emily and slump about until I find Eric and Krista.

Fortunately they're ready to retreat from the masses. Eric suggests that we walk to the Areopagus, the area often called Mars Hill, to discuss the apostle Paul's time in Athens. We're finally getting into the part of the world that is Eric's element. His master's degree in Ancient Near East first-century backgrounds has stuffed his head with savory knowledge. We sit on a craggy rock overlooking the Agora, with the Parthenon above us.

"Paul came to Athens around 50 C.E.," Eric starts out. "The book of Acts records a snapshot of his time here." I rummage through my daypack to pull out my little black Bible and a smashed protein bar to share. Eric flips to Acts 17. "This passage actually gives us a glimpse of people's view of the gods and how Paul responds to them." He reads from the middle of the chapter: "Paul . . . was greatly distressed to see that the city was full of idols. So he reasoned in the synagogue with the Jews and the God-fearing

Greeks, as well as in the marketplace day by day with those who happened to be there."

Gazing at the Agora below us, Eric mentions, "One of the things that always grabs me about this passage is how comfortable Paul felt in the midst of the crowds of the marketplace. The Agora was the epicenter of Greek life. It was where the masses gathered to barter, hear news, greet strangers from every corner of the Empire, debate philosophy and politics, listen to speeches, vote, exercise, compete in games, participate in festivities and worship. It's clear Paul felt very much at home in a cosmopolitan environment." He continues reading.

A group of Epicurean and Stoic philosophers began to dispute with him. Some of them asked, "What is this babbler trying to say?" Others remarked, "He seems to be advocating foreign gods." They said this because Paul was preaching the good news about Jesus and the resurrection. Then they took him and brought him to a meeting of the Areopagus, where they said to him, "May we know what this new teaching is that you are presenting? You are bringing some strange ideas to our ears, and we want to know what they mean." (All the Athenians and the foreigners who lived there spent their time doing nothing but talking about and listening to the latest ideas.)

Eric turns and looks up at the Acropolis behind us. "I'm fairly confident that Paul's feet never touched the steps of the Propylea. In fact, as a devout Jew, probably his time here on Mars Hill was the closest he ever came to Athens's sacred precinct.

"People often look at this passage in the New Testament and get the impression that Paul was a Jew well-acculturated to Greek culture, comfortable quoting Greek philosophers and the like. But something about Athens was really getting Paul's Jewish goat. A Hellenized Jew he might be, but don't get the impression that he was Hellenized enough to easily come up here to the Areopagus. The Greek philosophers have to pull Paul from his element. They wanted a clearer hearing in the place *they* felt more at home in. Paul, of course, was happy for the invitation but his time with them takes some surprising turns." Eric turns again to the passage from Acts:

> Men of Athens! I see that in every way you are very religious. For
> as I walked around and looked carefully at your objects of worship,
> I even found an altar with this inscription: TO AN UNKNOWN
> GOD. Now what you worship as something unknown I am going to
> proclaim to you. The God who made the world and everything in it is the Lord of
> heaven and earth and does not live in temples built by hands. And he
> is not served by human hands, as if he needed anything, because he
> himself gives all men life and breath and everything else.

"Paul may have not spent his days dealing with philosophers, but he was
savvy when he spoke with them. His statement bears a twinge of light-
hearted sarcasm. The Epicureans and Stoics actually shared Paul's contempt
for showy, sentimental religiosity; to them the gods—if they existed at
all—were unencumbered by the affairs of men. They taught, in fact, that
it was useless to entreat the gods for favors, much less their images. When
Paul critiqued the Athenians on the abundance of idols, he would be gar-
nishing the support of those philosophers.

"So at this point, Paul has the audience at the Areopagus on his side. He
then spotlights how these philosophers' view of God lines up with the God
he had traveled to Athens to proclaim." Eric reads further.

> From one man he [God] made every nation of men, that they should
> inhabit the whole earth; and he determined the times set for them
> and the exact places where they should live. God did this so that men
> would seek him and perhaps reach out for him and find him, though
> he is not far from each one of us. "For in him we live and move and
> have our being." As some of your own poets have said, "We are his
> offspring."

Eric's demeanor is more engaged than I've ever seen it as he continues
elucidating the text. "Paul's audience, following in the tradition of Plato, believed that God is the distant 'unmoved mover' who sets all things in motion

and orders the cosmos with his thoughts. The ancient philosophers, especially the Stoics, believed that the primordial divine thoughts of God were open to anyone with a heart to understand them. In fact, they believed that since we all have reason within us, we have embers of the 'divine nature' within us, and we have the ability to discover the thoughts of the Mover in ourselves and in the world around us.

"Surprisingly, Paul did not refute this Stoic conception of the divine nature in his dialogue with the Athenian philosophers. Paul, in fact, stakes his argument on the unquestionable existence of a universal quest to pursue the thoughts and heart of God. Like many Jews of his day—including Jesus—he gave surprising deference to the Gentiles on some matters. But he *does* challenge their notions of God in two distinct ways. First of all, Paul's Divinity is a Being who longs to be known by humanity, a God who shakes up, scatters and generally"—Eric laughs—"irritates folks to pursue him into an eternal relationship. The striking difference of Paul's conception of the divine nature, the sign of God's presence, from that of these philosophers, is that he regarded it as a sign of a beckoning God."

As Eric pauses, it's as if my belief in God is making itself more at home in my soul. I have deeply believed that God pursues us. Yet I've questioned whether my experience has been tainted by my own sentimental hopes that God would want to be close to me. Here's Paul, an ancient apostle and scholar, saying it is so.

Eric continues, "Paul's parting shot, the second thing that would have challenged the Stoics and Epicureans, was his teaching about the resurrection. Here's how Paul ends his time with the philosophers."

> Therefore since we are God's offspring, we should not think that the divine being is like gold or silver or stone—an image made by man's design and skill. In the past God overlooked such ignorance, but now he commands all people everywhere to repent. For he has set a day when he will judge the world with justice by the man he has appointed. He has given proof of this to all men by raising him from the dead.

"The quest of the Stoics and Epicureans," Eric goes on, "was simply to achieve serenity in one's lifetime through the careful cultivation of reason and self-discipline. Theirs was the science of living the well-lived life. Guidance was provided by the 'divine nature' within. As a scholar once put it, their ideologies were 'the tranquilizers of life.' It's easy to see why some of the philosophers sneered at Paul's statements. The Stoics and Epicureans belived that life was in the here and now, nothing more. The Epicureans, in particular, coined the saying *carpe diem,* literally, 'Pluck the day,' as one plucks a fruit to enjoy. Paul's science of living for the life to come—as opposed to the present one—would have understandably undermined their quest for 'serenity' in many sectors of life.

"So Paul's remarks right here where we're sitting created quite a stir. His description of God as a Being personally engaged in the affairs of humanity and a relational Being that could be known for eternity challenged conventional wisdom and the thoughts of the Athenian erudite. No wonder many were perturbed and few were won over."

As Eric wraps up his thoughts on Paul and the Athenians, a collection of Americans plop down close to us on this rugged rock. I introduce myself; they tell me they're on a study trip for the Maryland Institute College of Art. While they need to climb down the rock in a few minutes, they're open to me asking them a question.

"So, how do you describe God?" For a moment there's a dam of silence, followed by trickles of nervous laughter. Then Ryan, a twenty-one-year-old, turns the conversation into a deluge of thoughts. "I was raised in an antireligious household. I don't think I'm old enough to respond. Right now I don't know what I believe. I can't define it, but I'm open."

Kim, from New Jersey, jumps in. "I grew up in a bicultural household. I was Catholic, but I haven't gone to church since confirmation—when supposedly you move closer into the church family. I kind of just thought of God as mostly a belief, a human belief. I felt there might have been something of a worldly thing at one point. But it was mostly because people kept telling me about karma. Bad things happen, good things happen. Everything's supposed to be on the same level.

"I feel like God is something that people just need to have." When Kim says this, her friends say, "What?" Kim regroups. "I mean, every culture has created one so far in history, except if you are atheist. I basically want to think of it as a universal thing"—Kim pauses for a moment—"so everyone could be happy." She laughs nervously as she says it. "It should be something nobody would be against."

I turn to another student and ask her, "Are you wired the same way?"

Jenny thinks for a moment and says, "I don't know. There are people at my school who are religious. My roommate is Baha'i and she is psychocrazy devout. It's funny, I'm really not sure quite what I believe in. I've taken in what she says, like most religions, but then I forget. I don't know. I don't know what I think either way."

Jacob, from Rochester, New York, dives into the conversation. "I was brought up in a bicultural family as well. My mother was Buddhist; my father was Catholic. I never really went to church. My first time going was Easter last year. Both of my parents came from rather poor families. I guess the main thing I got from them was to work hard to do something you love. That's why I'm in art. But in a way, hard work is kind of like God. It is kind of like a love for what you're doing. I was taught that God is love."

I ask if anyone else wants to jump in. Just as they are standing up to go another student says, "I took a philosophy class last year. We discussed the nature of God, what is God, who is God. I started thinking about those things. I could talk for hours, but I don't know—"

His friends are all leaving. He says he has to go. As we join them clambering down the rock, I wish I could have talked more to the last student. I wonder where all his study and contemplation of the nature of God has left him. Has it made a difference? Is he left with a sense of an Unknown God? Does he hope that a Divine Being can be known and is actually pursuing him with extravagant love and sacrifice? I wonder how he would have responded to Paul's words right here. What would he say about a God whose Son was resurrected from the dead?

It's such a treat to have Eric take the lead today. My questions continue to tumble out as he guides us down to the Agora. He explains that Athens was world-renowned for the exuberance of its religious festivals. "Chances were very good that Paul had numerous occasions to view the Panathenaic Procession of priests and priestesses and devotees and revelers. He likely watched them parade votive offerings and garlanded beasts through the Agora toward the Acropolis. The procession was the apex of Greek religious expression and the pride of Athens. Athens was the Jerusalem of the Greeks.

"In fact, when Paul looked up at the base of the Acropolis, with its huge pylons and the ceremonial entrance of the Propylea with the smallish Temple of Nike on its dramatic pedestal, he would have been hard-pressed not to remember his beloved Jerusalem, where he was trained as a rabbi in its most prestigious academy. I think the resemblance of the Acropolis to the Temple Mount in Jerusalem is what was getting his Jewish goat."

"I thought you said that the Athenian elite did not put much stock in religious festivities," I respond. "Why such enthusiastic worship in Athens?"

"Well," Eric replies, "religions, even if you don't put much stock in them, offer a wealth of side benefits. The Epicureans, for example, basically saw religion as a way of creating harmony within the culture. While ritual could be empty, it was not devoid of purpose. What mattered was that you took things in stride in your thoughts, and that you didn't grant things greater importance than they're due. Friendship and community—now that was important!"

Eric smiles and points to the building just ahead of us. "That long building with the arcade in front of it, called a stoa, represented the happy fellowship of mankind. No doubt in my mind that Paul loved that place. In the stoas strangers were expected to interact with strangers, common folk were expected to greet blue bloods and vice versa. Besides shopping, here was where you heard the latest gossip, where you debated matters of politics and war—where, in fact, you cast your ballot in elections and referendums, paid your taxes and whatnot. Here is the center of civic life in Greek culture.

"It's no accident that democracy was birthed and flowered in this space. We call this in the architectural world 'liminal space,' where folks interact with others at the same level. It's not hierarchical space but a space of interchange."

I get so excited hearing Eric describe liminal space. That's our sacred bench! How would relations between the East and West be different if nations and neighbors embraced a sense of mutual learning and exchange—if negotiations took place on the sacred bench?

But how does liminal space work with my description of God? Are all views of God equal? For Paul they weren't, but I'm starting to wonder if one's view of God matters. If you love God and others, is that what's important? I disregard my questions and go back to reveling in this place that has had so much influence on my concept of faith and understanding of the world.

We walk through the stoa and museum. After hours of thinking about ancient marketplaces, we're ready to enter the fray of twenty-first century commerce, so we venture to the *Monastiraki* district and split up to shop. I purchase the obligatory T-shirt, a respectable tribute to Greece's *Hellas* soccer team. Then I'm off for the serious purchase. I will splurge on an icon.

I find a shop that has an extensive collection of icons. I wait for minutes for someone to help me. When the guy finally offers to assist me, the items he shows me cost over a hundred euros. I ask him about less expensive icons; he seems offended and uninspired to help. I mumble a "thank you" and leave. How rude! Where's the customer service in this continent? Maybe I won't get an icon. Should something so sacred be reduced to an impersonal transaction? I pass a shop with a large bead collection. Yes, beads! That's what I'll buy.

A portly man smiles broadly and asks if he can help me. I tell him I'd like to buy some prayer beads.

"These are actually *komboloi,* 'worry beads.' They look a lot like prayer beads, but the sultans brought these beads over from Turkey. They'd have them around as a symbol of wealth. The Greeks took to carrying them, something to finger when you're talking or sitting around."

I introduce myself to this kind shopkeeper. "I'm Jorge. I was born in Chile, but I'm Greek." I tell him about our pilgrimage and he becomes curious, so right there in the middle of the shop I ask him to describe God.

"Creator, Father," Jorge responds. "He provides for me. He looks at me. He blesses me and directs me. He lives in a Spirit. He can't be contained." Jorge's gentle eyes grow more direct. "You accept him in your heart and a power comes in you. He comes to touch the deepest part of your heart. You change when you come to him. When you have God, you have everything."

Jorge longs to go into religious service. He's working at this shop right now to save toward that. "I desire to work for God in a mission. I am waiting for God to soon use me." As I go to pay for my *komboloi* I notice small, exquisite icons. Jorge helps me find one of Jesus. The painting is done in Byzantine style. Jesus is portrayed with sharp features against a gold background. This tiny icon is framed with silver; the design looks like an arch. Jorge turns it over and shows me the mark of authenticity. Greece takes its production of icons very seriously.

On my way out, with beads and icon in hand, Jorge asks me, "What do you do back in the States?"

"I work at a Presbyterian church. Actually I'm one of the pastors on staff."

Jorge's broad smile widens. That's a reaction I never expect when I say I work for a church. I rarely mention I'm a pastor. *Pastor* is a label that frequently feels foreign to how I understand myself, one that carries connotations I can't control. Jorge, however, excitedly tells me that Presbyterians invited him as a youth to go to church in Chile. "They were so kind and showed me Christ."

I'm learning to see that these sacred encounters are like living icons, revealing to me Jesus again and again. I say *yassou* ("thank you") to Jorge and exit his shop into the stream of strangers.

Our ferry creeps toward Turkey in the dusk. We face the region of the world where the apostle Paul earned his reputation as a church planter. First, however, we will stop on an island where another apostle spent his time mending nets and chatting with criminals. I pull out my worry beads and icon, both wrapped in dainty blue and white paper with the symbol of the Acropolis stamped on it.

I unwrap the worry beads first. Larger than any of my prayer beads, they look like white marbles strung together. They share the same elegant strength as Athena. I finger them one by one. They're cool to the touch. The beads move from thumb to index finger faster and faster; they're distracting and centering all at once. I can imagine how these beads could be addicting, a solution to anxiety and boredom right in one's hands.

I slowly remove the paper from my little icon. I stare at the detail. Jesus seems to be stepping out of the silver arch to be with me. In one hand he holds the Bible open, like he wants me to read it. His other hand forms the sign of blessing. Yet it's his eyes that beckon me. He gazes at me as if he were at my level, as if we were both standing in the stoa.

What was it that Jorge said about God? Oh yes. "God looks at me. He blesses me and directs me. He lives in a Spirit. He can't be contained."

14

PATMOS, GREECE

A shrill crackling explodes like a bomb in my eardrums. I scrape myself off the ground. The awful noise blares through antiquated speakers as the image of a ship's foghorn shows up on our ferry's video screen.

I strain my eyes to locate Krista and Eric; both of them look disoriented and irritated. I don't know what would inspire someone on our night ferry to Patmos to wait until the majority of the passengers are asleep to play a poorly produced welcome video. Perhaps the person is working through revenge issues, or ran out of her Zoloft, or maybe inadvertently hit a wrong button. Anyway, the horrible video has awakened us to the reality that we are all sleeping on the filthy floor of a less-than-classy cruise ship.

Oh well.

A couple of hours later another foghorn rouses us. We've reached Patmos. I dust myself off, grab my pack and look at my watch. It's 2 a.m. We haven't made arrangements for a room. Will we have to sleep on the streets tonight? Will it be colder than our bus ride to Belgrade? Will we be safe? Though this ferry's floor is a tiny bit foul, we do have a roof over our heads. I slow down my pace as we exit the boat.

A man approaches us as we debark. "Do you need a room?" We pile into his little Fiat and wind around in the dark. We are dropped off beside a small collection of one-story rooms with front patios. We collapse on our beds, too tired to be thankful or scared.

⇒⇐

The liquid sun of the morning slowly seeps in. We climb out of sleep and tumble down to the water's edge, where we eat our breakfast facing the Aegean Sea. Salt air and coffee gradually revive us.

Eric fought to put Patmos on the itinerary. I didn't know Patmos still existed, but it didn't take much convincing for Krista and me to want to come as well. Not only is an island-stop hard to argue against, John—an apostle and perhaps Jesus' closest confidant on earth—spent time here.

John didn't come to Patmos for a holiday. He was banished to this tiny isle off the coast of Asia Minor, today a sleepy Greek island with a little over three thousand residents. When John was here in 95 c.e., he was very old, perhaps in his eighties. The Romans used the place to sequester political exiles and religious prisoners. I wonder what it was like for him to come. John would have likely been in his element by the water. He grew up fishing; it was his profession until likely his late teens or early twenties, when he met Jesus and his life's trajectory took a dramatic twist.

I ask Eric what he thinks John was like. "He was called 'a Son of Thunder,' so he must have had a strong presence. I envision him with a hearty laugh, a full beard, the capable hands of a fisherman and a zest for life. Leonardo da Vinci's painting of the Last Supper is unfortunate; we feminize and enfeeble John because of it. I see John as a man of strength and a true mystic.

"When you read John's Gospel you see he had a fine eye for detail. His imagery is elaborate and lush. He was also a keen listener and always thinking of the Old Testament. I see him as a passionate soul."

I am looking forward to exploring this place where John lived and wrote the last book of the Christian Bible, Revelation. Even though it starts out with a blessing—"Blessed is the one who reads the words of this prophecy, and blessed are those who hear it and take to heart what is written in it, because the time is near"—I grew up scared of it. When I was a kid I watched some movie at church about being left behind when Jesus returns. I spent much of the movie with my head in my lap and scared to death. I had nightmares thinking that Jesus had come and collected my mom and dad and friends; I had been left to live in a world going up in flames.

I also remember sitting in a college chapel service at the start of the first Persian Gulf War. The speaker used the book of Revelation to lay out his theory that Saddam Hussein was the antichrist. I didn't read Revelation for about a decade after that.

Despite my complicated history with John's apocalyptic letter, I have a deep affinity for his Gospel from my days of chatting about it with Eric in Jerusalem. So I'm game to have a fresh look at Revelation.

However, there's one problem with my new openness of mind. In order for us to get to the cave where John wrote Revelation, we must ride bikes. I'm scared of riding a bike. Throw me out of a plane with a parachute or take me into a potential war zone and I think I can hold my own, but riding a ten-speed completely freaks me out. I've been splayed on the ground before because of a bike. My shaky skills knocked me off our family scooter on multiple occasions. Argh! I try to hide my fear from Krista and Eric. Bike phobia *is* ridiculous after all.

The route to John's cave is a vertical climb with sharp switchbacks. The road is so steep that both Eric and Krista suggest we walk our bikes up the mountain. I oblige. We arrive at the Holy Grotto of the Revelation gross, but alive.

The complex is minute compared to Meteora's monasteries. I have difficulty locating a priest, so I descend the stairs to the cave. It feels like Narnia's wardrobe; in this small, dark space the most colossal vision of Jesus came to John. I sit on a bench carved out of the rock and try to imagine the scene. John writes that he heard a voice and turned around.

> Among the lampstands was someone "like a son of man," dressed in a robe reaching down to his feet and with a golden sash around his chest. His head and hair were white like wool, as white as snow, and his eyes were like blazing fire. His feet were like bronze glowing in a furnace, and his voice was like the sound of rushing waters. In his right hand

he held seven stars, and out of his mouth came a sharp double-edged sword. His face was like the sun shining in all its brilliance.

Jesus, according to John's account, put his hand on his right shoulder and said, "Do not be afraid." I realize I currently have a river of fear rushing through me. I'm really afraid of plummeting down that hill on my rented ten-speed. Maybe I just don't like losing control and getting hurt. And with that confession a torrent within me releases. I'm afraid of getting my heart broken or breaking another's. I'm scared of not loving someone I should, of falling for someone I shouldn't.

Wow. I didn't realize I had such fears dammed up inside.

Perhaps I'm most afraid of failing on this journey—that I'll make it to Jerusalem and find I wasn't worthy of this pilgrimage. I wonder if Helena was ever afraid of failing? Maybe she was liberated enough not to worry about that. I look around this tiny, dark grotto. Did John confess his fears to God in this little cave? I light a candle for "the brothers." The flicker slices a swath through the darkness. Did the Light of the World come to John here, bringing courage?

Lord, grant me courage today.

Sunlight strikes my eyes as I exit. Eric has promised Krista and me that he will share with us more about the background of Revelation. The fears that flooded me in the cave dry up in the light of day. The thought of getting to learn makes me feel bold and hopeful.

A stone wall becomes our bench. The three of us sit side by side as our legs dangle above a terrain that plunges toward the sea. Eric tells us about the apocalyptic book of Revelation. "Embedded in its story line is a tale of survival. This was one of the deadliest periods of persecution that the church had ever faced. It was on the brink of extinction and perhaps wouldn't have survived as we know it if the book had not been written.

"In 70 C.E., after the Romans destroyed the temple in Jerusalem, droves of Gentiles around the Empire ironically became fascinated with Judaism and, by extension, Christianity. Gentile conversions were skyrocketing. The Jews were actively proselytizing throughout the Empire, and it must have been compelling to see how courageously they persevered against Rome in their desire to be under no dominion but God's. Christianity benefited from this increased interest in Judaism and was also propelled by its own evangelistic energy. However, the Roman emperor Domitian became increasingly the Jews' and Christians' nemesis."

"So what was Domitian's deal?" I interrupt. "Was he feeling threatened?"

Eric laughs. "He did have a god-complex. In fact, when some Stoic senators refused to address him as 'Lord and God,' he had them killed. And he once introduced his wife to the senate as someone fortunate to visit his 'divine couch.'"

Krista guffaws. "I bet his 'divine couch' was quite chilly that night."

"Well, as you can probably imagine, when Gentiles converted to Judaism or Christianity, life became quite tricky, since the second of the ten commandments bans idolatry. Calling the emperor 'Lord and God' didn't quite fit into the faith. Domitian made it increasingly difficult for Jews and Christians to participate as citizens. The Romans had always granted the Jews the right to abstain from idolatry, but following the suppression of the major revolt in Judea, Vespasian—Domitian's predecessor—required the Jews to pay for such exemptions, including a privilege tax called the *fiscus Iudaicus,* or the Jewish Fund.

"In the early nineties, Domitian demanded that all people who practiced or adopted any kind of Jewish religious practice (which would include the Christians), whether openly or secretly, pay the *fiscus Iudaicus.* If they failed to come forward, the state would confiscate their properties. Domitian began to reward informants who exposed tax evaders, and then many tax evaders started to pay off these informants to avoid persecution. Blackmail spiraled into rampant proportions. In the year 95 Domitian banned secret conversion to Judaism and outright conversion to Christianity. Suddenly conversion was a capital offense.

"John, being Jewish, had probably always paid the *fiscus Iudaicus* and so was likely off the hook for charges of impiety. However, since he was one of the key evangelists in the Christian church, Domitian had him exiled to Patmos in 95 C.E., right around the time conversion was outlawed. John might have already witnessed some of the troubles his fellow Christians were now facing in the mainland—such as losing their properties and going to trial for imminent execution."

"So," I say with a bit of impatience, "how did the book of Revelation encourage the Christians?"

Eric is in no hurry to skip to the beauty in this story. One more tragedy occupies his mind as he looks down the slopes below us. "The frictions Domitian inflicted on the Jewish community became the wedge that drove the synagogue and the church apart. A few synagogues refused to protect the Christians, exposing them to Roman persecution. The wound never healed, and the next generation of Christian leadership slid into anti-Semitic apologetics as a result. Revelation may have contributed to the growing divide; it contains harsh language against traitorous synagogues. This tone is not unwarranted, though: one of the greatest sins in Judaism is to betray your fellow Jew, or God-fearer—a potential Jew—to the authorities."

A silence blows through us as Eric wraps up his insights on the divide between Jews and Christians. What a jagged mountain range of hurt and distrust. I glance back at the church and think of how heartbroken and perhaps afraid John must have been, knowing that the future of the church and the bond with his Jewish people was in jeopardy.

My thoughts go to an annoying place. How flimsy my fears must have sounded, voiced in John's grotto. I wish my fears were more noble, more global, more compassionate, less selfi—

Fortunately Eric interrupts my silent blabber. "But in the end, this is a story of beauty from ashes. Jesus gave John a potent reminder that God had a larger story line at play than the persecution the church was enduring. There was a world of evil forces, but more importantly there was a God committed to and capable of redemption.

"The message of Revelation spread through Asia Minor, the very area where Christianity was transformed from a Jewish sect into a full-blown world movement. Had the jolt of hope and encouragement and promises of Revelation never arrived in Asia Minor, I doubt that the church would have persevered so steadfastly through the grueling second and third centuries of its history—or spread around the world so amazingly."

"But Eric," I ask, "if Revelation was such a straightforward message of encouragement, why was it written in such an obtuse way?"

"Revelation is actually a letter meant to be circulated among the churches of Asia Minor. I believe it was designed to be memorized; the couriers themselves were the 'letter.' The text itself hints that it should be transmitted by word of mouth; an angel commands John to eat the scroll of the vision. It's full of memory aids that make it easy to memorize. The vivid imagery carries implicit double-meanings that a well-learned Jew would find poignant and would be able to unpack for the congregation. The pervasive scriptural symbolism and references, especially to the Prophets—books very important to Jews facing difficult times—would have been known by rote in those days.

"But probably most importantly, Revelation is *extraordinarily* structured to facilitate rapid memorization. It would have probably only taken a couple of readings for a well-trained Jewish scholar to have the entire message committed to memory through embedded structural handles. That may sound fantastic and improbable to us, but the ancients were masters at memorization; after all, writing was at a premium in those days, and the least expensive way to 'copy' something—monetarily and timewise— was to memorize it.

"In other words, Revelation is a message that was intended to disseminate with blazing speed—to get to the largest audience possible in the fastest way available. It's an *urgent* letter."

I let my legs swing against the wall as I try to absorb Eric's words. I think about how much I've tried to avoid this "urgent letter." It has often seemed so inaccessible, so bewildering, so . . . scary. How curious that this urgent letter draped in apocalyptic imagery was a call for encouragement. And, how ironic that Domitian, in his grand attempts to squelch Christianity, provided John with a cave and some time to receive a vision of Jesus that kept the church going. A story of ashes and beauty it is.

We reclaim our rickety ten-speeds and push them further up the mountain.

Krista struggles with the enormous doors of the Byzantine Monastery of
St. John the Theologian. It must be the monks' day off, so we trade our
monastery tour for a restaurant expedition and locate a sophisticated bistro
clinging to the edge of the mountain.

"We are hosting a wedding party," the maitre d' tells us apologetically.
As we deflate, the gentleman says, "I'll ask the bride and groom if they mind
if you join them." In the States I'd perhaps protest, but here I'm delighted
to risk rejection. The maitre d' returns grinning. "Come! Come!" He leads
us outside to a charming deck that eyes the ocean. We are offered a prime
corner table surrounded by the view and the wedding party. Laughter flows
as gently and abundantly as the wine. The bride wears a simple white silk
gown; her long, dark hair is swept back with tiny white flowers. She is both
exquisite and at ease. The groom looks just as comfortable. He talks with
his friends and then turns to glance at his bride with an expression of "I can't
believe my good fortune." She seems just as pleased.

The couple appears as young as the midmorning sun. I wonder what made
them want to spend the rest of their lives together. Why did they fall in love?
The union of marriage is considered a sacrament in the Greek Orthodox
church—an act of sacredness and mystery. Looking at these newlyweds,
marriage takes on a holy naturalness.

Their wedding party is small, but everyone seems genuinely happy for
the couple. The maitre d' embraces his role as host, treating the couple like
he is the proud father of the bride. As the meal progresses, he even comes
to us, offering dessert liquor on the house. We soak in the stunning view of
the water and the contagious laughter of the wedding party. Krista, Eric and
I need not exchange words; we each recognize that this has to be one of the
most glorious meals we've experienced together.

My mind drifts to the apostle John. During his time on this island he
probably never partook in a wedding party; perhaps that was one of the experiences he missed most while in exile. However, John's apocalyptic vision
ends with a wedding feast.

The Spirit and the bride say, "Come!" And let him who hears say,

"Come!" Whoever is thirsty, let him come; and whoever wishes, let him take the free gift of the water of life.

I savor the thought. Thirsty people meander in and are greeted with "Come!" The finest of libations flow forever. Laughter and ease and adoration know no end.

I stroll out of the restaurant in utter bliss. Then I spot my ten-speed and immediately panic. At least my last meal was a good one. I try to regroup and begin positive-affirmation therapy. "I can do this. I am a good bike rider. I am full of courage. I'm competent; I'm in my thirties for goodness' sake!"

The island breeze brushes through my hair. The sparkling sea and glowing sun seem united in celebration of my journey. I speed along a switchback, poised and at one with my bike. What was I afraid of—should childish fears still hold power over me?

Real fear is the fear of being squeezed out of society by politics and pushed out by religious persecution. Real fear is the fear that a religion of love has been misinterpreted. It's living under the threat of anti-Semitism. It's being exiled from the sounds of laughter and celebrations of loved ones. Real fear is—

Oh no! Car! Coming at me! I grip the handlebars. I jerk my body and the bike to the edge of the lane. I pinch the brakes. The car swerves. I lurch. I tumble to the ground. My adrenaline sends my limbs into a frenzy. I stand and attempt to steady my voice as I call down to Krista and Eric, "Wait up. I'll be right there."

My arms and legs shake like an earthquake. My heart pounds like a hurricane. My entire being feels like a natural disaster. Yet all around me is eerie calm. The car has sped up the next switchback. Eric and Krista are not in sight. The breeze gently blows, the sun glistens, and the ocean waves haven't stopped their ebb and flow. I too must continue. I collect my quaking limbs and place my bum on the little seat. I breathe. I pray. I pedal. And I make it down alive.

"Please be quiet. Please." I mumble under my breath. I am so tired. Today's experiences were exhilarating but tiring. The wedding party, followed by the near-death experience on a ten-speed, have made today feel like eight hours straight on a roller coaster.

"Would you shut up? Don't you know people are trying to sleep?" I'm not sure if I'm screaming those words right now or simply dreaming I am. Some guy from Canada and some girl from England are laughing and playing cards and talking about acting classes right outside our bedroom window. They must be on the shared patio, but it is *so* past midnight. "Come on!"

Morning shows up like an unwelcome guest. In a dazed state we pack, go into town and climb on a ferry heading east. Before I'm even fully awake, our ferry docks in Samos, Greece. We have two hours to get to the other side of the island to catch another ferry to Turkey.

As we walk through Samos, we pass a guy sitting on a park bench. He looks familiar. Oh my gosh, it's the Canadian who kept me up last night. I introduce myself to him again. Though he's been living in Montreal for the past couple of years, twenty-two-year-old Gabriel is actually from Guatemala. He wears a straw hat, a gray short-sleeve silk shirt, black pants and a leather necklace. Somehow the crazy combination makes him look like a suave hipster.

I ask Gabriel about his time in Patmos. I refrain from a biting remark regarding his exciting nightlife on our patio.

"I went to Patmos because I desired to see where John wrote the book of Revelation. I sat in the cave and read the entire book. I was struck once again by the beauty of the symbolism. Though I don't know the exact meaning of the book, it gives me hope that there is a purpose to this world. I have a sense of trajectory and a belief that One is guiding time."

Gabriel's pensive reflections flow out naturally. He tells me that he has been studying communications and theater. He's taking time off to travel the world. He's a Baptist, and his understanding of God has been deepened in his travels.

"I have not felt alone in dark times on this trip. When I've been in need, people have taken care of me. Though I'm traveling alone, I haven't felt lonely."

I ask Gabriel to describe God and his dark brown eyes lighten. "God is my Creator. He's the one who reminds me to be a better person every day. He's the one who listens to me no matter where I am or what I'm doing. God's the one who protects me and guides me and the one who is waiting for me on that glorious day."

Gabriel looks up at the sun and says, "God's my Father. He's the light of my path, the smile behind my tears." His mom, he tells me, is a woman of faith, the one responsible for the man he is becoming. "Patmos was such a godly experience for me. I've decided not to go to Mykonos"—an island famous for its wild parties—"because I don't want to lose what I've gained from Patmos."

As we go to leave Gabriel tells me, "This is the first conversation about faith I've had in two months of traveling." I wave goodbye several times. Less than twelve hours ago Gabriel was just an annoying voice keeping me up at night. Now, Gabriel is a fellow pilgrim, a sacred journeyer, a person I'm destined to share one eternally gorgeous wedding feast with!

Ashes to beauty, indeed.

15

EPHESUS, TURKEY

"Practice walking with it," Jimmy suggests.

"Oh yah," Krista jumps in. "If you grab one handle and I get the other, I think we can do this."

Krista and I walk around Jimmy's expansive shop with our two 4' x 8' Turkish silk rugs folded in a duffle bag. The bag is remarkably lighter than one would think, we tell ourselves. How rare and gorgeous our carpets are! How strong and smart we both must be!

"There's one minor issue, Jimmy," I say with hesitation. "We don't have much money. We have hardly any."

"That's not a problem," Jimmy replies. "I take credit cards. You can even purchase it on a payment plan. I'll help you out."

"Thanks, Jimmy. We're almost certain we'll buy these two carpets. We just want to sleep on it."

Only a couple of hours ago we arrived in Selçuk, the modern town on the edge of ancient Ephesus. We've already walked the whole town, so to stave off boredom Krista and I have resorted to spending an evening looking at hundreds of luxurious carpets at the store owned by our hostel, Jimmy's Place. Jimmy is a charming host and a passionate salesman. He's explained how the colors in the carpets express meaning, and the symbols reveal where they were made, and the tightness of the knots per square inch indicate quality. We report what we've learned to Eric. "Can you believe it? We're going to be owners of genuine Turkish carpets."

"You're what?" Eric asks, aghast.

"Carpets. Isn't that wonderful?" I respond.

"There's no way I'm going to carry them for you." Eric speaks with a tone of determination that I've never heard from him.

"I know. Krista and I already practiced walking with them."

I go to bed dreaming of my beautiful, old carpet. Certainly I deserve to splurge every once in a while. It will be my reward for trekking all this way. Every day I can tromp barefoot on strands of silk purchased from one of the most important regions in antiquity.

Ephesus was home to the Temple of Artemis, which was considered to be one of the seven wonders of the world and the largest edifice in the ancient world for a time. By the end of the first century, the city had close to half a million inhabitants, making it the largest city in Roman Asia. It was famous for its intellectual atmosphere and commercial influence. Eventually it became an epicenter for Christianity; the apostle Paul made Ephesus his base for church planting, and the apostle John and Mary, Jesus' mother, are believed to have lived out their final days here. All of this intriguing history will be easily recalled every time I look at my salmon and olive-green silk rug lying majestically on my living room hardwoods. How lovely!

I awake with a burst and venture up to the buffet breakfast, included as a bonus with our less-than-ten-dollars-a-night hostel room. As I devour my bread, tomato, olives, boiled egg and watermelon, I read the book of Ephesians. This letter, written by the apostle Paul to the church here, has been one of my favorite pieces of spiritual literature through the years. Since I was a teen I've read and recited portions of it hundreds of times. Its intimate and encouraging words have invited me to hope in a world beyond myself and dream of a love larger than my imagination.

I flip back to Ephesians 3 as I finish my third cup of coffee. This prayer of Paul's for the Ephesians has been a mainstay for my restless soul. The few times I've had the privilege of officiating weddings, I've always included Paul's prayer as a blessing for the bride and groom. Some weddings have gone better than others, but they all seemed rescued by the magnificent benediction in Ephesians 3.

> I pray that out of [God's] glorious riches he may strengthen you with power through his Spirit in your inner being, so that Christ may dwell in your hearts through faith. And I pray that you, being rooted and established in love, may have power, together with all the saints, to grasp how wide and long and high and deep is the love of Christ, and to know this love that surpasses knowledge—that you may be filled to the measure of all the fullness of God.
>
> Now to him who is able to do immeasurably more than all we ask or imagine, according to his power that is at work within us, to him be glory in the church and in Christ Jesus throughout all generations, for ever and ever! Amen.

As I gulp my last sip of caffeine, I wonder what inspired Paul to pray this prayer for the Ephesians. Why was he so adamant that they comprehend the love of Christ?

After breakfast, Krista and I lug our monstrous backpacks to the front desk to be stored for the day. As we teeter down the stairs we simultaneously proclaim, "Are we idiots?" There's no way we're going to survive a trek through the Middle East heaving a separate bag of carpets. What were we thinking? Last night we were obviously tired and lacking the logic-inducing drug of caffeine. We regretfully inform Jimmy we can't buy the antique, storied, gorgeous and oh-so-slightly cumbersome carpets.

Jimmy's coworker drives the three of us to the Ephesus archaeological site. We're dropped off in a sea of ruins and tourists. Most people congregate in puddles around tour guides holding up umbrellas under an arid sky.

Eric resumes his role as tour guide. First he paints a picture of the vastness of the city. "Ephesus was so extensive that at one time it had two agoras—one for commerce and a separate one for state dealings." I think of Paul, and how he must have been in his element soaking up all the sites for banter and serendipitous interactions. Eric leads us along the Curetes Way, which means "Priest's Way." As we pass one column and stele after another, Eric keeps squatting to read the writing. "Hmm . . . very interesting."

"What are you discovering?" I beg.

"There are a lot of inscriptions." Before I can get a proper explanation, Eric's eyes and the rest of him move only inches away from another piece of stone. "This is remarkable," Eric notes in a reverent tone.

"Eric, please let us in on what you're finding," I say impatiently.

Eric steps back and takes on the posture of a professor. "See this two-story façade of columns? This is what is left of Domitian's temple. He sure was a narcissist." The inscriptions Eric's been noticing honor the patrons who constructed the monuments, statues or buildings. The majority of the benefactors of public buildings were emperors; however, some were magistrates or other wealthy individuals. Domitian used funds from the tax system to build edifices for publicity. He tried to have his name on as many public places as he could.

"While Roman emperors expected to be gods after their death, none before Domitian declared themselves to be a deity while they were alive. Building a temple dedicated to himself was unprecedented in his day," Eric continues. "This building was a huge display of hubris. Only the gods had temples dedicated to themselves. Domitian disrupted the status quo by forcing himself into the pantheon of the gods.

"And can you imagine?" Eric gasps. "Can you imagine what it was like to be a Jew in Ephesus at the time this temple was being constructed? You pay the Jewish Fund over there," Eric says pointing back at the administrative district, "and then as you walk by here on your way to conduct your business in the lower agora, you notice this new building being built. You ask the workers, 'Who is this magnificent edifice being dedicated to?' And they respond, 'The emperor is building this temple in honor of himself.' The thought of it! The very tax you thought was buying you the right to abstain from idolatry was going to finance probably the most egregious example of it!"

As Eric leads us toward an expansive and elegant façade at the end of the Curetes Way, I wonder what it was like for the apostle John to see Domitian's temple after Domitian's death. Did John revel in the poetic justice of the fact that Domitian got his fleeting moments of fame on earth, only to spend an eternity discovering he's no god? John doesn't seem the vengeful type. I suspect he would have been deeply saddened by the misguided nature of the emperor, rather than being consumed by revenge.

We reach the base of what Eric tells us is the Celsus Library, a magnificent two-storied façade with sophisticated Corinthian-style columns. "Gaius Julius Celsus was once the governor of the province of Asia. He's said to be buried below the building. This is another example of benefaction. In academic circles, it's actually called *evergetism*. When the library was built in 135 C.E., it was the third largest in the world. It had the capacity to hold more than twelve thousand scrolls. See the statues in the niches of the columns? They symbolize the supposed traits of Celsus." Eric squints to read the inscriptions and points as he says, "There's *Sophia*, that's wisdom. *Episteme* is knowledge. That reads *Ennoia;* I think that's intelligence. And then there's *Arete*, which is virtue.

"It may seem shallow and completely unethical to buy one's own honor and power. But we underestimate the impact of Jewish sensibility on Western culture. Jewish ideals have given us the impulse to credit God as the ultimate source of our good fortune. Archaeological evidence has revealed that Jewish donorship lists underplayed the role of the individual and placed the focus on the community. Jewish donors even credited their gifts to Providence.

"Jesus' teachings deeply reflect this Jewish sensibility. He taught that those who received praise from others for their acts of righteousness received their full reward on earth, rather than gaining a heavenly reward later. So it comes as some surprise that Jesus, in Revelation, promises the faithful several rewards that sound suspiciously like the honors benefactors gathered for themselves. This shows up most vividly in the letters to the seven churches in the first part of the book.

"Jesus offers a crown to those in the church in Smyrna. The Pergameme devout are given the hope of 'new names.' The lowly Thyatirans are promised a rod of iron to rule the nations. The Sardians are even promised to have their names proclaimed in the heavenly throne room, much like being conferred an honorary title. The overcoming Philadelphians are also promised new names, the Laodiceans get to sit with Jesus on his throne, and the Ephesians are invited to eat of the tree of life, which is in the paradise of God."

Eric's synapses seem to be firing like rockets. One of his great gifts is weaving themes together. It looks like some of his thoughts are coming together for the first time.

"Revelation's model of benefaction throws the patron-citizen relationship on its head. Jesus, the ruler of heaven, shares his rewards with the faithful citizens of his kingdom. The letters actually represent a drastic leveling of the honorary distance between the ruler and the ruled in Greco-Roman society. In fact, the promises indicate that the servant-citizens of Jesus' kingdom are to fully share in the act of government! The 'poor' and the 'powerless' are the very ones who are to sit on Christ's own throne.

"The apocalyptic vision reveals that God is always the benefactor. He inscribes *his* name on the faithful overcomers. They become the pillars of *his* temple. God's civic project is our lives. The honor that is due to himself, he inscribes on us."

I have to sit down. I'm hot and thirsty, and my mind feels like it has just run a marathon. After sprinting through centuries of ruins that tell the story of power-grabs after power-grabs and one calculated PR move after another, I'm worn out.

I can't help but think of celebrity culture in light of what Eric has told us. Today's celebrity culture turns teen pop stars into demagogues, actors and actresses into personas, athletes into "brands." Has creative expression been tainted by capitalistic greed from the beginning of human history? And how do I distinguish between marketplace agendas and personal motivations to make a difference? Why do cynical questions arise whenever a billionaire starts a foundation to help the poverty-stricken and the AIDS-afflicted, or a superstar adopts a child from Africa?

I gulp from my Nalgene bottle. I let more water pour than I can swallow.

It's one thing to try to sort out human proclivities toward self-promotion. It's another thing to try to grasp Jesus' approach to power. How do we relate to a God that defies societal norms of power and promotion? I suspect this context of self-promotion has to do with why Paul was so bent on the Ephesians comprehending the countercultural love of Jesus.

I rise from my seat on the steps facing the library and attempt to climb out of my head. I introduce myself to a tour guide named Ozzy. He's buff, twenty-five years old and from Istanbul.

"Ozzy, how do you describe Allah?" I ask.

"I visualize someone powerful. Allah has some effect on me, some influence on me. I believe, but I'm not a good Muslim."

"Why do you say that?"

"I don't do all the practices."

I change direction. "When you give tours in Ephesus, do you have any spiritual feelings?"

Ozzy's whole demeanor shifts. He becomes simultaneously relaxed and energized as he tells me, "I'm at home here. I studied architecture, so this is like a laboratory. I love it here."

Ozzy must reconnect with his group, so I approach another tour guide. It seems like the library area is where the guides and tourists temporarily take a break from each other.

"My name is Sibel. It comes from the goddess Artemis or Cybele." Sibel is tiny-framed, with copper hair and the complexion of a young beauty. She too is from Istanbul, and happens to be my age. She describes Allah as "a unique and big power. He is the one who forgives. And he gives everything you want."

"Wow!" I blurt out in amazement at the thought. "Does this place have a spiritual effect on you?"

"Yes. Many people have been here through the centuries. There were temples here. Whether you have the beliefs of those people or not, it feels special. You can feel the history here. I've been a guide here for five years. I'm here almost every day, and I never get bored."

I thank Sibel and leave. She seems gentle-spirited and genuine. It was inspiring to hear how much she loves her work. I turn back and glance at her again; she looks nothing like her namesake Artemis. Artemis was depicted as a many-breasted, mummylike honeybee. It's curious that Ephesus emerged as a major city because of her. Apparently the first idol of Artemis was carved of wood and set in an oak tree here by the Amazons. Soon it became a place of pilgrimage.

One temple succeeded another on the site. Thousands of people served in the temple. Huge sums of money were poured into keeping the cult of Artemis alive. In fact, the temple complex became the major banking center of Asia. Not only was Artemis the guardian deity of Ephesus but she was also seen as a savior goddess.

I wonder how Sibel's description of Allah would line up with the reputation of Ephesus's ancient goddess. Did queen bee Artemis give people everything they wanted? Did women get her assistance in childbirth? Did her devotees get rescued in life? Did she care for people in death?

I try to meander outside my head again and force myself to speak with two teenage girls from Puerto Rico. They looked at other faiths but still embrace the religion of their families, Catholicism. They feel something special here, yet it doesn't compare to what they feel when they pray to Mary.

I then have a chat with a couple from the Netherlands and with one from Australia. Both couples are overwhelmed by my question; both are agnostics. However, they greatly appreciate the history here.

I'm really hot and exhausted. I'm finding it difficult to be present to people. I just want to sink into an oversized couch with a big bowl of mocha almond fudge ice cream and watch a *Seinfeld* marathon. Instead I find Krista and Eric, and we venture to the theater, which has remained surprisingly intact through the centuries. Perhaps at the end of the day the Greeks prized their theaters more than their temples. Well, I don't know about that, but maybe their plays have had a greater impact on Western society than their religion. It's the Greeks who spread the tradition of tragedy. They gave us the word *theater*, which comes from their verb *theaomai,* meaning "to view" or "to look upon."

Their theaters were usually built into the side of a hill as an open-air structure with a semicircle of stone seats, typically seating five thousand. Every audience member was positioned to view the play, and every play was performed by only three actors, who acted all the various roles. We decide we'll sit in one of the rows and read about Paul's stay in Ephesus, especially how a mob in this theater that seats twenty-five thousand almost tore him apart.

Krista turns to Acts 19 and reads aloud about Paul entering the synagogue in Ephesus, spending three months bantering about the kingdom of God. Some people become obstinate and malign Paul for his beliefs in Jesus. So he trades his conversations in the synagogue for discussions in Ephesus's famous lecture hall. For two years Paul goes to the hall day after day, and—according to the account in Acts—"all the Jews and Greeks who lived in the province . . . heard the word of the Lord."

Wild miracles apparently were happening during Paul's time in Ephesus. Even Paul's handkerchiefs were used to heal people. The name of Jesus became revered throughout the city. In response to the teachings of Jesus, people burned magic scrolls apparently worth as much as 50,000 drachmas, roughly equivalent to 137 years' wages.

The burning of the scrolls reminds me of Savonarola's bonfires of the vanities, but Paul doesn't go on to enforce morality. Rather he commits himself to teaching the Ephesians about the love of God. Nevertheless, after the scroll burning, the silversmiths who sold idols of the goddess Artemis became nervous that Paul's preaching would cause them to lose their business. A mob formed in the theater.

As Krista reads the end of the chapter, we notice a familiar face. It's a guy we met in Croatia. Last time we saw him, he was disheveled and sluggishly searching for a hostel in Dubrovnik. I found his apathy about finding a place to stay intriguing.

We reintroduce ourselves to Brian. He has dark brown eyes that seem to take in all the color of life around him. He speaks with a voice like a personal trainer talking you through a cool down. My heart rate slows as he tells us about his year studying in Florence.

"My time there gave me a great start to seeing the world. Whenever I had a chance to travel, I did. I went to Amsterdam and Paris, Prague and Moscow. My view of the world has really changed."

Krista, Eric and I talk with Brian some about the challenges of moving back to the States after an adventure abroad. Then I ask him, "How do you describe God?"

Brian seems taken aback by the largeness of the question, but he rallies. "I am still in the early stages of trying to figure that out. God, it's very abstract. It's all around us, if you think about it. It's in you, in the sky, the clouds, the trees. It's creation; it's love. It's that energy that sort of keeps a peaceful order. It's not an order by force, but something invisible we all have inside us. We all have the capacity for love.

"I'm not very good with words, but I'm trying to keep it together. But, ah . . . I don't know. I mean, mankind has a lot of hope, you know."

I ask, "Why is that?"

"Everyone has the capacity for love. Unfortunately, there are a lot of people in power missing that point, you know, which I think is the point of life: to share the love, to be happy. I don't know. God—it's Mother Nature. It's in the galaxies, in the cosmos; it's a positive force that orders things, or at least has the capacity to."

"Ephesus has a lot of spiritual history. Have you had any spiritual feelings here?" I ask.

"Yah. I see that people in their own way here were looking for that kind of order. I was told that St. Paul preached here, preaching the message of Jesus. Jesus had a wonderful message, but I think it has been perverted in many ways by the church. You had guys trying to fix that, like St. Francis, you know, trying to bring things back like it really should be, as opposed to building lavish churches. You know, spending all this money for robes and gold.

"Jesus was just a simple shepherd guy. He rode a donkey around town. He didn't have his own pope-mobile or jet. You know . . ."

"What was Jesus' message for you?" I ask Brian.

"Love, essentially. It was being good and living the good life. There are a lot of religions. I think every religion shares that philosophy, whether it's Islam or Buddhism. Whatever deity you have, that deity is an example to follow. Someone to sort of guide you. I don't know. I forgot my point."

It strikes me that Brian cares deeply about these matters. "Is this something you've thought about a lot this past year?"

"Yah, I think so. I've always had it in mind, but seeing other possibilities out there, seeing other ways to live has had me thinking about it more. I was talking about this last night with some others. In the States there's so much stress in the freeways and on television. You have shows like *COPS*, and there are two million people behind bars. The U.S. is a beautiful country. It was built on beautiful ideals. It's got so much potential. But it falls so far short of that; you know what I mean? There's so much good we could be doing in the world, as opposed to starting wars and getting stuck in Iraq. People keep on dying. We could have gone in with peaceful means rather than going in and bombing the sh*t out of it. And, in the process there's been the killing of a lot of innocent people, which makes people more pissed off at us. And the anger just continues.

"What if this all-powerful country—where we teach love and peace—would put its weapons down? That would be a wonderful example to follow. It would be like following Jesus and his message. Yet greed and selfishness take over, and that is unfortunate. It's not how it is supposed to be."

Brian stops himself and asks, "What was your original question?"

"How do you describe God?" I reply, with a smirk. Brian embarks on another response to the description of God. He talks about the importance of learning from history and the mistakes the Romans made, and how that was carried on by Constantine in the church. We chat with Brian for about an hour. He's an obvious thinker, desiring to pursue paths of peace in this world. While he says he's still trying to sort out his understanding of God, his musings left me with questions.

What would the world be like if Jesus' message of love moved through the ages uncorrupted?

How would the church that Paul worked so hard to help start look today? How would that affect the world's struggle with peace and greed?

Eric's words earlier today collide with my questions. "God chose to make us his glorious civic project." While the civic projects in ancient Ephesus were motivated by self-promotion, the libraries and waterworks and government buildings did help better Greek society. I believe that is what followers of Jesus are supposed to do all the more: in promoting God's love, we are to contribute to the needs of those around us.

God's glorious civic project: what if that was what the church was known for?

We get back to Selçuk, and Eric and I hike up to the ruins of St. John's Basilica, which lay scattered on a hill. Four columns mark the place where John, the confidant of Jesus, is thought to be buried. Eric and I move like two little slugs through the maze of stone remnants of John's final days.

Perhaps John wrote his Gospel right here? Maybe John had dinner parties over there? Would he have welcomed us young strangers to come in and mine his mind? I would have loved to stop by. But out of all the places for John to move after he was released from exile in Patmos, why did he chose Ephesus? I wonder if it has to do with Jesus' words to the church here, which John recorded in Revelation: "I know your deeds, your hard work and your perseverance. . . . Yet I hold this against you: You have forsaken your first love."

Was that the worst tragedy of all for John, to know that some of his people were working really hard to be good, were living counterculturally in a sea of paganism but somehow were letting love slip away? Perhaps even in John's last days, even after a difficult exile in Patmos, he was intent on helping others know and experience God's love.

Eric and I make a few circles around the ruins and sleepwalk back to find Krista. We have less than half an hour to catch our bus. So we dash to collect our baggage from the hostel and say goodbye to Jimmy. He was such a generous host. I feel bad that he spent all that time showing us carpets and we didn't buy one. But there's no way we could run with our carpets, and we seem to always be running these days.

As our bus chugs on to Izmir, ancient Smyrna, I say a little prayer to ask God to help me remember the story of Ephesus. That carpet would have been a gorgeous reminder of the ancient city and of Jimmy; I'm afraid the idea of being "God's glorious civic project" may become more elusive when I get back home.

I'm learning so much, but there are so many more experiences left to be had before I get to Jerusalem. Will I be up for the journey?

16

IZMIR/SMYRNA, TURKEY

"My family wouldn't even say the word *Turkey* for the longest time. So when I told them I was moving here, it put them into shock."

Nancy, a forty-something acquaintance of Eric's from his MIT undergrad years, is an Armenian American running an Internet café in Turkey's third largest city. We sip cappuccinos around a small table in Nancy's café in Izmir after our fifty-mile bus ride from Ephesus. Lyrics from a song by the British band Delirious, "I'm not ashamed of the gospel," play in the background as she shares her parents' shame at her decision to live here. Nancy never would have imagined her story taking this twist.

Today Izmir is known for its thriving university, global trade and liberal lifestyles. However, this progressive place's extensive urban history dates back 3,500 years. For over two millennia the city's name was Smyrna. In the first century, the church here was the recipient of one of the seven letters in Revelation.

Smyrna was renowned for its advancements in science and medicine, and for its majestic buildings. It was also famous for its alliance with Rome; the city actually petitioned Emperor Tiberius to allow them to build a temple to his deity. The city proved its devotion to the Caesar cult in grand form. When Domitian came to power, nondevotees to the emperor—especially the Christians—suffered in Smyrna. The synagogue here didn't provide safe haven for followers of Jesus, so Christians found themselves on the margins of both the dominant and the minority communities.

Polycarp, a disciple of the apostle John, was arrested in Smyrna and urged by a sympathetic Roman proconsul to offer a small pinch of incense to Caesar's statue and say "Caesar is Lord"; by doing so he would escape a painful execution. Polycarp responded famously, "Eighty-six years I have served Christ, and he never did me any wrong. How can I blaspheme my King who saved me?" He was subsequently executed. Here in Smyrna the blood of the Christian martyrs was spilled in the streets.

While I've only known Nancy for less than an hour, I've gained immense respect for her. She strikes me as a woman of great courage and conviction. As the Soviet Union dissolved, Nancy was one of the first Americans to move to Armenia, her family's homeland, working with InterVarsity Christian Fellowship to start a Christian student movement there. During that time, electricity and other basic services were sporadic. Yet she worked energetically, and the student movement grew and grew. When she returned to the States she was welcomed home as a hero by her Armenian community in Washington, D.C.

"Coming to Turkey has been a tragedy to my parents. They went from having a daughter heralded for helping the homeland to then seeing me go to the land of the enemy, the country that exacted genocide on our people." I can't imagine how difficult Nancy's journey has been, to go from being thought a hero to being called a traitor, all while following what she saw as God's direction for her life.

I learned about the Armenian genocide when I lived in Jerusalem. Posters lined the ancient alleys of the Armenian Quarter, declaring the murder of 1.5 million Armenians. A catastrophic genocide had occurred in the early 1900s and I had not even known about it. I began to grieve for the Armenians and went on a quest to learn more. I made friends with the Armenian historian in Jerusalem. I read government documents and academic papers. I discovered that the king of Armenia was the first Christian king in recorded history, years before Constantine. Armenians through the centuries built beautiful churches and superb hospitals. The Armenian Evangelical

Movement was established in 1870 and continued up to 1915. It was said that because of the Armenians there wasn't a city in the Ottoman Empire that didn't have a Christian witness.

I learned about the death marches and destruction of ancient Armenian churches, the blood and the bodies that flowed down the Euphrates during the dark days from 1914 to 1917. I became infuriated with Turkey and outraged at the international community of that day.

"People in Turkey still deny the genocide," Nancy tells me. "They refer instead to the departures and deaths of the Armenians as 'the cultural wars.' Maybe Turkey was threatened by Armenian culture or faith. Or maybe the use of the term 'cultural wars' simply has allowed the populace to sleep at night. It wasn't just a 'cultural war' that caused my grandparents to flee their home. It wasn't some theoretical disagreement that compelled so many other Armenians to leave Turkey.

"But how could I deny what I believe has been God's leading for my life—no matter how difficult the assignment? We who have Christ struggle with forgiving others; how much more do those who haven't known Christ's forgiveness? The Turks need to experience God's grace and forgiveness in order for a spiritual awakening to take place."

Nancy came here in the hope of showing Jesus' love and forgiveness. However, she has to be careful how she shares her faith. She operates an Internet café and runs English conversation classes. Christian posters hang on the café wall, and Christian music plays through the speakers. Yet during her classes she doesn't mention Christianity. Her students discuss current affairs and challenges in the world.

"The university scene here is very secular. Because of the legacy of Atatürk, education takes on a socialist atmosphere. Students are encouraged not to have any expression of faith. So for some students, when they come into the café they are meeting Christians for the very first time. People walk in and say they feel something different. I believe what they feel is God's Spirit. Though Turkey is typically closed to Christianity, I find that it's very easy to talk about spiritual things with the students."

Many of the students, Nancy finds, seem disappointed with Islam. "They don't really get instruction about it. Though the Qur'an has been published in Turkish, many see reading it in any language other than Arabic as hypocrisy. The students don't know Arabic. They memorize sections of the Qur'an in the holy language but don't understand it.

"Sometimes students will stay after classes and ask me questions about my faith. I tell them about my relationship with Jesus and that I pray for them as well. Many seem amazed that the God of the universe—whom they fear—would actually have an interest in their lives."

Nancy looks down pensively at her empty coffee cup for a moment. She resumes by saying, "It's very difficult to change one's religion in Turkey. This country is all about group identity. If the group doesn't go for it, it's extremely hard for people to choose faith on their own. There is a student I know who reads his New Testament every day and is trying to follow the words of Christ. He says that his professors and others tell him Christians are evil. The ties to family and friends are so strong; it takes incredible courage to become a Christian believer here.

"There are lots of misconceptions about Christians in this country. And the church has a tenuous status here. Unless the church has been recognized by the state, it is a nonentity, and nonrecognized churches can't own property, pay taxes, et cetera. Yet churches pop up. They are not *illegal,* but because the law is so ambiguous they are not completely *legal.* It's not clear, and it's frustrating. People do what they do, but the authorities don't like it."

Nancy doesn't lead a church, but she's had to deal with a court case regarding the café's status. "I've been told they're going to do everything they can to kick me out; I've even experienced death threats. The police are constantly watching. The terrorist police, who monitor the Kurds, also monitor the Christians. They've barged into the café several times. However, since we've had a court case going for two years, we've been freer to do what we think we should do. I guess it's because there's less to lose."

Nancy seems fearless as she talks. "There are over a thousand Christian workers in Turkey, but there hasn't been a lot of movement. People aren't courageous enough with their faith. If Turkey is rejected by the EU, there will be greater persecution of Christians, but perhaps the church will grow in the midst of it, like it did in its early history and recently in China."

In light of Nancy's story, I'm curious how she will describe God. Her faith in God has led her to the land of her enemies. It caused her to exchange her identity of hometown hero to foreigner struggling with authorities. So who does Nancy know God to be?

Nancy's demeanor relaxes when I ask her. "I believe I am following a God who is out to redeem history. God is a glorious and hopeful God. He's also very much a God who sacrifices and suffers. People don't understand that our God is both the Savior who suffered on the cross and the Savior who rose from the dead. We tend to fixate on one aspect or the other of God's character. In Armenia and Turkey I've seen people who are stuck in the sufferings of Christ on the cross. My friends in the States tend to focus on the God of the resurrection. To them life is great and they have no sense of people's pain.

"It's when you say that life is unjust and see the pain"—Nancy stalls for a moment, perhaps images of pain play out before her—"There are times when I go home and just cry. Yet God is a God of hope and joy. There is mystery in both sides. God lives in both realities, in the suffering and hope. I've experienced a lot of pain and sacrifice. I've found God to be very much in the midst of that. I see his fingerprints in those times. I've also known great joy. I'll tell you, there's no greater joy, life and relief to the soul of the students when they get to know Christ."

As Nancy has been describing God, Jesus' letter to Smyrna comes to mind.

These are the words of him who is the First and the Last, who died and came to life again. I know your affliction and your poverty—yet you are rich! . . . Do not be afraid of what you are about to suffer. I tell you, the devil will put some of you in prison to test you, and you will suffer persecution for ten days. Be faithful, even to the point of death, and I will give you the crown of life.

I can't help but think of how God would describe Nancy. I imagine he wouldn't hesitate to say, "I know your affliction and your poverty—yet you are rich!"

Nancy suggests we go to her favorite pizza café for dinner. I'd go eat rocks with Nancy if she wanted to—anything to get more time with this strong, courageous woman.

Over steaming flatbread vegetarian pizza, Nancy shares that Turkey is in the midst of an identity crisis. The university cities, such as Istanbul, Izmir and Anchora, have an air of secularism. In the rest of the country the women have their head covered and the men are religiously conservative.

"How is it to be living in Turkey as a single woman?" I inquire between bites.

Nancy graces us with a candid conversation about her struggles with singleness and the gifts that have emerged from it. "Are you sure you must leave this evening?" she asks us.

"Yes, we need to be in Istanbul by morning," I respond.

She looks like she wishes we'd stay. Perhaps she would enjoy the company this weekend. But she offers to drive us to the bus stop.

My comment about needing to get to Istanbul was half true, and half not.

We originally planned to be in Istanbul tomorrow. However, Eric made arrangements for us to stay in Izmir tonight. Krista and I were open to it; that is, until we arrived at the hotel Eric booked and found out that it was a hundred dollars or more per room, which might as well have been a million dollars or so. Our exhaustion from walking around centuries' worth of ruins in Ephesus all day made logical communication elusive, so we've yet to sort out the money situation. The bill was destined to go on my credit card, so suddenly it became imperative we get to Istanbul. We canceled our hotel rooms. I got mad at Eric and Eric got frustrated with me.

I have a budget and a return flight already booked. Time and money must be respected; or, at least those are the staples I've grown up on in my Western world. This journey keeps challenging my notions of what's important.

People have been so generous to me; they've given me time and even gifts, and I've struggled to receive.

Receiving isn't my only struggle, I guess. I'm finding it hard to give, when giving calls for sacrifice. As I look at Nancy across the street waiting in her car to make sure we get our bus, I'm sad. I feel selfish for not being willing to disrupt my budget and inconvenience our agenda in order to stay an evening and get to know her more, perhaps even encourage her on her journey.

Nancy's description of God comes to mind. Hers is a God "glorious and hopeful"—as well as one "who sacrifices and suffers." Am I like some of Nancy's friends from the States who just focus on the resurrected God? Does my Westernized view of God inhibit me from making sacrifices?

I silently mouth a prayer, *"Suffering and hopeful God, I, like Turkey, am in desperate need of your love and forgiveness."*

17

ISTANBUL, TURKEY

Some days I wake up and want sex. Other days I want nothing else. Today is the latter.

Maybe it's just Istanbul—the city's clash of cultures creates an intense sexual energy. At its essence Istanbul exists in sturdy contrasts. Spread across the *Bosphorus,* or the Istanbul Strait, Istanbul is the only metropolis that embraces two continents, clasping hands with both Europe and Asia. It exudes the libido of a teenage boy while maintaining the elegance of a refined woman. The city is clothed in the finest of European fashion, bejeweled with the best of Eastern architecture and perfumed with the scent of the sea. And so it seems like every gulp of its air is saturated with sexual tension.

The last time I breathed Istanbul's sultry air, I had to rally all of my reserves not to have sex with a random Turkish fine-leather coat salesman. He was Italian Turk, which made matters even more difficult. My friend and I had gone to Istanbul for a long weekend. Every night we had been asked out by men, and every night it became progressively trickier to resist sex.

Tony the Turk was working at the posh boutique where my friend bought her leather jacket. He was charming and attentive, and offered to call his brother and take us out for a proper last night in Istanbul. How could we say no?

We dined in the happening *Taksim* district; we were dazzled by a night-tour of the city; well past midnight, we arrived at a quaint bar situated along the *Bosphorus.*

Tony's declarations of affection increasingly became blunt requests for sex, accompanied by soft kisses to my neck. Every pheromone in my body was screaming, "Yes! Yes!" He was attractive, and attracted to me—at least for that moment.

It had been so long since I had felt pursued. Actually, the guy I had gone out with the night before was much more my type—intelligent, funny, cultured, dark-haired, respectful. We had danced in a reggae club and then in a club that played *good* American eighties music. He knew all the lyrics, and he knew how to spin me. We just didn't share the same faith. So when he asked to kiss me, I knew I couldn't linger.

But here was Tony, and here I was even more sexually frustrated than the night before. Beside us my friend was making out with Tony's younger brother. I couldn't kiss Tony back. If I did, it would be all over for me.

I awoke the next morning in my hotel bed, alone. I was somber. I knew I had come close to having sex for the first time.

This visit to Istanbul should be quite different. I'm searching for the sacred this time. I stare out the window and see the skyline appear like a field of flowers abloom with minarets and domes, towers and a few crosses. Krista, Eric and I have exchanged our bus for a taxi and are traveling toward the flat occupied by a guy my dad took a Greek class with and who now lives in Istanbul. The guy is traveling, but his wife has offered to host us.

Lisa, a petite woman with brown hair flowing down her back and a voice like a bubbling brook, welcomes us. Her personality transforms our travel-weary moods like a shot of carbonation pumped into soda syrup. She's pure zest. Although she hasn't even met my dad—let alone Krista, Eric and myself—she has organized her busy life to host us for the next couple of days. After replenishing us with food and drink, she takes us downtown.

The tram is packed with people. I gaze out the window as we return to the heart of the city along the same route we'd come only hours ago. As I stare anew at Istanbul's edifices I wonder how this city's history might be told as a love story. I imagine it would start with the powerful Constantine, sweeping the poor but beautiful Byzantium off her feet.

Byzantium, today's Istanbul, was virtually unknown and untouched in the early fourth century when Constantine declared her *Nova Roma*. In 324 C.E. Constantine won his final victory over Licinius at the Battle of Chrysopolis on the *Bosphorus*, ending the civil war between the Roman emperors and consolidating Constantine's power over east and west.

Constantine had ruled from Rome for over a decade, but the city was too removed to exert influence over the eastern regions of the Empire. So Rome became Constantine's starter wife. Perhaps Constantine was already looking to move on; Rome was losing her sex appeal due to spates of flooding and outbreaks of malaria. The city could no longer provide the needed playground for the rich and famous. Constantine was likely getting a bit bored with his city.

Then came Byzantium, poised to become Constantine's trophy wife. Constantine could create her as he wanted her, he could easily defend her, and—perhaps best of all—he could Christianize her, unifying the churches of the east and the west. Constantine claimed to have a vision that God led him to her. Certainly God wanted Constantine to be happy.

So Constantine claimed Byzantium as his own. Immediately he went about adorning his new lover with jewels. If this new city were to be a place of power, elaborate amenities would have to be built in great haste—even if it meant that the raw materials of columns, marbles, doors and tiles had to be absconded from the temples of his other cities. Nothing in Constantine's vast Empire seemed to be off limits for his *Nova Roma*. The finest of Greek and Roman art suddenly appeared in her squares and streets.

Constantine created a few incentives to attract a population worthy of an emperor. He promised people land and food if they moved to Byzantium. As with Rome, in Constantine's new city approximately eighty thousand free food rations were doled out every day from over a hundred places around the city.

Soon *Nova Roma* had sophisticated gardens, military fortifications, the royal court and a church. In 330 C.E., the year Helena died, Byzantium was declared the new capital of the Roman Empire. Seven years later, upon the emperor's death, the city took his name. For the next thousand years she would be known as Constantinople.

≽≼

Lisa's tour of the city begins with the Hagia Sophia, the diamond of Constantinople in its glory days and the epicenter of the most tragic tales of Constantinople's relationship with Christendom.

We walk through the front gardens, which have millennia-old columns and marble pieces strewn on the ground. Apparently this space was the site of a pagan temple when Constantine came to town. He had a church, the "Great Church," built on top of the ruins. It was later burned in riots, and another was built on top of it; that too was eventually destroyed.

In 532 C.E. Justinian I started building something with a little more staying power. Emperor Justinian enlisted a physicist and a mathematician to be the architects. They created a dome like no other during its day. It took a construction team of ten thousand workers to get the project off the ground. When it was completed in 537 Justinian said ever so humbly, "Solomon, I have surpassed thee!" For over a thousand years the Hagia Sophia was the largest cathedral in the world and housed, before they were stolen and distributed to churches throughout the West, some of the greatest relics of Christian history—bones of heralded saints, the shroud of Jesus, a stone from the tomb of Jesus and the Virgin Mary's milk.

As I step into the edifice it feels like I am walking into a cold cosmos just after the separation of light and dark. The grandeur of the place is inescapable, but the ethos of it is confusing. My eyes are repeatedly pulled to the ceiling. I squint to see extreme details of design. Crosses are painted over with geometric designs. Mosaics of Christ and the names of Allah mingle together. Despite the wealth of religious imagery, it feels more like a museum than a place of worship.

The Hagia Sophia is no longer the epicenter of worship for the Greek Orthodox Church, the seat of the Orthodox patriarch of Constantinople or the primary setting for Byzantine imperial ceremonies—like it had been for almost a millennium. Nor is this edifice, the model for so many other mosques built in the sixteenth century, any longer the dominant mosque in Istanbul. Its almost five-hundred-year history of being a mosque came to an end when Turkey's first president, Mustafa Kemal Atatürk, turned it into a museum in 1935, as my admission ticket unabashedly tells me.

I had hoped it would feel different here—or at least that I would. I've been here before, and it felt like a cold cosmos then as well. I try to adjust my expectations once again and approach it like an object of curiosity, one that I'm emotionally detached from, one that I can professionally observe.

My professional detachment disintegrates when I walk past the Tomb of Enrico Dandolo, the doge of Venice. I want to spit on it. I wouldn't be the first; the dear doge with his posse of Crusaders carried out the Sack of Constantinople in 1204, raping and pillaging the beautiful Hagia Sophia. The Fourth Crusade, originally launched to reclaim Jerusalem, turned into the capture of Constantinople—perhaps the most obscene story line in Christian history.

Pope Innocent III championed the Fourth Crusade to stop the spread of Islam and reclaim Jerusalem for Christendom. The Great Schism of 1054 had split the church of the East and the church of the West, and now the West envisioned itself rescuing the East and coming together against a common enemy. The mission was trumped, however, by economic and political agendas, a scenario that has happened time and again in the church's history. By the time the doge and the Latin Crusaders made it to Constantinople they had disregarded the pope's pleas not to desecrate the Hagia Sophia.

The doge had his own monetary motivations for pillaging the treasures of the church, and many of the Crusaders had collected a chestful of hatred toward the Greeks that compelled them to rape this sacred space. The crusaders murdered Orthodox clerics, violated nuns, destroyed paintings, smashed silver iconostases, and demolished icons and holy books. They even had a whore sit upon the patriarchal throne in the Hagia Sophia and sing coarse songs to them as they drank wine from the church's holy vessels. Upon his death, the doge was entombed in the church.

The endeavor was a disaster—an utter failure in both premise and execution. After the Sack of Constantinople the Greek Orthodox were convinced that the Turkish Muslims would not have been as cruel as the Latin Christians. The Fourth Crusade ultimately was a victory of Islam.

When the Byzantines recaptured Constantinople from the Crusaders and won back control of the Hagia Sophia in 1261, a line of Greeks formed to spit on the doge's tomb. I refrain from casting my saliva in solidarity, and climb upstairs to look at the mosaics.

In the mosaic *Virgin and Child flanked by Justinian I and Constantine I,* Mary is oversized and Jesus is a contented baby boy sitting on her lap. The Christ child gives a blessing with his right hand and holds a scroll in his left. Emperor Constantine presents Mary with a model of his beloved city; Justinian gives Mary a model of the Hagia Sophia. I liked the mosaic the last time I saw it. This time it seems prosaic, maybe untrue. I can't set myself up as judge of these emperors' motives, but emperors holding churches and cities makes me slightly squeamish. Perhaps what bothers me more is the image of Jesus as a little kid compared to those emperors and Mary. It's nothing like the image of Jesus that shows up in John's revelation. Maybe the proportions of the mosaic tell the real story.

I've had enough. I need to see green grass, a wooden bench and twenty-first-century people who will tell me about their own proportions of God. I approach two couples standing in the courtyard.

Costos, a strapping thirty-something, responds to my request to describe God. "For us Greeks, you can't find words to describe God. It's something you believe, something that gives us power."

"What did you feel when you were inside the Hagia Sophia?" I ask, wondering if he experienced anything different from a cold cosmos.

"I was very disappointed." Costa's energy deflates as he shares. "This was our greatest church, and they have made it into a museum. All these people come in there and they don't know the history of this church and what has happened here."

I thank Costa and approach a few others, but they say they can't describe God because the Divine is indescribable. Anyway, it's time to meet up with Krista, Eric and Lisa.

We venture to another of Justinian's feats: the Basilica Cistern. While Eric and Krista take a tour of the underground cistern with its ancient forest of columns, Lisa and I chat. Lisa and her husband left a comfortable life in the United States a couple of years ago to do exhausting and at times dangerous humanitarian work mainly with Kurds, a minority population in Turkey. They've spent a significant time studying the culture and language. Lisa seems to love the adventure, even in the midst of great challenges.

"Turkey looks Western on the outside but tends to be more fanatical at the core," Lisa tells me. "Superstition is a powerful force here, even among the educated. Witchcraft and spells seem to work here. I have a friend who hadn't been able to sleep. She tore up her pillow and discovered a curse. There are neighborhoods with coffee shops that have future telling. People gather to read tea leaves and tarot cards.

"Women have less access to the truths of Islam than men. They don't often read the Qur'an and aren't taught by the imam. For some, their faith has been formed by the hadith"—the oral traditions of Muhammad's sayings and deeds—"and shaped by folk elements of Islam such as the idea of the Evil Eye and the fear that demons enter the orifices. Syncretism still exists between Islam and the tribal religions.

"In the midst of the superstitions and curses, I believe there is something larger at work. The demonic world feeds on people's fear. On the flip side, I believe God has used dreams and visions to help the Turks get to know Jesus. Many of the Turkish believers I know had dreams that started them on the path to Christ. Someone comes to them in a dream and tells them to speak with a certain person who happens to be a Christian. The people just know that the person in their dream is Jesus."

As Lisa speaks, memories of my formative years accost me. Some people I knew growing up claimed to see demons behind every corner. Counseling and medication were often ignored in favor of a more spiritual cure for various issues.

I've swung to the other extreme. I prefer not to think about an unseen world of evil. I guess, when it comes to the supernatural, in my gut I want a God who acts in ways I can understand and predict.

Yet Lisa is telling me about a God who works in the most unpredictable ways here in Turkey. "There's a guy my husband and I met at an Internet café. We struck up a friendship with him. He then went to the fortuneteller, who told him that he had made friends with an American couple and that they are good and he needs to get to know them more. This culture seems to respond to dramatic expressions of faith. The younger people, however, don't like to talk about religion as much. Atatürk gave society a sense that religion is a private matter. Nevertheless, there's a strong integration of nationalism and religion."

Before I can ask Lisa about how that integration plays out, Eric and Krista return. The conversation shifts to the fabulous pictures Krista was able to take and where our next meal might be eaten. Lisa decides we should go to İstiklal Avenue and Taksim Square, Turkey's equivalent to Times Square in New York. On our way we duck into one of Istanbul's historic wine bars located in the embassy district. Surrounded by dark wood walls and early 1900s craftsmanship we sip local wine, savor an array of cheeses, bread and fruit, and discuss global issues. I feel refined, enlightened, European. I accidentally start talking with a slight English accent.

Endowed with a lovely meal and a sense of internal wealth, we strut along the İstiklal Avenue. I notice an iron gate with a sign indicating it's a Catholic church. Lisa, Krista and Eric are game to explore it.

The inside of the church is barely lit and almost empty. I make a quick circuit and go back outside to see if any of the people pleasantly loitering on the steps would be willing to be interviewed. Yasar introduces himself. When I ask him to describe God, he looks reluctant.

"I'm not so religious. My ID card reads 'Muslim,' but I'm agnostic. I don't think so much about religious things or God. So I describe myself as agnostic. I can't make a description of God for that reason."

"OK." I respond. I consider thanking him and leaving. It seems no one in this city wants to describe God. Instead I ask, "Were you religious at one time?"

"No. Never."

I plow forward. "Why are you here on the steps of a church?"

Yasar turns to the people he is with. "We are just visiting here. It's a very beautiful place. It's a place everyone should see. I was born in Istanbul and I went to university here. I studied economics, now I'm looking for a job—maybe with the military."

"Do you think Istanbul is a very religious city?" I may be pushing my luck that Yasar will want to continue the topic.

"It changes with the population," Yasar responds. "I think young people are not so religious. The people are living with popular culture, and there is no religion in popular culture. I don't know."

Yasar's "I don't know" carries an unusual conviction. After a substantial pause he continues. "I do not deny there may be a God. Yet I can't place myself in a religion for now. Maybe it will change in the future."

A teenager walks up. Yasar introduces me to her. "This is my niece Ebru. She is studying English." Ebru is sixteen years old and likes English. She is taller than Yasar and has the confidence of a young woman who knows she's attractive. Since she is still learning English, Yasar kindly agrees to translate my question.

"I believe Allah created everything in the world. There is a saying from Turkish that Allah created everything from nothing."

Yasar adds, "She believes more than me." He then continues translating Ebru's response. "Allah was not born. I believe after death you go back to Allah. I believe, but I do not do the religious practices."

Yasar decides to offer commentary on his niece's beliefs. "Many people here aren't practicing. They may believe like Ebru, but if you ask them 'Do you practice?' they don't. It's ridiculous to me actually, as an agnostic. If you believe you must practice. You can't say 'I believe in just words'; if you believe you must do it. Maybe that's why I say I'm an agnostic. If I'm not living out the practices of my religion, I can't say I believe."

Ebru, who obviously hasn't understood what Yasar's been saying, jumps in with her final comment. "Islam represents peace."

With that we all say goodbye. But as I thank Yasar, I think about what wisdom he has. I imagine Jesus would have said "Amen!" to his frustration about those who say they believe and don't do. In fact, few things I can think of made Jesus more riled than a heap of words void of action—especially in the name of religion. Once Jesus healed a blind man on the sabbath, and some of the people blasted him for violating the holy day of rest. Jesus suggested that those who lack compassion are the truly blind.

Jesus risked everything to live out his words about loving God and others. I can't imagine the pain and disappointment God has endured when he has seen people wearing breastplates with crosses and swinging swords to kill in his name. Constantinople's tragic love story was perhaps one of God's saddest moments.

My mind staggers briefly back to Izmir. I get so angered over the Crusades and frustrated—like Yasar—about people saying they believe in something without backing it up with actions, and yet I realize it's easier for me to dole out generous, well-meaning sentiments than do gritty, self-sacrificing good deeds. I suppose I'm as vulnerable to what Jesus characterized as hypocrisy as anyone.

Lisa, Krista, Eric and I sally back down the İstiklal Avenue catwalk. The sky is spattered red with dusk's glow. By the time we arrive back at Lisa's flat, night has settled into blackness. I'm physically exhausted from weeks of travel and emotionally wiped out from the tragic love story of this city. I collapse into bed so very tired.

I awake tired. I slept well, but right now I could sleep for days. The sun and moon could switch places again and again and again while I lie in this bed talking to no one, walking nowhere, doing nothing. Perhaps then my fatigue would feel satiated.

I hoist my body up from the bed and gaze out the window. Gray. The gray outside doesn't strike me as the flat gray of Belgrade. Here the gray is more mysterious, more unknown.

I grab my Bible and lower myself back in bed. I read the proverb for the day, Proverbs 19. I underline the beginning of verse 22: "What a man desires is unfailing love . . ." I read, but I can't gather the words to pray for divine encounters.

"Oh my gosh! Elephantitis! My ankles have turned into elephant parts overnight!" Krista's words shatter my meager attempts to ease into the day. As I'm about to accuse her of being overly dramatic I glance down. Oh yah, I'd be alarmed too. Her ankles are *huge!* "How did that happen?"

Hours of walking, twelve-hour overnight bus rides and our two-country-per-week pace. Oops.

Lisa is a gracious and intuitive host. Observing Krista's freakishly swollen ankles, my fatigue-slathered face and Eric's current comatose state, she declares today a "Day of Rest." She serves us breakfast, waits for our food to properly digest and then escorts us to a fishing village along the *Bosphorus*. OK, it isn't a fishing village. It's just one of Istanbul's charming neighborhoods along the sea, one with a mosaic of cafés, restaurants and vendors selling silver rings and cashmere wraps. Everyone seems appropriately sleepy and hardworking. Perhaps they'll all move to a fishing village when they retire.

Lisa offers to collect us several hours later. Krista, Eric and I scatter, but not in our usual manner; sketching, photography and interviewing are far from a given. My legs drag me to the sea. I spot an outdoor café and order a cappuccino. In an ocean of tables for two, I sit alone in conversation with God.

Perhaps the thing that has disturbed the "god of my gut" the most has been my singleness. I'd describe God, as so many on this pilgrimage have, as loving. Yet I was created with such a healthy sex-drive and have yet to marry—and I have committed myself to celibacy in my singleness. There are moments when my gut is inclined to describe God as less than loving—"the Divine who entices but doesn't deliver"; "the God who gives others good gifts, but not me." Oh, and "the God who is waiting for me to get my act together until I am worthy of a man."

I look down at my cappuccino cup. The coffee has been drained. There's only froth left: my favorite part. I hear a familiar voice that has whispered to me in moments of silence, contented or desperate: *My daughter, I love you more than you know. You are beautiful to me. You are loved forever by me. I will never leave you. I will never forsake you. You can't out-trust me. I won't reject you. You aren't going to be made a fool for believing I am good. I love you.*

I pay my bill. I meander through the stalls of silver rings and cashmere wraps. I walk about as one loved, loved entirely.

I locate Krista, who shows me the silver ring she bought. She has great taste in rings. We find Eric and then Lisa and dine together. After a scrumptious Turkish meal, I retire early. I sleep as the moon and the sun switch places. I walk nowhere. I do nothing. I talk to no one. And yet I'm not alone.

"They don't look too bad" I tell Krista. Her ankles are still freakishly large, just not as elephanormous as yesterday morning.

Today we are bound to do more walking. We have one day left to explore Istanbul before we climb into an overnight bus headed to Cappadocia, Turkey. We say our farewells to Lisa and take the tram one last time downtown. As the Hagia Sophia and the Sultan Ahmed Mosque across from it come into view, I can't help but think more about Constantinople's tragic love story.

Some fifty years after the Fourth Crusade, the Orthodox Christians recaptured Constantinople from the Latin Christians, but so much damage had been done. How does one go on after such betrayal? How does a city regain its sense of self after such death? Constantinople was only a shadow of her former self. Islamic Turks were gaining more and more influence in the city, and the Greek Orthodox seemed to be losing more and more heart.

In 1453 the Ottoman Turks captured Constantinople. One of their first acts was to turn the Hagia Sophia into a mosque. Before the official conversion could take place, however, the Hagia Sophia had to undergo a thorough makeover. The once glorious church had gone into utter disrepair; even some of its doors had gone missing. The sultan ordered her to be scrubbed and then made to be a proper Muslim house of worship. Fresh plaster was placed over her mosaics of Jesus and the saints. (In Islam, as in Judaism, images of humans are not used in worship, and it is considered a sacrilege to depict God in human form.) The crosses were also covered. A mihrab was added and a minaret was built.

The city became known as Istanbul. Constantinople's bitter divorce with Christendom was finally official. The once cherished maiden who had become the abused wife was now the possession of a new lover.

For the next few centuries Ottoman edifices bloomed all across the city. The Hagia Sophia served as a model for several new mosques built in the sixteenth century, including the Sultan Ahmed Mosque, constructed directly across the road. Krista, Eric and I stand in its courtyard right now. Though it's drizzling, hundreds of other tourists join us in this vast space. The Blue Mosque, as it is often called because of the twenty thousand tiles of blue ceramic that adorn its interior, is one of Istanbul's most popular tourists sites.

We follow the crowd to the portico, where a line forms to enter the Muslim holy site. There's an impressive setup for preparing people to experience the Blue Mosque. A system of managed chaos enables each of us to remove our shoes, gives each of us a plastic bag to carry them in, and provides head coverings for Krista and myself. Within minutes we go from looking like Western tourists to resembling observant Muslims from the East.

As I step barefoot into the Blue Mosque, I feel like I'm seeing the sun rise over the Atlantic Ocean. Unlike the Hagia Sophia, the Blue Mosque is awash with warm morning light, flowing from windows and spilling out of dozens of chandeliers. A sea of space is reserved for prayer, and even though most of the people here are tourists, this is no museum. It's unequivocally a house of worship.

I sit down on the base of a column in the tourists' section. It becomes my bench and place of prayer. I whisper, *Thank you, God, for this adventure and for your generous love toward me. Oh yes, would you give us divine encounters today? Amen.*

Upon exiting the Blue Mosque, Eric sets off to sketch, while Krista and I meander the courtyard. A lanky middle-aged man dressed in a blue oxford shirt, maroon tie and navy slacks approaches the two of us. He offers to give us a tour of the city, and a few compliments as well. We decline his tour, but he graciously accepts my request to describe God.

Mehmet tells us, "In this Muslim religion, life is written on the head so one can't see what's to happen. But we do know that all good and all bad comes from Allah. There are no guarantees for tomorrow or for the next ten years. You don't eat sweets all day long. You change what you eat—sometimes sweet, sometimes sour. What is hard strengthens you for life."

Mehmet is balding, wiry and passionate, and his navy pants swallow up his scrawny legs. His smile appears unbroken, but his words seem rife with difficult years. He reminds me of someone—oh yes, Christopher from Macedonia, blue-eyed Christian Christopher.

I wonder what sour experiences Mehmet has had to eat through the years. I wonder what he thinks about Allah handing him both good and bad. In those moments when the sweet switches to sour, how does Mehmet relate to Allah?

It starts to pour, so we thank Mehmet and run for cover. For our final couple of hours in the city we separate. I'm on sensory overload, so I enter a pub and attempt to write. My thoughts act like a middle-school girl after a slumber party—delirious from lack of sleep, hyper from all the sugar and determined to tell others about how thrilling the pillow fights were. I begin writing. "Embracing both continents, Istanbul is forever committed to the East while it whispers promises to the West . . ."

I set down my pen. I can't write in this state of mind. I stare out the tiny wood-framed window of this two-story pub. Perhaps I wouldn't be sitting here if Mustafa Kemal didn't found the Republic of Turkey in 1923. Kemal, known as Atatürk ("Father of Turks"), had a vision to raise Turkey to the level of modern civilization. He was a reformist to the core. He supported the abolishment of the offices of the sultan and caliph, adopted the new Turkish alphabet with Roman letters, encouraged men to wear European clothing, ended the required Islamic tithe, and promoted equal rights for women.

Atatürk had the Qur'an translated into Turkish, and though Islam prohibits the consumption of alcoholic beverages, he cheered on the domestic production of alcohol. He even established a state-owned spirits industry. Thanks to Atatürk I can sit in this pub and order a beer instead of tea.

I guess in a way, Atatürk stepped into Istanbul's love affair with Islam. Although the Republic of Turkey is approximately 99 percent Islamic, it's the only country in the Muslim world with a constitutional provision for secularism. Istanbul seems far from a divorce with Islam, but the scent of secularism's cologne does seep into her skin on occasion.

I finish my beer, leave a tip, gather my journal, and meet Eric and Krista for a quick meal before our bus leaves. In the midst of eating we look at the time and realize our bus is about to leave. We pay our bill and run like we are being chased. Our packs stab us in our backs every other step. It seems iffy whether we'll make our bus when, gasping for air and risking crosswalk violations, we see our bus from afar. Others are still loading onto it. Yes! Another travel disaster averted.

I claim a window seat and breathe deeply. Dusk settles on the city like glitter. My eyes follow the skyline of Istanbul to the very last gaze. Tonight's city tour bedazzles me even more than the one with Tony a few years ago. I wonder, *How will Istanbul's love story end?*

18

CAPPADOCIA, TURKEY

A while back, perhaps three million years or so ago, the earth convulsed and spewed its fiery contents right where I've flung my backpack. Thanks to wind, water and a series of natural disasters, the lava and ash created whimsical rock formations and multistoried caves. And thanks to an industrious guesthouse owner, one of those caves is now our bedroom.

I turn to Eric to exclaim my delight in getting to stay in a real, live cave. But my remark is lost in a machine-gun round of sneezes. "Allergies?" Eric's face is red, his eyes are swollen, and his nose is running. "Just a little."

Our windowless cave is, well, slightly moldy.

"Check this out!" Krista calls from two feet away. "There's no door for the bathroom." She holds up the thin scrap of material that separates our communal accommodations from our private world.

It looks like Cappadocia may connect us to the experience of the ancients more than we anticipated. We're staying in the town of Göreme, an area densely populated with cave churches. The Christians in this region were known for their ascetic lifestyles. Many originally came here seeking safety in the caves, fleeing persecution from the Romans in the second century and Arab invaders in the seventh and eighth. Others were drawn here by the austere landscape, hoping it would help them focus more on their faith.

We didn't travel all this way to understand how early Christians lived,

though. Our sacred trek leads us here to explore what they thought. For a
time Cappadocia was the epicenter of early Christian theology. Three guys
known as the Cappadocian Fathers, and the woman who taught them, may
have had the greatest collective impact on how Christians describe God.

I'm curious what effect this other-worldly terrain may have had on the
formation of the ancients' view of God. But even more, I look forward to
seeing how God is described by the people here living some sixteen hundred
years later.

We've arranged for guides to introduce us to the region. Rosie and Bedo
take us to a valley that looks like something Walt Disney would design if
he got real estate on the moon. We gaze at rocks shaped like camels, babies
and mushrooms. Rosie, a petite and vivacious twenty-something, walks us
through how the rock formations, named "fairy chimneys," came to be. In a
high-pitched and happy voice she begins. "Fifteen million years ago volcanic
activity commenced in this region. Two major eruptions interspersed with
periods of calm, and smaller volcanoes emerging through the millennia
caused superposed layers of dust to form in varying density."

As Rosie talks about thousands of years of erosion, shifting geological
plates and constantly evolving landscape I realize how scientifically ignorant
I am. While today my view of God seems to expand with each glimpse of
scientific insight, I grew up with a deep connection to nature but with the
notion that God created the world in one workweek. That was that. I suspect the Cappadocian Fathers would be amazed that science and theology
ended up in different schools of thought.

Bedo leads us on a hike through the Rose Valley. Bedo is buff—built like
a linebacker—but his passions are a little less menacing. He is enamored
with foliage and Islamic history. It's been a long time since I've listened to
a brawny man talk about plants or God. He's excited to tell me about how
ancient people used the juice from red oaks to paint symbols on caves and
how Islam taught the people here to live a life of devotion.

As captivating as Bedo is, I'm hot. The sun has been assaulting us this past
hour. We're all shellacked with a layer of sweat. Rosie makes the brilliant
call that it is time to go underground.

Soon we are in a labyrinth of subterranean passages. The original underground cities were likely built by Hittites around 1200 B.C.E. while playing hide-and-go-seek with the pesky Phrygians from the Balkans. Christians took the Hittites' idea and literally ran it into the ground to escape persecution during the seventh and eighth centuries. As we snake through one tight tunnel after another, I wonder how these Christians viewed God. In the darkness, how did they see the one called Light of the World? Did they wake up each day expecting God to rescue them, or did they feel powerfully cloistered in their faith? Whatever these people were thinking, one thing is obvious. They weren't sitting around; they were busy. These tunnels seem to have no end. There are six to seven levels, filled with living quarters and wells, wine cellars and chapels.

As we climb back up I'm jolted by the light. I can't imagine spending chunks of life in the dark and in the damp. Staying in our little cave-room has given me enough insight to know that I'm not cut out for underground living, so when we return to our hotel, I immediately head back out to explore Göreme.

As I venture into town I see a beautiful woman weaving a carpet. Her fingers move across the threads like a classical guitarist strumming a masterpiece. A tall, handsome man invites me to sit down beside her at the weave, and she teaches me how to grab one bright strand over another. After a few minutes of direction he offers me a cup of tea, and I follow him into a covered stone courtyard, situating myself on a bench lined with ornate handmade pillows.

Beldad asks me why I am here. Before I can ask him any questions he starts to tell me about Turkish culture. "We are different from the Arabs and the Europeans. While we are easily influenced by a number of cultures, we can observe the distinctions quite well. The common value that brings us together is Islam. It serves as a peace between the different ethnicities. Let's say you're traveling to the East and you don't have a place to stay. Before you have to ask, someone will offer for you to lodge with them. It's the religion that brings people together like that."

Beldad's tone is straightforward and winsome. I remark, "So it's like a brotherhood."

"Yes. We call each other brothers and sisters. The main reason is that we've all come from the same family, with Adam and Eve as parents. Prophet Abraham is also our father." Pointing to me, Beldad says, "This is something we share in common. Jesus came from the Isaac side and Muhammad from the Ishmael side."

Hospitality seems to be a significant value to Beldad. He continues talking about it. "If you have someone over to your house for dinner, you don't expect them to return the invitation. And, if you are working in the field and someone doesn't have money to pay you at the moment, you continue working."

I'm so impressed with Islam's brotherhood, but I'm also befuddled. It seems like we move through life with so many agendas. Does this Islamic generosity really come without one? I consume my last swallow of tea as Beldad says, "Human needs are quite basic. There are only three things you must have to satisfy your stomach. You need food, sleep and sex. If you have these things you are happy on this side of life."

Oh no! So here it comes. This lovely conversation is going to devolve into a proposition of sex. It's a popular idea that Western women are indiscriminate connoisseurs of sex. I've had more than one pleasant discussion with a shopkeeper in Jerusalem that turned into an overt request for physical pleasure. As I suspected, everyone seems to have an agenda when it comes down to it.

Before the conversation goes further a man brings me another cup of tea. The three of us chat for a moment and then Beldad launches back in, making no more mention of basic needs. "This side of the world is quite different from America and Europe. I can understand that the Europeans aren't ready for Turkey, or Turkey ready for Europe." I'm surprised to hear Beldad say this, as Turkey is currently in the international news as a candidate for inclusion in the European Union. "It's not only financial reasons. On the backside there are cultural and religious differences. We have a totally different way of thinking about life. Although some say we are talking about the same God, Christianity has been corrupted."

I ask, "How do you see the corruption?"

"Christianity has brought a new religion, a pagan religion. In our religion, Jesus is a prophet. He is not a god. Most Christians see Jesus like a god. In Islam, God isn't human. God doesn't have any gender. He is a being above all, which you could never shape.

"It is a very difficult and very dangerous subject to think you can describe God. Describing Allah is dangerous because your mind can never work it out. We live in a world of logic, dealing with what we can see. But we can't see Allah."

Beldad's comment about not describing God has been made by many along this journey. The more devout someone seems, the less apt he or she is to describe God. "What we know about Allah comes from what Allah has done. We have ninety-nine different names of Allah. They are in the Qur'an, such as 'Allah is Almighty,' 'Allah knows everything—past, present and future.' These are ninety-nine objective names given to us by Allah."

I'm on my third cup of tea as Beldad talks about his desire to go on a pilgrimage to Jerusalem because Muhammad went there in a dream. Then Beldad pulls out his Bible. "Though I subscribe to the Qur'an, I read the Bible. I like to read." He wants to show me something, so he flips to the book of Deuteronomy and reads an obscure verse that mentions the Lord shining forth from Mount Paran. "Mount Paran is Mecca. I believe this is foreshadowing Muhammad. I'll tell you what the prophet Moses is like: the prophet is like a Pentium One computer. Technology moves forward, and also the prophets."

Beldad's reasoning both resonates with and clangs against my beliefs. I love reading the Hebrew Scriptures and see glimpses of Jesus foreshadowed in the images and stories that pack their pages. I strongly believe both Old and New Testaments tell one grand epic, yet I wonder what Jews think when I say that.

Converting to another faith seems impossible. Our filters can be so strong. It certainly takes more than convincing arguments. When we start talking about Jesus' return to earth, Beldad brings up a great concern. "When Jesus comes to earth everyone will see and pray to him and believe. But that is unfair. What about the people who aren't alive when he comes, who didn't get to see him and didn't believe?"

Before I can attempt to respond to Beldad's question, he continues verbally processing. "When Jesus comes back only the faithful will see him. Not all people will. But to be honest I don't know where I stand on that. I don't know if I am a faithful person or not. I try to be a good person." Beldad's voice seems to be filled with both longing and uncertainty. Then he adds, "But maybe Jesus is walking on earth now and I don't see him. I believe it's the faithful ones who will see. It's the ones who do what the religion says, including what Allah says, or what God says, they are the ones who will see.

"But look at all of us. How clean are we? I don't know your life. Each of us must assess ourselves: How clean am I? How ready am I for the other side? But none of us are clean. None of us are pure."

I'm nodding my head. Beldad has nailed the human dilemma. "Yes," I interject. "If we are really honest with ourselves, we are confronted with our own selfishness. I know that I tend to keep things for myself when I know I am to give to others. But the story of Christianity is that humanity couldn't make ourselves good enough—clean enough—to relate to God. So God in his mercy sent Jesus."

Beldad shouts something. I'm a little confused, then I see he's calling for someone to bring me my fourth cup of tea. Beldad's still on his second cup. It hits me that as long as I'm drinking, they'll keep pouring. I really need to cut myself off.

When my tea arrives Beldad lets loose. "I've asked several people this question but no one has given me a satisfactory answer. Maybe you can." I immediately get a sense of being trapped, but—optimist that I am—I have a twisted hope that I can be the one to break free of his conundrum.

"What about the people who are born in remote tribes who never hear about Jesus? And what about the babies who die, what happens to them?" That is consistently a good question, and reveals a longing for a God that is just, a God that treats people fairly. And I think underneath it is a desire to know God can show compassion. But Beldad doesn't wait for me to respond. He has other questions he's been storing away, questions that need to be set free.

"I don't get the way Christians talk about forgiveness. If you come in and rob me, kill my wife and my son, and then the next day you ask God for forgiveness, how is that right? I can't look the other way like that. And here's another thing I don't understand. You have homeless people in the United States, right? And, you have Christians living in million-dollar houses, right? If you say Jesus cares for others, why are there homeless people in the United States? With all the Christians, there shouldn't be homeless people."

I'm sad. Beldad's questions are so good. They reveal his desire for justice and his commitment to generosity. I shuffle around in my backpack, pull out my little black Bible and turn to the book of Acts.

"Beldad, what I think you're looking for is what the early church was about." I read the initial chronicles of the church captured in Acts 2:42-47. "All the believers were together and had everything in common. Selling their possessions and goods, they gave to anyone as he had need." I feel a pang in my stomach. I have had such rotten run-ins with my selfishness on this sacred pilgrimage.

Beldad asks, "Where is a church like that?" Before there's even a pause, his colleague comes in with a customer. I get up and thank Beldad for the conversation and the boatload of tea. He makes me promise that I will return.

As I walk back up the hill to our cave-room, I wonder once again if our description of God even matters. The Cappadocian Fathers fought so hard to get the church to embrace the divinity of Jesus. Beldad doesn't subscribe to Jesus' divinity, yet he seems to live out Jesus' mandate to love others more than I do. If I'm not hospitable and generous to others, do my thoughts about God have any value?

My questions follow me around like a despondent new friend. They keep interrupting as Krista, Eric and I consume loaves of steaming-hot flatbread and laugh about our cave accommodations. They linger until late into the night.

Glorious! The sun is already drenching this city of stone. I'm on the patio overlooking the rest of Göreme and savoring my morning feast. A guy with a contagious smile asks to join me.

Bassa is an attractive twenty-six-year-old doctor from South Africa. He is practicing community service medicine in Cape Town. "The past few months I've been working with people in unimaginable poverty, dealing with devastating diseases. It's been rewarding but exhausting." He asks what I am reading. Proverbs—ancient wisdom. He invites me to read some. I read the second verse of Proverbs 22: "Rich and poor have this in common: / The LORD is the Maker of them all." Bassa tells me, "I grew up living to the hilt. I spent lots of money on partying, drinking and drugs. I almost died from an overdose. After miraculously surviving I prayed to Allah and then resolved to devote my life to finding and living truth."

Today Rosie and Bedo take us on a marathon tour of churches in the region. I'm thrilled to find out that Bassa is joining our group. Our first stop is a fifth-century cave church; to enter we must climb up a rope ladder a couple of stories. My motor skills are disastrous, but I love climbing. I make it, remarkably unscathed, into a cave chapel smaller than my bedroom. The walls are covered with simple frescoes of saints, each with their eyes scratched out.

Bassa is terribly inquisitive, which I adore. Before I can ask, he has Rosie explaining the eyes. "The majority of the frescoes in this area are damaged. During the time when icons were outlawed—the iconoclastic period— many were marred. But the eyes were actually scratched out by superstitious locals fearful of the evil eye."

We head off to Göreme Open Air Museum, which strikes me as a curious name for a complex of ten chapels built by monks between 900 and 1200 C.E. The first cave I walk into is called the St. Basil Chapel, named for one of the Cappadocian Fathers.

This dark, small cave offers little indication of the significance Basil the Great had on this area, and on Christendom as a whole. The monastic rule he wrote still governs how many Greek Orthodox monks and nuns live today. But his reach goes beyond the monasteries and convents. When the early church was still being shaped and its theology of the Trinity was quite nebulous, St. Basil articulated a philosophical formula that continues to clarify the mystery: "three persons *(hypostases)* in one substance *(ousia)*."

It's difficult to know for certain if St. Basil would be known today had it not been for his big sister, Makrina. Schooled in philosophy, she had overseen Basil and her other brothers' education. When Basil returned home from university and started acting uppity she challenged him to use his mind in the service of God. Makrina apparently influenced Basil, two of his brothers and a friend of theirs from university, together known today as the Cappadocian Fathers.

Makrina's influence might have gone undetected in history if her brother Gregory of Nyssa had not written *The Life of Makrina.* I look to see if there is a St. Makrina Chapel. There are no signs of her existence here.

I'm grateful to learn about Makrina, but I wonder how many other women have contributed anonymously to the church's understanding of God. How would our collective notions of God be different if women had a more active role in theology through the centuries?

Our tour ends with the *Tokali Kilise* (The Buckle Church), the most expansive and ornate church in the "collection." Built in stages, it contains one of the finest ensembles of frescoes from the early Middle Ages. However, the church is packed; Rosie has to shout over the other guides describing the paintings that depict different scenes in Jesus' life.

I'm frustrated that all these churches have been turned into soulless museums. I decide to interview people, but they all tell me they don't believe in God, or they don't want to talk about God, or they don't speak enough English to describe God. It's not a total loss; a kind shopkeeper gives me a book on Islam, and I find a guy selling ice cream.

I offer to get Krista a cone but she's starting to look green. By the time we get to the cave-room she's, well, officially sick. With only that thin scrap of material for a bathroom door, Eric and I decide to leave Krista to sort things out on her own.

We find Bassa and climb a cliff. As we watch the sun slip through colored clouds, dive down below the stone mountains and fade into oblivion, Bassa shares with us his description of God. "Only Allah can describe Allah." Happily, Bassa doesn't stop. "I believe God is greater than any perception, more distant than we can imagine and at the same time closer to us than our jugular vein. That's from the Qur'an," he adds. We all sit in silence for a moment. The sun's spectacular descent beckons our attention.

After a few minutes Bassa resumes, but in a more conversational tone. "Whenever I need Allah, he is there. His plan for me is better than I could have planned. His plan, as it unfolds, perpetuates his neverending wisdom and mercy. All I have to do is raise my hands, think or feel, and I know he is there." Bassa is quite animated at this point. "God is personal. He knows me better than I know myself. Whenever I have wanted something and didn't get it or I've gotten something I haven't wanted, I've tended to become angry and blame God. But later, when I've gotten to see the big picture, I realize God's plan has been better than I could imagine."

The sky is gently turning pink and gray. Bassa no longer faces me but sits beside me to see the sun's finale and share his concluding thoughts. "Look at nature. Every ecosystem untouched by man is perfection. When man tries to take on the role of God, we see imbalance and disharmony. The only way to regain the balance is to acknowledge God. See the awe and be struck by the majesty of God."

As Bassa and I sit next to each other beholding the splendor of our surroundings, I realize how deeply content I am. I'm amazed how much my appreciation for Muslims has grown and how my prejudices have dwindled. Bassa feels like a kindred spirit, a true brother. What a gift!

We say goodbye to Bassa, and I return to the room with Eric. Krista is sleeping, but she still looks terribly pale.

Morning breaks, and the room has the distinct feel of an infirmary. Krista is trying to digest a banana. Though we had planned to leave today, it appears we'll need to stay and let Krista regain strength.

Eric and I escape the deathtrap with a sense of mission. Today we will search for a "living" church. We pray for divine encounters and are on our way, walking all over Göreme, asking around. Finally, after a friendly chat with a guy at lunch, we have a lead. His mother-in-law knows of a church.

He has his brother walk us to the edge of town; his nephew will meet us and escort us the rest of the way.

We meet up with his nephew in a dusty, seemingly deserted area. The twelve-year-old boy takes us up a hill, kicking rocks in that totally bored preteen way. We scrape for conversation. A kilometer or two later we come upon the cave of our new friend's mother-in-law—our new friend whose name we can't remember at the moment. That doesn't seem to inhibit this woman's hospitality. She points to the couch and prepares tea.

We scope out the place. The cave walls are covered with ornate wall hangings. By her chair are stacks of pillowcases hand-decorated with gold and silver design work. She indicates that she's sewn them all. We sip our tea and converse in that way you do when neither party speaks the same language. Then Eric and I look at each other and in stereo say "Church." "*Kilise.*" Soon the nephew is back, accompanied with an older man. They are to take us to the church. I buy a pillowcase on my way out and can't help but wonder if this woman has any idea why Eric and I showed up at her house.

The nephew and the older man direct us to a dusty hiking trail. Within a few minutes we're scaling a small cliff. The nephew says in broken and bored English, "Climb up in that hole. That's the church."

When we get inside the old man holds out two tickets, the raffle ticket kind. The nephew asks for three New Turkish lira (about two U.S. dollars) from Eric and me. I confess, I'm pissed. It's just another cave church with frescoes of figures I don't recognize, all with their eyes scratched out. This church doesn't even have a rope ladder. It's not a living church. I pay the three lira, but I am not a satisfied customer. I ask, "Where is a church with people, one where people pray, one with Christians?"

The nephew responds as if I have asked a very silly question. "There are no churches like that here."

Eric and I find our way back to the city along the barren hiking trail. We don't say much. We don't need to. When we return to the room Krista's color has returned to her face. We sit out on the patio soaking in the sun, and a young passerby asks if he can join us.

Jerome is twenty-three years old, from Singapore. We have such a fantastic chat we invite him to come to dinner with us. "We know a place with delicious oven-baked flatbread."

Jerome has an easy laugh and a near-constant smile. During dinner he tells us he converted from Buddhism to Christianity just four months ago. When I ask him to describe God, he says, "God is all-powerful, all-knowing, all-present." Then he starts laughing. He's caught himself sounding pedantic. In a more earthy tone he continues. "God loves us so much. He knows we'll do bad things, but he still loves us. He has a purpose for each of us. And we are equal in his eye. He can't see a road sweeper as less important than a lawyer."

Jerome speaks in a way that suggests a lifetime with God. "God is good. Even though bad things happen to us, he wants us to grow through them. He guides us and gives us strength. He desires good from the bad things. I'm so grateful to know him."

Jerome tells us about his conversion and then goes back to his description of God. "People ask what happens to those living in faraway tribes or babies who don't know God. But God is just."

It's so curious: Jerome mentions one of the questions Beldad asked about Jesus. As Jerome speaks I wonder, would so many people be asking questions about God's justice if Christians were living out mercy? I just wonder. While we didn't find a living church today, meeting Jerome certainly felt like a divine encounter.

I rise out of bed with sudden regret. What were we thinking? Feeling weak, I blurt out in the morning silence, "Why did we go back to the same restaurant after Krista got sick?" I sit back down on my bed.

Krista and I decide to find a pharmacy. Maybe we both have food poisoning. Right in front of Beldad's shop, I throw up. Then I momentarily pass out. This is annoying on many levels.

I had not planned to vomit on anyone's threshold during this trip—but particularly not in front of Beldad. To be honest, I have been avoiding him. I don't even know exactly why. Maybe I felt exposed by his generous spirit.

Maybe I'm still questioning whether he has another agenda. Does he want me to buy a carpet? Does he want me to convert to Islam? Is he truly seeking answers to his questions about Christian spirituality? Is his kindness really without strings?

Beldad sits me down on the bench with the ornate pillows. He has someone bring me water. He talks with Krista as I recover. He tells us where the pharmacy is and what we should get.

Though we really need to leave Cappadocia, now I'm too sick to travel. The day is a blur until my senses are awakened by the sound of drums and a soulful voice wafting up from the valley. Our guesthouse owners tell us the music is a wedding singer.

We've gotten close to the owners of our guesthouse during the past few days. Like our hosts in Macedonia, they've told us to call them Papa and Mama. Papa invites us to join him for the fete. Eric stays back, but even in our weakened state Krista and I can't resist going.

We load into Papa's little car and follow the music. The bride-to-be and the women are having their celebrations on one side of the street; the groom-to-be and the men on the other side. Krista and I are greeted by the groom. A host offers us hand sanitizer, cigarettes and candy.

We enter the back garden filled with over fifty guys; we're told we can have the pick of any. We choose to simply enjoy the passionate songs of the traditional Turkish singer as we drink tea and chat with two kind older men. I ask the gentleman next to me when the Christians left Cappadocia. "The Christians and Muslims lived side by side up through the Ottoman times," he tells me. "It was when Atatürk came to power the Christians from this region began to leave."

The subject gets changed but my mind continues to try to sort it out. So much of the makeup of Turkey changed in the early twentieth century. Between 1914 and 1917, over 1.5 million Armenians in this country were killed. But I don't think the Cappadocian Christians experienced genocide; I think they were a part of the two-million-person population swap with Greece in the 1920s. I look up. The sky is a black box displaying Venus and Mercury, yet sadness invades the glory of the night. I am caught between the realities of the generous Turkish hospitality and the realization that a city of churches no longer has Christians living in it.

Papa kindly takes us back to our cave hotel, but the sounds of our singer follow us. I can still hear his voice and the drums as I edge into sleep. The music from the valley mingles with my thoughts.

I'm so grateful for the people I've met here. Beldad, Bassa and Jerome exuded such a compelling love for God and others. Once again I question whether one's description of God matters if one's actions are not loving.

I wonder what Makrina and her Cappadocian brothers would say about that?

19

ANTIOCH, TURKEY

I don't mean to be crass. It's just that I'm constipated and my innards feel like gobs of Silly Putty. And—I don't mean to be negative—on top of that, I'm just tired and disappointed that out of the cornucopia of churches in Cappadocia, none were active houses of worship.

In this miserable state I exit the bus at the Antioch station and realize we have no idea where we'll spend the night. We simply start walking, hoping to see signs for a hostel, hoping not to choke on the exhaust posing as air.

I stumble behind Krista and Eric, bloated and irritated, yet I'm not the first to enter this city bedraggled. Around 34 c.e. a horde of people straggled into Antioch, having run for their lives from three hundred miles away. One of the leaders of these followers of Jesus, Stephen, had just been stoned to death in Jerusalem, and the threat of greater persecution was gathering.

Antioch was an obvious place of escape. After Rome and Alexandria, it was the most important city in the Empire. Surely they could slip into the frenzy of this cosmopolitan center unnoticed. Antioch also had a substantial Jewish population, with a large number of Gentile converts, so there would be a built-in sense of home.

With all of Antioch's assets, it had a few liabilities. The city had a reputation for being rowdy. Commerce and ideas flowed in and out, from Europe and the Euphrates, but so did drifters, whores and the morally lax.

In this raucous atmosphere the followers of the way of Jesus were labeled "Christians," meaning "little messiahs." The name stuck, like those nicknames people get in junior high that somehow wind up on their gravestone. Both Jews and Gentiles joined the way of Jesus, and soon the church in Antioch had become a center for study and for sending Christians to other parts of the world. It was also renowned for its generosity, providing funds to the people of Judea during a famine. That was their future, however; in 34 c.e. these followers of Jesus stumbled into Antioch with no idea what awaited them.

Right now I just wonder if we'll find a decent, cheap place to stay. After being waylaid in Cappadocia, our overly ambitious travel schedule is descending in a tailspin. Somehow I had neglected to factor "sick days" into our sacred trek. According to my itinerary we should be in Beirut, but we are two countries away. We really should leave first thing in the morning, but I have the sense that there's a story here.

Tomorrow is Sunday. I am hoping we can find one church in Turkey where we can worship. This country used to be a critical force in Christian thought and mission. Now locating an active church here feels like searching for a contact lens in the ocean.

We happen upon a two-star hotel that is willing to take us. We decide to splurge by eating at a real restaurant. The selection is impressive, the welcome from the owner and chefs is warm, but do I really want to pack my ever hardening midsection with more food? I tempt fate and order a spinach pastry and a colorful Mediterranean salad.

When we return to the hotel, we see a map in the lobby. Together we spy out one, two—no, actually *three* churches on the map. We ask the manager whether our sightings are accurate. While he doesn't know any information about the churches, he confirms that they exist.

Yes! We all agree we have to stay at least through the morning. We head back to the bus station and purchase tickets to leave for Aleppo, Syria, tomorrow at noon, giving us the whole morning to church-hop.

I fall asleep with a boulder in my belly and a pile of questions on my lips, all leading to just one: "What divine encounters will we come across in the morning?"

The sun has woken up much earlier than I; its perky greeting causes me to go into a mild panic. I overslept again, as did Krista and Eric. We were supposed to awake early, have some significant experience in Antioch and then be out of here. *Great.*

We finally get ourselves together and stake out a plan for the two hours we have left. First we'll hit the Protestant church, then the Orthodox church, then the Catholic church. Who knows when the services are held, but it's encouraging to think this city still has a few churches.

As we tear out the door, we remember something: our prayer for divine encounters. Though my body feels like a big ball of apathy, for some reason the rest of me has an extra sense of excitement about today. We give the big wooden map hanging on the wall one last stare, then set off. We find the Protestant church within a few minutes. It's Korean, which seems surprising and slightly random. A kind woman lets us in. Their service doesn't start until noon, and the pastor will not arrive until 11 a.m. Why do we have to leave at noon? We plan to return around eleven to at least chat with the pastor.

Now to find the Orthodox church. I see a woman walking a few paces in front of us; I try to be subtle in my attempt to accost her. "Excuse me, do you speak English?" She replies, "A little," so I ask directions to the Orthodox church.

"If you are just looking for a church, I live near the Catholic church. You can follow me there," she offers. She leads us through a labyrinth of cobblestone alleys and leaves us at a sign: *Turk Katolik Kilisesi.* The arrow points to a large door seamlessly connected to the stone alleyway. We ring the buzzer, and Father Domenico invites us to sit with him in a serene garden.

We slip into conversation without effort. "What is the Christian community like here?"

"There are only about a thousand Christians in Antioch. The majority are

Greek Orthodox who speak Arabic. The Catholic community has about fifty to fifty-five people. But for the past sixteen years the Orthodox and Catholics have celebrated our major religious holidays together, such as Easter. Since the Orthodox are the majority, we celebrate according to their calendar. And because the Orthodox celebrate Sunday Mass in the morning, we wait to have our Mass until the afternoon. We respect each other. It's not competition. We also work together to help the poor—especially during Lent. And we commemorate feasts together. Next Wednesday is the Feast of St. Peter and St. Paul, so we will celebrate together in the Grotto of St. Peter. It is a very important time to have ecumenical prayer with the Orthodox."

I take a deep breath as Father Domenico tells of a church marked by unity and not competition, one that prays and reaches out to the poor together. My anxious questions about the viability of the church relax a bit. Like in Athens, my faith feels like it can make itself a little more at home. I simply utter, "That is very encouraging to hear."

"Yes. If one thousand Christians can't come together, it is very sad for all the Christians. It is very important for us to continue in the way of the first Christians here. As you know, in the beginning of the early church the Christians had their meetings in private houses. We are so grateful to have our church in this private house in the Jewish Quarter, just like those in Antioch so many centuries ago.

"Though the Catholic community is small, pilgrims from all over the world come to visit our church. They are drawn to it because Antioch is where the church as we know it began. It was in Antioch that the pagans first became Christians."

When I ask Father Domenico to describe God he tells us, "Jesus Christ gives us the possibility to experience the presence of God in the world. Because of Jesus, the Word of God speaks to us. He shows us the love and mercy of God. For example, we say that God is love and mercy. When you see Christians living out mercy and love, you can say 'There is the presence of God.' Normally people don't love each other, especially if they are different or if they are enemies. But if people show mercy and love, it reveals that God is present with these persons."

My mind travels back to the Balkans on the wind of Father Domenico's words. What would it have been like for Sead and Eldad to encounter Christians showing mercy and love during Sarajevo's hellish siege? Would Belgrade's story line be any different if the church had taken on that role? What about Christopher—if he were surrounded by Christians living out mercy and love, would he pine for a deceased dictator?

And oh, how I wish Beldad could see this church. This seems like what he was looking for—a church that serves as "God's glorious civic project." I ask, "Since the Christian community is small, are you and your church challenged to live this out?"

"We are a small community; that's true. But for about the last fifteen years the Catholics and the Orthodox have met to study the Bible together. I believe it is possible to have a religious experience as one community, one church. I don't think it is important that we are only a thousand people. Jesus said, 'When two or more people meet together, I am there.' It is necessary for us to see if that is true or not. In a small community where there is the Word of God and prayer, you can see that people begin to love each other, to show mercy. So this is what is important. Here in our Catholic church, we provide the Orthodox a place to pray. We have icons for them. If we can see that the Word of God is true in one church, then we can take hope for the whole church. It is necessary to see if we can love each other. We've got to live this out!"

"How beautiful," I interject. "It seems like the spirit of the original church."

"Here in Antioch we continue to try to live out the experience of the first Christians. So, we focus on the Word of God. Even the Muslims here are interested in the Word of God. They want to see—in concrete—whether it is possible to live the Word of God. I believe the Word of God is for all humanity. It's not for just our little group, but our little group does have the opportunity to experience that the Word of God is true."

"How are the interactions between Muslims and Christians?" I ask.

"I think personal dialogue with Muslims is possible, but not discussion about religion. I am Christian, and my faith is this. You are Muslim, and your faith is that. I respect your faith, and I ask you to respect my faith.

Our faith is different. If we come to discuss it, there are divisions. It is said about Antioch that we are a city of dialogue and respect. When Pope John Paul II died, we had a time of common prayer. Orthodox, Catholics, Protestants, Muslims and Jews came together in our church. I think this is important. Every confession prayed in their own language and tradition. It was a very interesting experience. As Pope John Paul said, dialogue and respect provide a path toward peace. That is true. The pope also said that God's greatest work is in humanity. We share this common face. But when we experience God, maybe it is possible to be different?"

Eric has a question. "You said it was special for you to be in the Jewish Quarter. Is there a relationship between Christians and Jews?"

"Yes. Very nice. The chief of the Jewish community calls me brother, and I call him brother. I gave the rabbi a Turkish Bible, and he found it very interesting that it was the same as his Hebrew Scriptures. He didn't know that. He was very, very glad to discover that. He said to me, 'You know the Christians read the same Bible as we have!'"

Father Domenico then offers to show us the church. The walls are lined with dark wood adorned with icons. "Because we have restored this historic private home, many people come to visit, including Muslims. Sometimes they ask about our faith. We have these icons here so we can explain what we believe. We believe that Jesus Christ was crucified and rose again on the third day. That is our faith. We have this icon of the Virgin Mary with the angel Gabriel. The Muslims know the Virgin Mary from the Qur'an. We share with them that Jesus is the Word of God; with Jesus we can have an experience of God. He is our friend. And Jesus tells us I am the way, the truth and the life. I am with you until the end of time." He looks back at the icon. "I find that very interesting to share with them."

Our tour concludes. Father Domenico ends our time together by saying that the church is open to any Christians. "It's not a problem if they are Orthodox or Protestant or Catholic. They are welcome to have celebrations here and come and pray."

Something feels profoundly true about this place. The church seems radically hospitable to different traditions and even faiths, and yet it is certain of its devotion to Jesus. As we step back outside I turn around and take in one more look at the church. *God, help me not to forget this.*

We amble along, captivated by the spirit of Antioch. While we don't have long before we must go to the bus station, we've got to get a glimpse of the Orthodox church.

"Excuse me. Can we go into the church?" The woman I am asking clearly doesn't understand what I'm saying, but I continue. "Is it OK for us to go in?"

"Do you need help?" A gentleman in his forties steps up and asks.

"Yes! We were hoping to visit the church briefly."

"Come with me. My name is Joseph. Where are you from?"

"America."

"Very good. I like Americans." Before he opens the door to the Greek Orthodox basilica, he asks, "What tradition are you?"

"Protestants," we say. "But ultimately we're Christians."

"Good. Me too. I'm not Orthodox, or Catholic, or Protestant. I am Christian," Joseph declares. Liturgy is already being chanted as he leads us to a pew. The fiery, flowery incense still lingers from the procession of the priests. I make my bloated body comfortable in the pew, even though I'm afraid of getting too comfortable; we should leave in about ten minutes if we want to see the Korean Protestant pastor before dashing to the bus station. Yet the chants are too hauntingly beautiful not to stay just a little longer.

My eyes scan the basilica. There sits Father Domenico. I pull out my Bible and flip through the book of Acts, searching out the biography of the church in this city.

As the Antioch church moved beyond Jews and Gentile God-fearing converts to include pagans who had been entranced by the love of Jesus, church leaders from Jerusalem started to notice. The apostle Peter, Paul and Barnabas spent significant time in the city. While here, Peter championed interactions between Jews and Gentiles, regularly taking part in the church's revolutionary practice of Jews sharing a meal at Gentiles' homes. This act challenged Jewish kosher laws, but the early Christians felt it was vital for the unity of the church.

Peter actively encouraged it until he faced personal critique from some fellow Jews. When he pulled back from eating with Gentiles in their homes, Paul publicly confronted him. A candid and difficult exchange took place. In the end, unity between Jewish and Gentile converts won out. That unity seems not to be taken for granted today.

People are shuffling in their seats like a rising tide. They file out of their pews and stand in a line in front of the priest. He looks glowy and kind. I long to join the others, partaking in this mystery of oneness with Father, Son and Spirit. But I can't. I'm not Greek Orthodox. Only those who are baptized as Orthodox Christians are supposed to take Communion in their services.

Joseph motions to us to come. I mean to shake my head no and respect the centuries of Orthodox church doctrine, but instead I give Joseph the "Are you sure?" look. He motions again and we all climb out of our pew. He hands Krista and me each a white lace scarf to cover our heads. We are among the last in line.

As much as I want to believe in the ecumenical spirit of Antioch as I approach the priest, I suspect that in a moment I'll be publicly declared as a heretic. I don't even attempt to cross myself. The priest asks my name. Here it comes. He plans to announce that some American Protestants have invaded their holiest of moments. But he doesn't. He blesses me. "Ta-mar-a," he whispers, as he dips his spoon into his chalice and gives me a piece of bread dunked in wine.

As Mass ends, we face a choice. We can take off like Olympic sprinters, grab our bags and make our bus. Or we can scrap our agenda and get to know Joseph a little more.

"I will be your host for the day," Joseph says definitively. He introduces us to his wife, Maryette, and tells her and us simultaneously the plan for the afternoon. "Maryette will go home and prepare a marvelous lunch for us as I take you to another church."

We follow Joseph to—I guess—the Korean Protestant church. As we walk along ancient cobblestone alleys he asks us about televangelists in America. I offer nothing about having grown up in the throes of televangelist mecca. Instead I simply say, "It's a very curious phenomenon."

Joseph's question quickly becomes a commentary on what he believes is true Christianity. "If you know a truth and you don't do it, then you really don't know it," Joseph says passionately. "If I'm not helping someone, then I don't have deep love for God.

"OK. We're here." Wherever we are, it is certainly not the Korean Protestant church. Joseph leads us toward what looks like someone's house. The sound of voices singing with a guitar greets us before we get to the door. Wait a minute. That song sounds familiar. We step into a room of people mainly in their twenties singing worship songs. We slip into a row in the back and join in. Though they sing in Arabic, we recognize many of the songs.

Joseph begins translating for us when a guy around our age named Ibrahim starts speaking. Ibrahim invites people to share anything they'd like about their faith. The atmosphere is casual and conversational. A few speak, then Ibrahim reads some Scripture. After the service everyone goes into the courtyard for coffee and dessert.

Joseph introduces me to Ibrahim and offers to translate. Ibrahim says he would be glad to share some of his life story with me. "I converted from Islam to Christianity three-and-a-half years ago," he begins. "I was a strong Sunni Muslim. I was like the Taliban. What do you call it?"

"A fanatic?" I offer.

"Yes, a fanatic. I read all the books of Islam, but I still felt empty. I read and read to fill myself. I would just pray and learn. For five years, when I was twenty-five to thirty years old I'd pray all the time, every day. I tried to do even more than the prayers required by Islam. Instead of praying five times a day, I prayed eight times. I tried to get close to God. I became like the Taliban, yet I felt like something was still missing. I worked so hard, but I felt I had nothing.

"Then I came to two roads. The first road told me, 'The God you wish for in your heart is not this one.' The second road indicated that there is no

God or I did something wrong—I made a mistake. Either there was something wrong with God or me.

"I had prayed and I didn't feel God. I felt so confused. So I decided to leave God. For one year I lived without God—no prayer, no religion, no holy books.

"One day I was so desperate, I tried to talk with God. I spoke very directly, very personally. I never did that before in my life, because I was ultrareligious. I said, 'God, come help me, or I am going to lose my faith in you and I am going to die. I want to know you.' Then I went to my room. Five minutes later my brother came in with a newspaper. I believe the Holy Spirit guided me to search the newspaper. So I searched, flipping the papers, not knowing what I was looking for. On the third page I saw a small advertisement that said, 'Do you want to know Jesus Christ?' The Holy Spirit told me: 'This is what you're looking for.'

"I kept the newspaper. I sent a letter to the address. I started to study with one of the Christian teachers through letters. For four or five months they sent me letters. Then someone contacted me and invited me to come to church. My brother, who was also doing the correspondence, responded 'Yes' as a joke. But our family went to church. I decided to go along to be like a bodyguard. I didn't know what to expect.

"My brother and I were so moved we asked to be prayed for. I experienced God and accepted Christ to be my Savior. From that first Sunday I believed, but life became very difficult. My brother went once and quit. I kept going. I knew a new God through Jesus Christ. I promised to follow him the rest of my life. Since then I have worked for God."

"Has your conversion presented a problem with your family?" I ask.

"Yes—too big of a problem. My family tried to kill me because I changed."

Ibrahim is now in hiding, a challenge faced by his whole Christian community. "All of the people here this Sunday are from Muslim backgrounds—except for Joseph. They are not accepted by their families and communities. Everyone tried to change my mind, to change my life, to get me to turn back to Islam. They tried to scare me; they even tried to kill me. They would never leave me alone.

"One day God told me that he appreciates my belief and he will guide my way. I prayed to God. I said I don't want money, house or car, but for God to give me my wife, save her. She was the first one against me. She was very conservative. She wore a *burka*.

"God told me to fast for one day and pray. So I didn't eat that day; I just prayed for her. I did it but she didn't know about it. At the end of that day my wife opened the Bible; she started to read and pray to God. She became a Christian. One month later she was baptized. I actually got to baptize her. I didn't want to pressure her to change her religion. She came to God on her own. I didn't want to tell her I had fasted and prayed for her. Now she is a strong Christian."

I am stripped of words, except only to thank Ibrahim and ask Krista to take a picture of him with his gorgeous wife and two children.

As we follow Joseph to his house I try not to speak. I just pray silent thank-yous for the humility, courage and generous spirit of those I've encountered here. I am so grateful that the spirit of the early church has survived some-where in the world.

Maryette welcomes us at the door. While their flat isn't extravagant, it is elegant. It's obvious that they have done well for themselves. Since we still have some time before the meal is served, I ask Joseph to describe God.

"God is holy and great; I belong to him. When I was young I felt like I was in the system of God." I ask him what he means and he replies, "It was like being a bottle of Pepsi." I guess I give Joseph a quizzical look; the language barrier has made describing God a creative challenge for many on this trip. He breaks down his answer for me. "I have felt close to God."

Joseph starts to tell us that he has wondered whether the U.S. govern-ment was behind the September 11 attacks, but then he stops himself. "I'm sorry. It's just that our media has referred to it as a conspiracy. American politics have made life harder for Christians in Antioch. People associate Christianity with America. Since September 11, the Christians here have had a hard time."

Joseph's words are so sobering I can't push out a response. I'm saved by Maryette's announcement that it's time for dinner. She first serves us salads, bread and hummus. Then comes her trademark chicken and rice dish. Heaps and heaps are placed on our plates. It looks scrumptious and smells savory. If only there was any room left in my innards.

I sit in silence as the others chat. I try to sort out the spirit of Antioch.

If Rome or Constantinople had fought for unity like Antioch, would there have been the Crusades? Would so much killing have happened in the name of Jesus? Would politics and power-moves have been such strong subplots in the church's history? What would other cities look like if their Christians fought for unity like those here in Antioch? I wonder if the spirit of Antioch could serve as a model for churches today. If the church lived out unity, concern for the poor, ecumenical prayer and Scripture reading, radical hospitality to those who don't identify as Christians, and a commitment to love and mercy, how might that affect everyone's understanding of God? I just wonder.

"Why aren't you eating?" Joseph catches me deep in thought and obvious avoidance of eating.

"I'm sorry. It looks so good; it's just that I haven't been feeling well for a while," I respond.

"What is wrong?" he presses.

"Well, uh . . . I'm constipated."

Immediately Maryette goes to the kitchen as Joseph declares, "Maryette has the perfect solution." She brings out the frying pan used for the chicken, scrapes off the oil and pours it directly into a cup. "Drink it," Joseph instructs.

I imbibe it obediently. My capacity for protest is limited these days.

Maryette smiles. Joseph instructs, "In a minute or so you will have to go." Then he leads me to their bathroom, a mere seven steps from the dinner table.

As I sit on the commode I can hear Joseph asking Krista and Eric about our itinerary in Syria. My mind becomes a playground for schizophrenics.

You haven't had a bowel movement in days: Go, go, go!

Do you really want to unload your intestinal baggage on such gracious hosts?

Who knows the next time you'll encounter such a hygienic toilet!

If you can hear them, they can hear you.

My body, meanwhile, is mute. Maybe it is protesting because of the cruel and unusual oil treatment, or maybe it is something more.

I return to the table, shaking my head right and left. The universal sign for disappointment spreads across each face. Joseph, an obvious optimist, promises that the oil will work within hours. He glances at Maryette lovingly and says, "This is a family remedy; it always works."

I feel like a loser. These people have been unbelievably generous, and I can't even appropriately honor their family remedy.

They offer to host us for the night, but we're so behind on our itinerary and I really want to make it to Syria tonight. Joseph arranges for a taxi to take us to Aleppo, and then hugs us farewell like we are family. I stare out the window of the taxi, waving to Joseph and internally chanting, "Long live the spirit of Antioch! Long live unity!"

20

ALEPPO, SYRIA

I clutch my belly full of oil and stare out as the sun sloshes over the horizon. I've so looked forward to visiting Syria, desiring to see its ancient cities, longing to consume its famous food and curious to discover how people describe God in what the U.S. government has labeled a "rogue state." But my eyes are hazy with pain. I hope I won't miss seeing the true Syria because my internal organs seemed to have disowned me.

Less than fifteen miles from Antioch we arrive at the Syrian border. As excited as I've been to visit Syria, I have been slightly anxious about the border inspection. Besides my American factor, on my iBook I have documents about Israel, and on my back I have a Hebrew tattoo. I meant to rename my documents and contemplated covering up my tattoo with a marker, but constipation has caused me to lose focus. I'm too bloated to be paranoid. Fortunately the border guard asks to simply see my passport; I offer him my best smile to seal the transaction.

We enter ancient Aleppo in the black of the night. I stumble out of the taxi feeling pregnant. Krista and Eric are ready for dinner; I never want to eat again.

Our hostel is located in the tire district. As we wind through two blocks of 10' x 10' stalls stacked with new and used tires, we hear the sound of laughter growing stronger. Across the busy intersection some kind of party is in full swing. The laughter is irresistible. Pimple-faced teens chat with middle-aged scruffy men. Arms flail with animated gestures, mustaches drip with sauce, yogurt drink flows like wine. Everyone holds an oversized falafel. Happiness must be in the falafels. I want a happy falafel too.

An English-speaking, lanky teen notices our unmet desire to obtain a happy falafel and directs us to a wrinkly, winsome man sitting on a stool with a metal box. "Give the old man thirty-five Syrian pounds"—approximately seventy-five cents—"and he'll give you a token. Order your falafel from the guys behind the glass counter, and give your token to the guy over there." I strain to pay attention. It seems very important that we get the process down. I recall the Soup Nazi from *Seinfeld;* one wrong move and it's "no falafel for you!" We approach the old man, and the proper routine collapses.

The old man's wrinkles disappear in an expression of wonderment. He sees we're Americans; we see that he is adorable. It's love at first sight. He pulls out plastic stools from some hidden storage area and motions for us to sit. He signals to another teenaged boy, and within moments, falafels are in our hands and the manager, Mustaffah, is welcoming us to his establishment.

Mustaffah looks to be in his early forties; he has thinning brown hair, hazel eyes and a wonderfully wide grin. His English is excellent; his persona genteel. After we consume our falafels Mustaffah ushers us into an open-air lift that lowers us down to the basement. As we descend, so does my falafel, submerging into the vat of murky oil I drank earlier in the day.

My happy falafel is turning on me like forbidden fruit. Why did I think I could eat without punishment? Mustaffah has no way of knowing this, however. He is treating his new American friends like royalty—and a little like health inspectors. He wants us to taste all the ingredients he uses, even the condiments. He pulls a ten-pound container of mayonnaise from his industrial-sized refrigerator and hands me a spoon. I don't make it a practice of eating globs of mayonnaise—on anything, let alone a la carte. But I want to make Mustaffah as happy as his falafels make everyone else.

The next stop on our condiment tour is the sliced pickles. But now the mayonnaise is meeting the deep-fried falafel in my belly. Their introduction is hardly cordial. I'm going to pass out. Krista mentions to Mustaffah that I haven't been feeling well, so he pulls out a plastic stool from another hidden storage area and beckons someone to bring me a cup of liquid yogurt.

I sit in this underground kitchen gulping the thick, cold drink, realizing that this is the most natural thing I can do in Aleppo. This city has a long tradition of hospitality. Its Arabic name, *Halab*, literally means "gave out milk," hearkening back to the ancient tradition of Abraham giving milk to travelers as they passed through the region.

After my yogurt drink, I find myself cheek-to-cheek with the old man who hands out tokens. We are in some kind of photo shoot. Krista, Eric and I try to pay for our dinner, but the old man tells us it is "on the house."

Since we dined for free we decide to splurge on some drinks at the renowned Baron Hotel. We sit alone on the terrace where European travelers once gathered in droves to swap stories and commence intrigues. From here, Agatha Christie absorbed the atmosphere and formulated her most famous thriller, *Murder on the Orient Express*. The Baron Hotel has hosted many twentieth-century world shapers—aviator Charles Lindbergh, explorer T. E. Lawrence (better known as Lawrence of Arabia), Turkey's founder Mustafa Kemal Atatürk, and Gertrude Bell, a British linguist who played a major role in creating the modern state of Iraq.

The air is sultry and seductive. Here—where celebrities and diplomats have rendezvoused, where shysters and the bourgeois have exchanged secrets—here, I think to myself, is the perfect place to have my last drink. But after a few sips of Syrian beer, I regain hope. With renewed optimism I enter the storied hotel looking for the bathroom. T. E. Lawrence's hotel bill is on display; maps of explorers and other memorabilia of the famous hang on the wall. Yet tonight the historic halls are empty, the place feels forgotten, and nothing happens in the bathroom. I return to our table a tad dejected.

Our waiter comes over for a chat. He speaks with a refined accent and expounds on the treasures of this city. He offers to drive us around tomorrow. We can't afford his fee, but the reality that we're in Aleppo begins to capture me. We've made it to one of the oldest cities in the world! We decide that right now we will explore the city by foot and take off in a straight line. We walk and walk and walk until we happen upon a crowd clumped around an ice cream stand. Everyone seems intoxicated with bliss. I want to be intoxicated with bliss.

I order a scoop of pistachio; Aleppo is famous for their pistachios. For good measure I have them top my cone with another scoop of chocolate decadence. Oh my, it's orgasmic! This must be the best ice cream I've ever tasted. I waddle behind Krista and Eric across the street. We enter a public park that has the feel of a civilized block party—with fountains and benches and alcoves for friends and families to gather. Couples walk hand-in-hand, little kids run about, some holding their own pistachio ice cream cones.

The atmosphere is festive; the people appear at ease. It's difficult to reconcile the images of this park with the words "rogue state." I don't want to be naive, however. Syria landed on the U.S. State Department's inaugural list of state sponsors of terrorism in 1979. It's remained there ever since. A police state, Syria is reported to have a chemical weapons program and is suspected of harboring people who help fund the insurgency in Iraq. The country is technically in a state of war with Israel. And Syria's government has been accused of assassinating Lebanon's former prime minister, Rafik Hariri, earlier this year.

Before coming here I was told we must be careful who we interview; we could endanger people's safety. We've heard that we might be followed. However, I wonder whether these couples strolling in the park and these children eating ice cream feel like they're living in a rogue state on the margins of an axis of evil. I don't know if I'll get to find out, but I am curious if their political situation influences their perceptions of God.

As I toddle back to the hostel with all my questions and all my discomfort, I make a vow to get better—even if I have to abandon pride in the process. I so want to find out how Syrians describe God.

Sleep offers solace, and the morning light a momentary relief. I awake with a renewed commitment to last night's promise. I will do anything to improve, anything to choose life. Though my innards are in rebellion, I resolve to honor Syrian hospitality and find out their views about God. And, if I can help it, I will not die of constipation in this fine country.

I greet the gentleman at the hostel desk, "*Salaam!* Excuse me, Sir, I haven't gone to the bathroom—the bathroom, b-a-t-h-r-o-o-m—in a week." Another guest is obviously listening. I turn and smile at him, determined that I will not be killed by propriety. The hostel worker recommends a certain medicine and writes it on a scrap of paper. The fellow guest chimes in with his sure-fire cure. It's a fruit juice, some fruit I've never heard of. I hand him the paper so he can add it to the list.

Then I ask the hostel worker how to get to the ancient Christian Quarter. Aleppo is a city rich in historic religious sites and diverse in faith. The majority of the population is Sunni Muslims; however, with 15 to 20 percent of its residents Christian, it has one of the densest Christian populations in the Middle East. There's a considerable Armenian population as well as many Syrian Orthodox living in the city. Before Israel became a nation, Aleppo even had a significant number of Jews.

What a feast for potential interviews! But right now I'm captivated by the discovery that if I hold my belly in place I can actually walk. Blocks later we spot a dapper-looking man walking toward us. He looks like the perfect man to describe God or give us some historical context to the Christian Quarter. I approach him instead with another pressing question: "*Salaam!* Excuse me, Sir, do you know the cure for constipation?"

The dapper-looking man seems slightly shocked and repeats my question back to me. As he does, I hear how far I've fallen. I hand him my scrap of paper and he graciously scribbles the name of another medical remedy beside the two others. We wander the streets looking for pharmacies. Krista spots a doctor's office tucked away among some apartments. We attempt to schedule an appointment, but the woman at the front desk says the doctor is on a smoking break; she doesn't know when he will return. We wait. Maybe he went to Cuba to get some decent cigars. We leave.

In our search for a doctor or legal drugs, we come across a church. The sign that hangs on the iron gate entrance signifies it's a Greek Catholic church. We meander down a marble colonnade until we happen upon a priest who doesn't speak much English. I make out that this church has a very important leader who has written many books. Father Ignace would be happy to speak with us; however, we'll need to speak to him in French.

Oh no! I love French, but oh how I feel like a loser when it's spoken in my direction. I can't speak French, even though I should be able to. After residing in Belgium for over two years, I became an official language loser. In a sea of French-speakers, I moved about on my little expatriate raft, working and living with all English-speakers. Maybe I didn't study as I should have or take the risks required to learn a language.

Father Ignace comes and greets us. He dons a long, crisp gray robe; his silver hair is clipped close to his scalp and his glasses are thick. He looks extremely smart—until he smiles, and then he just seems like a kid's favorite grandpa. I'm emboldened to launch in, "*Bonjour, Pere Ignace. Peut-être. Hum . . . Pouvez vous? . . . Hum . . . Vous parlez avec Dieu . . . Oh la la . . .*" Father Ignace patiently faces me as a jumble of disconnected, poorly pronounced French words tumble from my mouth.

Finally a form of "*Comment décrivez-vous Dieu?*" comes out. Father Ignace takes his cue. We walk back down the marble colonnade as the Father describes God. I could be in ancient Athens learning from Aristotle, or perhaps in ancient Ephesus talking with Paul, or even Cambridge conversing with a history professor. The only intruding factors to this scene are that I am having a difficult time translating Father Ignace's words, and I'm finding it hard to concentrate, being bloated and all. I think Father Ignace says, "Before our existence, God was reality. He was life. God, the Father, Son and Spirit, was the necessary Creator. He made humanity, but humanity searched for happiness on his own. God sent Jesus to reveal true love. He gave his life for man and woman to know real joy for an eternity. God is the God of history, the giver of life. We cannot comprehend God, but in him is hope, and life, and love, and brotherhood."

"*Merci, merci, merci encore.*" I give this generous sage a hug. Such grace. He didn't seem annoyed by my barbaric French. And when he spoke I sensed the joy and wisdom of God in our presence.

From what I could make out from the priest who greeted us, Father Ignace is well known in Aleppo and beyond as a scholar, a writer, a spiritual thinker. I wonder how his faith and understanding could enrich those of us in the West. In all my theological studies, I've never read a Syrian biblical scholar. I imagine the church is missing out because of our East-West divide.

I wonder if Father Ignace experiences vibrant exchange and learning in the midst of the city's Christian community. Is there a commitment to unity here like in Antioch? Does the government limit his expressions of faith, or is he free to carry on a centuries-upon-centuries tradition of being the church in the Middle East?

My musings abruptly end when we see a pharmacy. I produce my piece of paper with the recommendations scratched on it. They are all written in Arabic. I can't read Arabic. I ask the pharmacist to pick his favorite remedy. He seems pleased to help and hands me a large glass bottle of brown liquid. The normal dosage is one teaspoon but, he tells me, since my situation is so dire I can take four teaspoons. I need to wait until I am back at the hostel by the bathroom, because it is potent.

The logical next step is to return to the hostel and begin the regimen. But no. We have ventured almost two miles from our hostel and are close to the famous Citadel of Aleppo, the Great Mosque and a holy site where Helena visited—and one of the largest and oldest outdoor markets in the world. I can't go back just yet. So I shove the glass bottle into my backpack and scoot onward. Krista takes off toward the promise of cheap silver bracelets and perhaps a small Persian rug, while Eric and I move toward the Great Mosque.

The cobblestone alleys leading to the Great Mosque of Aleppo are tight, teeming with people. However, once we step into the spacious courtyard of the mosque, it's like we've entered a garden. The ground is adorned with marble geometric designs. An ancient ablution fountain serves as a focal point, like a lone tree in a clearing.

While the original mosque was built in 715 c.e., sacred sites have resided in this place for millennia. A Semitic temple was built here, then a Roman temple which later became the Byzantine Cathedral of St. Helena. The cathedral was then converted to a mosque and then a *madrasa* filled with young boys studying Islam.

Eric drifts away as I try to locate the place where Helena's church once stood. Apparently the Great Mosque was only built on the gardens and court-yard of St. Helena's, which enabled the Christians to still use the church until the twelfth century. When the Crusaders came through, the ruler of Aleppo was so mad that he had the cathedral converted into a mosque as a way to get revenge.

I wander into the former cathedral, saying a prayer where Helena likely once stood. I think of Helena's journey. She, like us, had traveled over a thousand miles by the time she arrived in Aleppo. Who did she meet in the churches and taverns she visited along the way? Did any of her conversations challenge her perceptions of the Divine? Did her description of God change from what it was when she started out in Rome?

I wish Helena were here and we could have a leisurely little chat. Besides hearing what she learned about God and others en route, I'd ask if she too had stomach troubles by the time she reached Syria.

I catch up with Eric as I sally through the prayer hall, which contains a shrine to Zechariah, father of John the Baptist. Supposedly his bones are housed here. We then make our way to the citadel, a twelfth-century fortress that crowns the city. Situated on a hill, it forces onlookers to crane their heads in admiration. It's possibly one of the most imposing medieval fortresses in the Middle East.

I'm impressed, but I'd prefer to use my final reserves to shop. I say a feeble goodbye to Eric and enter a narrow alley in Aleppo's legendary souk. I'm surrounded by carved stone façades and vaulted ceilings and pleading shopkeepers. For centuries this *souk* was a desert port along the Silk Road. Traders passing through from Asia to Mesopotamia came here to buy and sell goods. Now I join the fray.

A slight, friendly-looking guy invites me to come to his jewelry stall. I say "No" and then follow him. I assume it will be just around the corner. However there turn out to be miles of stalls. As we snake through tiny alley after alley, I hold my belly in place. Right before we arrive at our destination two guys warn me not to buy from the slight, friendly-looking man. They tell me he is a cheat.

I am becoming weak. My eyes are blurring. Everything feels surreal. In the jewelry stall there is a bench with a blue velvet-covered cushion. I sink down in it. It seems similar to the interior of a coffin. This would be a nice place to die. Oh, but I can't die. I made a resolution. The slight, friendly-looking guy interrupts my fight with death, asking me if I want tea or coffee. The word *coffee* comes through my lips like an automated response. He motions to a boy across the alley and starts pulling out drawers full of silver bracelets, then necklaces, then earrings. "Handmade from Bedouins." "Genuine silver." I say I have very little money. True. And, I am a student. Half-true. I did *just* graduate. I tell him I have only fifty dollars to spend. True enough. He says he will give me a discount if I kiss him. I guess I say "Yes." I'm not feeling particularly pretty as I'm dying of constipation. He must be joking.

By the time the Turkish coffee arrives I've spent my fifty dollars on eight blue velvet bags full of loot. The bags match the cushions of my would-be coffin. I give another man my credit card. It's obvious that he is the real jeweler. He has a crooked nose and kind eyes. On his desk are strewn small pliers and beads. He must also be "Bedouin." He does the work while his friend lures the ladies in for the sale.

When I get my credit card back, the slight guy sits down beside me. I ask, "What are you doing?"

"I'm ready to kiss you."

"What?" I mumble, aghast.

"I gave you the discount for a kiss," he asserts.

"I thought you were joking. I don't make it a practice of kissing strangers in exchange for jewelry discounts," I rebut. He seems taken aback. As I get up to leave, I realize I am completely disoriented. I have no idea where I am or how to get back to my hostel. The jewelry guy—the one who wants the kiss—offers to lead me in the right direction. I say "No" and then follow him. I am too delirious to rally reason.

Within minutes I'm in an alleyway with no one in sight except for my dubious guide. He starts talking dirty to me. I tell him, "I'm not that kind of woman" and give him a look like I will slap his slight body with all my bloated might if he tries anything. Of course, both of my hands are holding my belly and I don't know what would happen if I removed them. Fortunately he backs off and gets me to the falafel stand, which becomes my home base.

I locate Krista and Eric and together we go to say *Shucran* to Mustaffah. I plan not to eat but when I see how happy everyone is holding their falafel, I cave. Once again we're offered plastic stools and falafels "on the house." But as we eat, Mustaffah looks preoccupied. He keeps getting up during our conversation. Then after we swallow our final bite, he says he has a surprise for us. As we stand, a taxi driver pulls up. Mustaffah is taking us across town to see where the actual falafel balls are made.

On the way to the falafel factory, we almost die. Our taxi driver drives with a death wish; we come within inches of oncoming traffic. Mustaffah tries to engage us in pleasant conversations about our families as the taxi driver yells at trucks and mutters something about "Bush" and the "U.S. government." I comfort myself: *A car wreck is a much more respectable death than croaking from constipation.* I arrive alive enough to sample raw chickpeas and cumin, and have another photo-shoot with falafel-scented gentlemen.

When we arrive back at our hostel I dump the contents of my backpack on the bed. There's the bottle of medicine. It's warm, almost hot. I hope I wasn't supposed to keep it cool. I toss the bottle to the side and open up my eight blue velvet bags of silver jewelry. Krista looks over at my booty and chuckles. "I bought the same necklace," she declares. We have a history of going to foreign cities separately and buying the exact same merchandise. I'm curious about my "kiss-discount," so I ask her how much hers cost. She paid almost fifty dollars. The price of all my loot combined.

I measure out my four teaspoons of warm, brown liquid. I make sure each teaspoon brims. We turn off the lights and the trauma begins. I grunt. I scream. I whimper. I feel like I am having a baby—I've never had a baby, but in my world of assumptions this is what having a baby feels like. I camp out on the commode, but nothing significant happens. False labor. I wish I had died from the yogurt drink. I wish I had died in the alley with the jewelry guy. I wish I had died in the taxi.

≥ ≤

The hostel worker brings me chamomile tea in the morning. He looks at my medicine bottle and shakes his head. Obviously the pharmacist didn't choose his favorite remedy.

Before we depart to Damascus we have breakfast in a little café full of windows. I order rice pudding and jasmine ice cream. The breakfast tastes gentle and divine, like a healing balm even in the midst of pain. As I relish tiny bites, one after another, my thoughts begin to line up. I don't sit here solely in bliss, nor do I slump solely in pain at the moment. Who I am is a complex combination of the two—which reminds me of Syria.

I imagine Syria is not entirely full of Mustaffahs handing out free falafels to American tourists. Nor is it filled with jewelry salesmen talking dirty to women. It's not all couples strolling in the park and sage priests reflecting on God. Nor is it simply a police state or a country which sponsors terrorists.

How can we engage one another—as individuals and as peoples—in a way that honors our totality? How do we not categorize the entirety of nations or a person as either bad or good? Labeling can make the world so much simpler. Stereotyping can give us a sense of order. But when we do that, how much do we miss?

I look out the window as the last bite of jasmine ice cream comes to my lips. A man in a business suit walks briskly by; a woman wearing a hijab holds the hand of her young son as they wait to cross the street. How does God view Syria? How does he look upon each person here?

21

DAMASCUS, SYRIA

We're invited to pull down the shades as a movie starts. A gentleman makes his way down the aisle distributing cups of water and Coke. Bus travel in the Middle East is filled with surprising amenities.

Ominous music seeps through the bus stereo system as white words roll across the black screen: "Lost in America." The opening scene is of an Arab man sitting in a plane seat. A flight attendant brings him a Coke. He looks nervous. The real trouble begins when he lands in the States. His wallet is stolen at the Los Angeles airport. In it was the address of where he was staying. The American taxi driver is no help; he ends up dropping off the guy in some place like Compton. The Arab immediately gets mugged. Then I fall asleep.

When I regain lucidity I am in a taxi heading into the heart of Damascus. After hours and hours of sleep, I'm groggy. But when our taxi driver pulls up at the hostel and announces the fare, I bolt wide awake. "That is ridiculous! You're ripping us off!" I growl like a lion disturbed from a siesta. I discuss the matter with our hostel host. Yes, we were taken. I *hate* being ripped off.

Even more, however, I hate missing out on excitement. Eric and Krista suggest I stay in and continue my sleep marathon, thinking that might cure me of my constipation, but I know it will kill me to miss out on the intrigue of Damascus just because my bowels are in lockdown.

We meander the ancient cobblestone streets. Damascus is one of the oldest continuously inhabited cities in the world; since 4000 B.C.E. people have collected themselves in this desert plain watered by two rivers. The Damascus of old lies several feet below these cobblestones. Yet such places as Straight Street, reported in the New Testament as the location where the apostle Paul's eyesight was restored after he was struck blind by the resurrected Jesus, still exist.

I grew up hearing about the apostle Paul's infamous journey "on the road to Damascus." Paul stumbled into this city—down this corridor—after an encounter with Jesus changed the trajectory of his life, and perhaps the destiny of the church. As we make our way through the covered souk on Straight Street, my eyes dart from one stall to another. An array of hijabs cover one stall, while the next sells household cleaners and hardware. Another displays exquisite clothes. On that day when Paul stammered down this street he wouldn't have seen the vendors or their wares; darkness gripped his sight. But what was going on in his mind?

Paul, known at that time by his Hebraic name Saul, had studied under a highly respected rabbi and seemed to be on the fast track in Pharisaical circles. Apparently obsessed with seeing an end to the "Followers of the Way," he cheered on the stoning of the Christian leader Stephen and then went house to house dragging Christian men and women off to prison.

Acts picks up his story again with him en route from Jerusalem to Damascus in order to make more arrests of Christian leaders. What would compel him to travel 150 miles, a five-day trip, to cart strangers off to jail? Perhaps this was a way for Saul to prove himself as a religious purist in order to climb the ranks. Or possibly Saul truly thought these followers of Jesus had such a wrong view of God that he was obligated to put an end to their misguided souls.

"Why?" is the very question the resurrected Jesus poses to Saul on the road to Damascus. A light from heaven flashes. Saul drops to the ground, and a voice booms, "Saul, Saul why do you persecute me?" Introductions are made and instructions are given. Saul is to go into Damascus and wait for further word.

Saul, utterly blind, is led by hand into Damascus. For three days he goes without food or water. Ananias, a Christian leader in Damascus, gets a vision of Jesus telling him to go to Straight Street and pray for Saul to receive his sight. Ananias is well-acquainted with Saul's reputation and designs to persecute followers of Jesus, but the Lord tells him, "Go! This man is my chosen instrument to carry my name before the Gentiles and their kings and before the people of Israel. I will show him how much he must suffer for my name."

Then Ananias went to the house and entered it. Placing his hands on Saul, he said, "Brother Saul, the Lord—Jesus, who appeared to you on the road as you were coming here—has sent me so that you may see again and be filled with the Holy Spirit." Immediately, . . . [Saul] could see again.

I wonder what that first look between Saul and Ananias felt like. Saul had planned to throw people like Ananias in prison; the thought of such people had likely made his blood pressure rise three days previous. Now this man was the means of Saul's healing and likely the closest connection to his newfound faith in Jesus.

And Ananias! I'm astounded that Ananias calls Saul "brother." The gravitas of that kind of love and forgiveness amazes me. It makes me wonder how Ananias would describe God.

We continue east and come to the Ananias Chapel. My gait is anything but straight right now. I stumble and sway, but I really want to visit the historic holy site. Once Ananias died, his house apparently was converted into a chapel for Christian worship. In the second century the Roman emperor Hadrian tore it down and built a pagan temple on top of it. He, like other emperors, had developed this habit of demolishing churches in an attempt to erase the memory of the tradition. Once Christians regained power under Constantine, they built a cathedral on the site. In the successive centuries it vacillated back and forth between being a church and a mosque. For chunks of history it was a shared space. Both Christians and Muslims have come here to pray for healing.

As I mull over Paul's sight being restored, I realize I want to be healed too. We enter Ananias's courtyard and descend a tiny but lengthy flight of stairs to the church, which is more like a series of caves. In the first cave, Mass is being celebrated. I sit in the back; I will wait for the priest to finish and ask him to pray for me. I will leave healed, just like Paul.

I become impatient. I just want to be healed, but the priest keeps on speaking and speaking. Every time I think he is wrapping up, he turns another page of his liturgical book. I fess up to Eric and Krista: I am in loads of pain and need to return to the room. My stomach is having visible spasms.

We pass several restaurants on the way back. The very scent of food violates my intestines. When we arrive at the hostel Krista places a cool washrag on my forehead. I wake up eleven hours later.

I've survived one more day without dying in this country. I feel strangely optimistic.

Today we will travel to Sednaya and Maaloula, two towns in the Syrian hills where people still speak the ancient Aramaic used during the days of Jesus. Apparently there are a couple of convents and monasteries in the region. Maybe today I'll have the strength to ask people to describe God. Maybe today I'll get healed.

I put my flowing sundress back on. It ties at the top and then streams down—no interference for my belly. I've worn it four out of the last five days.

George, our driver, has a wide nose, sun-baked skin and a gregarious laugh. I imagine before the day is done he will know the details of my "situation." We load in George's white van and spend an hour increasing elevation.

Our first stop is the village of Sednaya. One of its attractions is apparently the area where Cain slew his brother Abel. To get to the town's convent, we have to spiral up a hill. When I finally get a view of the place, I'm stunned. I was expecting a quaint, little, run-down chapel. This looks like a fortress.

George says he'll wait in the van for an hour as we tour. We have to hike more stairs to the entrance. I support my belly with each step. When we make it through the convent doors, I'm shocked. It's more packed with ladies than a Macy's shoe sale. There are young women, old women, all shapes of women, and precisely two men, including Eric.

I think this freaks Eric out because he disappears. Krista and I move with the masses and are swept into a small chapel where we exchange our shoes for headscarves. The lighting is solely from candles. Paintings of saints and biblical stories wallpaper the place from floor to ceiling. The ambiance of holiness is tangible, more visceral than my pain.

Then we are directed into a larger chapel. Candlelight illumines the women's faces. Each has an expression of saintliness: some somber, others crying, still others caught in wonderment. Does my face stick out? In the midst of this beautiful sacredness, can others perceive my constipation?

I realize that the crowd I'm traveling with is actually a line. I peer around and notice it is leading to a small vat of oil in front of an icon. Two nuns flank it. I begin to study the transaction so I will be ready to imitate when it's my turn.

The icon is of the Virgin Mary. It looks very old. My Western Protestant background hasn't exactly prepared me for this encounter. But I try to do what I see the other women doing. I take a cotton ball from the nun on my left and dip it in the hot oil. I bow my head reverently as I receive a small Ziploc bag from the nun on my right. I want the nun to pray for me, but the room is packed and I don't want to hold up the line.

I tuck my Ziploc bag in my backpack and exit the chapel. My shoes magically appear in a stack in front of me. But Krista has now disappeared. I see if I can speak with any nuns.

A lovely nun named Juvana leads me back through the church to show me their impressive collection of icons. "St. Luke painted four icons of Virgin Mary; this is one of them." Juvana speaks in the tone of a proud mother showing off her children's artwork. "Here is the icon of Jerusalem from 1175. And this one is of St. Tekla from Maaloula from 813."

The convent currently has forty girls and about fifty sisters who come from Syria, Lebanon and even Jerusalem. The girls are orphans in need of a physical and spiritual home. Juvana leads me up several flights of stairs—this place is enormous—to a large office where the head nun runs the operation. I'm given a book on the history of Our Lady of Sednaya and am introduced to a lovely big-boned woman in her sixties.

She tells me she is simply "a servant of Our Lady, St. Mary." She offers me brightly wrapped chocolates and seamlessly starts sharing with me about how her parents used to bring her here as a child.

Now the nun is chuckling. I can't wait to hear what she has to say. With an innocent smirk she tells me, "I used to convince my parents to let me spend the night right in front of the icon of Mary. Early on I knew the best life was near the Virgin Mother of Christ. Finally when I was twelve, my parents let me move into the convent. I have lived here for fifty-four years."

I still can't fully grasp having such a deep connection to Mother Mary. I lack the framework to engage the Sister about her relationship with Mary, but my assumptions of those who pray to Mary have been repeatedly challenged during this trip. I turn the topic to familiar ground. "How do you describe God?"

"God is over everything," the Sister begins. "People here really love God and Mary. They come from all over the world. Every day there are miracles with St. Mary. About eight days ago a man came from Iraq for healing. He had cancer, and he couldn't get help in Baghdad. He then went to Damascus and they couldn't help him. The man knew a Christian family and they said, 'Come. We will take you to the biggest doctor in the world!' The man came here and prayed, and knelt and took the holy oil. He was between life and death, but a couple of days later he was healed! He could eat and the doctors in Damascus told him there was no cancer! They came back here; his wife brought food for the orphan girls and the man wrote his story in our book of miracles.

"Many Muslims and even Jews come to pray. When they see the icon, they believe. They may come in thinking one way but they leave thinking another way."

As the Sister says this something shifts in me. It must be my own description of God. I want to believe in a God of miracles, a God so bent on provoking humanity with his love and healing the sick and brokenhearted that he will use the most unexpected means. I ask the Sister to pray for me. I point to my stomach and say I've been having problems for a while.

I shuffle around in my backpack and pull out the Ziplock bag. I hand her the cotton ball dipped in holy golden-green virgin oil. I don't know exactly what she is to do with the cotton ball, but surely she knows. As she begins to pray, she presses the cotton ball to my forehead. The warm oil feels soothing. Words pour from her lips likes a mountain stream, confident and refreshing. I can't understand her as she prays powerfully in Arabic, but I know she is very close to God and that they must be having a significant chat.

I sense I am going to be healed today. I've been in such pain and so consumed with trying to find a cure, I've forgotten to pray about it.

"Amen." She looks at me with great expectation and says, "I hope to see you next year with your baby."

In the van, George explains that the convent dates back to the sixth century. "It's a popular pilgrimage site for infertile women. Christian, Muslim and Druze women from all over the Middle East travel here to pray to the Virgin Mary, asking God to give them babies."

It finally clicks; the lovely Sister thought I wanted to have a baby. I lean over to Krista and mention that if I get pregnant soon, it's not my fault. She looks confused, but I don't try to explain.

I was astounded at the idea of Muslims and Jews coming to Sednaya to be healed. I've been frustrated that so many Christian holy sites have been turned into mosques in the Middle East. Yet the Sister seemed thrilled to share her holy site with those of a different creed and see God's blessings spill beyond the Christian faithful. I imagine Jesus is pleased too. Jesus healed lots of people. Some knew him to be the Son of God, others didn't. He didn't take back their healing if they didn't believe. His love was generous enough, expansive enough to entrust it to even those who would reject him.

The expectation of miracles continues to challenge my orderly conceptions of the faith, and Mary veneration jars my Protestant notions. Nevertheless I'm growing grateful for places such as Medjugorje and Sednaya.

They remind me that my description of God is too boxy and the way I view others is too narrow. What a gift to get a glimpse of the largeness of Jesus' love by chatting with a Sister in Syria!

Our next stop takes us down one hill and up another. Maaloula is one of George's favorite towns; it has buildings with brightly colored paint and a convent built into a cliff. When we arrive at the foot of the convent, I notice a couple of buildings, and then my attention goes to Eric. Wow! He looks horrible. He says he's nauseated and awkwardly debarks from the van. As Eric leans against the door doubled over, George says with his gregarious laugh, "Look, there's a pharmacy."

Before we relay our symptoms, the pharmacist sizes us up and says, "I have exactly what we need." In clear English he continues, "Do you feel like you are going to pass out? Are you nauseated? Do you have diarrhea?"

Oh, just when I thought I was going to be healed today. But, then he adds: "Or, do you have bad constipation?" Yes! Yes! Yes! I almost kiss the man.

He pulls out two packets of tablets. He just got them in. "What you have is an amoeba!" What? "An amoeba. A very bad parasite." Excellent.

He says to take four tablets. We rip into the aluminum seals and chew the tablets right there on the spot. He tells us, "Only water and bread for the next twenty-four hours. This is very important."

Thank you, God! Thank you. Thank you. Thank you.

We climb up more stairs to the Chapel of St. Thecla. It is hot; my flowing sundress is sticking to me. The chapel is an airy cave with large windows. Water dribbles down one side of it. The water is reported to have miraculous powers, one of which is to cure flatulence. I hold my Nalgene bottle up against the cave wall and let the water trickle in. I don't want to miss out on any cures today.

St. Thecla was believed to have converted to Christianity after hearing St. Paul preach. The details of her life after that seem to get more mysterious and fantastical, many of which involve her efforts to keep her chastity. I interview Sister Agil, who looks to be in her early twenties. She is radiant as she raves about the miracles that happen here. Although her English is spotty, I sense we have a significant connection. I ask her to describe God. She tells me without pause, "We know Allah"—throughout the Middle East "Allah" is often used to refer to the Christian God—"is one word: Love. The other sisters say the same. Can you love God without loving your brother and sister? How can God see you if you don't love your brother or sister who you do see? Jesus said 'Blessed is the merciful; they will be shown mercy.'"

Her words are infused with conviction. She goes on to tell the story of the good Samaritan. "A man fell off his horse and into a ditch. If he didn't get help soon, his leg would have to be cut off. Religious men walked past him full of excuses. It wasn't until a despised Samaritan came by that the man in the ditch got help. Jesus says, 'Go and do what this man has shown us.'" She concludes her story by saying, "The love is the work. It is what you do, not just what you say."

On the way home, I sit up front with George. He tells me about his family; I tell him about being constipated all through his country. I tell him how I sensed I would be healed today, and how the pharmacist just got the amoeba medicine in yesterday and how I know I'm going to be better. As we talk I let my arm hang out the window surfing the wind. Having the strong air rush over my bare skin is one of my most favorite sensations. I tell George I am very glad to get to know him.

We slow down to turn a sharp corner and my arm feels like someone has dug into it with a dagger. I drag it back in the van. I inspect it. I can see the welt form and spread. I've been stung.

George looks over and tells me he'll get me help. In less than a mile he parks the van along the side of the road and motions to me to cross the street with him. We walk into a restaurant; everyone seems to know George. He chats with the manager and I'm offered a clove of garlic. I press the garlic to my bite like the nun had pressed the cotton ball to my forehead. By the time we return to the hostel the welt is diminished.

The hostel where we are staying is charming and cheap. The four-dollars-a-night cover charge has gotten us a bed and access to a bathroom down the hall. There's just a minor problem with the setup. Well, maybe a few:

1. The bathroom is shared by about forty backpackers.

2. The bathroom is such tight quarters that you have to hug your knees to your chest in order to shut the door. Eric claims that when he does that, the door still won't shut.

3. There is a two-foot gap between the door and the ceiling, so people can hear basically everything that happens.

Other than this it isn't that bad. Of course, I haven't really had to use the bathroom here. There is, however, a strong possibility that the amoeba extracting pills will take effect tonight. So I am at a juncture between reason, and, well, nonreason. Eric says he is checking into a real hotel with a real bathroom. I'm on a budget. Eric leaves. Krista and I stay.

Krista is hungry, so we go a couple of blocks to a five-star hotel. She orders an appetizer; I sip coffee and water. As we leave the restaurant two guys around our age follow us out. Once we cross the street they invite us to have a drink with them. We say we need to meet up with a friend.

Hours later we are at the intersection of Straight Street and some other road trying to sort out where we are. Savvy world-travelers that we are, we subtly stand on the street corner and hold open our three-foot-wide map. It's dark; we're two women without a male escort in the Old City of Damascus. Out of nowhere, the two guys from the hotel restaurant appear by our side. We ask if they know where the Whirling Dervish perform. I show them the location on our map but they say they don't know where that place is. They tell us they know of a fantastic restaurant that has live music.

Krista and I both mean to say "No," but as we look at each other "Sure, why not?" slips out of our lips in stereo. Alleys and alleys later we're at a stone courtyard, and through chunky wrought-iron gates we enter a tiled, palatial building. The ceiling must be forty feet high. There are tables scattered in a semicircle and more on a balcony. The décor is Mediterranean but when the two singers open their mouths the entire atmosphere becomes Latin. I've been slightly infatuated with salsa dancing, so I oblige when one of the guys offers to dance.

They order red wine, two bottles, and ask us about our stay. Then we all discuss Europe. The guy who attaches himself to Krista says he doesn't really speak English, so instead of talking he pulls out his videophone. It actually records for a couple of minutes at a time. He videos Krista sipping her wine, me dancing, his friend just sitting there. All this becomes highly annoying. When his friend asks him to put it away, moments later he has it out again.

The guy I'm seated beside speaks English fluently. He has a dark complexion, dark hair, dark eyes. Attractive. Articulate. Engaging. He asks me about American politics, the Iraq war, U.S. international policy, the global war on terror and whether I think Syrians should engage internal reforms.

I'm typically invigorated by political conversations. I could talk all night—and look into his eyes for hours—but every few minutes I repeat my inner mantra: *Tell him nothing, nothing, not even about my amoeba.*

They insist on buying us dinner. I know I shouldn't eat. I've already consumed too much wine. The words of the pharmacist ricochet around my brain: "Only water and bread. This is very important." I eat pita dipped in hummus that happens to be swimming in olive oil. I eat *tomboli.* I eat lamb; even when I have ample room in my belly I rarely eat meat. I guess I just don't want to offend another generous host.

They walk us back to the five-star hotel where we tell them we are staying, the one where they followed us out of the restaurant. They offer to meet us here in the morning. The non-English speaker wants to buy Krista some jewelry. We hide in a hallway near the elevator. A few minutes later we begin walking back to our one-star hostel. It's two in the morning and the only living species around are taxi drivers. One after another motions to us. We wave them off.

We tiptoe up the stairs of our hostel. The place is completely dark. I don't bother getting out of my sundress. It already feels like a nightgown.

My amoeba takes my lying down as the cue to vacate. I stagger to the toilet. The 2' x 2' room becomes my cell and liberator. I don't leave until my amoeba is evicted and my intestines are vacant.

I mumble a parting shot to my one-cell organism that has traveled with me since Turkey. "Goodbye, amoeba. Though you caused me great pain, you made me more attuned to the kindness of these Syrian strangers. Though you distracted me from my pilgrimage, in the end you made me desire the miraculous. Little amoeba, I think you enabled me to get a larger view of God. Thanks! Now, buh-bye."

I wake up to the words of other backpackers wafting through the halls. They are all asking who was sick last night. I change out of my sundress. I try to make myself look healthy, so as not to be found out. But I am weak. And I tell the kind lady at the front desk that I was last night's sick soul. She offers me a piece of bread.

Eric returns from his stay in a real hotel. He too looks like he had a bitter break-up with his amoeba. Before we leave, I ask the woman at the front desk to write down how much a taxi should cost to the bus station. I don't want to be had again. I shuffle along with Krista and Eric to the main street, and we fling our weary bodies into the first taxi we see.

We show the driver the piece of paper with the name of the bus station and the fare we should pay. Yet when we get to the station the driver wants to charge three times the fare. I'm weak and worn out, and now I'm also mad. I keep pointing to the slip of paper with the proper fare. He keeps insisting—now shouting—that we pay him more. I guess I'm shouting back as I get out of the taxi. Bypassers are gathered to watch; a police officer looks like he's about to come over. I throw my Syrian pounds at the driver. He screeches away.

We scurry into the station area to catch our bus to Beirut. I realize I don't want to leave Syria. There's so much we've yet to see here. We didn't even make it to the Great Mosque, a pilgrim site for Muslims and the reported home of John the Baptist's remains. We also missed a thorough tour of the ancient Christian and Jewish quarters. Yet this intriguing country—with its treasure trove of history and its hospitable people like Mustaffah, Father Ignace, the Sisters at Sednaya and Maaloula—has taught me much. To me Syria will always be the country where my God became the God of miracles.

However, even as my God has grown larger, I've hit my base-level. Fatigue, pain and attempts to control the gives and takes in my interactions with others seem to expose the most unseemly gut assumptions I have about life and God. I don't know what just happened there with the taxi. I'm in desperate need of a fresh start.

22

BEIRUT, LEBANON

We pull into Beirut in the blurry black. Headlights and fatigue obscure my sense of the city. I slump off the bus; heat hangs in the air, making the very atmosphere feel languid.

It's curious how your body can grieve the loss of the very thing that had been killing it. After my harsh break-up with the amoeba, I am left with little strength and less of an appetite.

In the days when I slept and ate and lived like a human, I was excited about coming to Lebanon. The Lebanon of my expectations was a land of sultry elegance, ancient adventurers, high fashion and gritty revolutionists. And a land with a visible population of Christians in a post-Christian Middle East. From Gilgamesh to the Hebrew Scriptures, the earliest of texts have heralded this land's snow-capped peaks. Lebanon's name derives from the ancient Semitic word for white, *laban*.

Lebanon is where many of those free-spirited Phoenicians called home and made a name for themselves. Once the strangling grip of the Egyptians and Assyrians loosened up a little, the Phoenicians became a people gone wild. Around 1000 B.C.E. they took to the sea, circumventing Africa, designing intricate pottery, trading fine wine and, in their spare time, scribbling out an alphabet that would teach the Western world to write phonetically.

Lebanon holds the title for the longest running nation name on record:

four thousand years. Yet ironically, it's Lebanon's modernity that seems to cause envy in the East. Lebanon, it is assumed, is where the best soap operas, trendiest fashions and hippest music in the Arab world originate.

Israel's most holy site, the temple in Jerusalem, was built with Lebanon's famous cedars. In exchange, the Phoenician royal family got a lifetime's supply of olive oil and wheat. Lebanon's current arrangement between politics and religion is more curious. The law mandates that the prime minister be a Sunni Muslim, the president be a Maronite Christian and the speaker of Parliament be a Shiite Muslim. This unique setup has presented a few challenges that in turn fueled a civil war and contributed to a revolution.

While religion and politics make this leg of the pilgrimage all very intriguing, at the moment, I care about none of it. I simply want to find our hostel and fling my body into bed. As I dream about dreaming I am surrounded by people who seem to have a more distinct plan to get to their beds than we have. People from our bus are kissing relatives, shaking hands with taxi drivers and leaving; the three of us are halted by lethargy, lacking any desire to kiss each other or anyone else.

Finally I drag out a crumpled piece of paper with the name of a hostel, a phone number, an address and our reservation confirmation number. After my fight with the driver in Damascus, I let Krista negotiate this one and ready myself for a smooth entry into sleep. The driver seems iffy about the address. He calls the hostel, talks to some lady and surmises that it's a wrong number. Is he sure? I got it from hostels.com; certainly it's just a typo. Our driver suggests we stay at another place. But I've paid a deposit, and based on the picture on my crumpled sheet of paper, the accommodations look great.

Now the circling begins. It should be right around here. No. Maybe it's down here. No. I get out and ask people. No one knows. Ugh! The taxi driver must have taken us down the wrong street. He's likely trying to gyp us.

An hour of "This way—no, that way" steals any human dignity I had left. I express my suspicions about the ethics of our taxi driver, aloud. I start adding up the fare, aloud. I think very mean thoughts, aloud. I now embody the bad name that Americans often get traveling abroad.

Our driver takes us to the place he originally suggested. He has an obvious relationship with the owners, and I have an obvious suspicion of that as well. The hotel workers refuse to tell us the price until we make our way up to the fifth floor with the manager to inspect his accommodations. My capacity for common courtesy had been consumed by the amoeba; I am now simply a transactional organism.

Fortunately my conscience is as fatigued as my body. I lose no sleep contemplating what a selfish and unsophisticated soul I am.

The morning begins with a distinct reminder that our room with cable, air conditioning and a private bath is more than we can afford. Hours later we are chatting with the custodian of accommodations more our style—cheap. He's brought us a big map and coffee. The moment is lovely. Then he informs us that we can't navigate this metropolitan city or charming country without a driver. And fortunately for us, he has one: his son.

A friend from Lebanon gave us a list of must-see places. I can't find the list right now but I know exactly where I want to go. It is a place we were advised not to go: Sidon, otherwise known as Saïda. My friend mentioned a possible safety issue, but our driver, Hussain, seems unconcerned. He looks slightly bored by our choice.

We scoot south through the city in our 1988ish, superbly maintained Mercedes, passing the place where former prime minister Rafik Hariri was assassinated only months ago. On Valentine's Day, Hariri and between sixteen and twenty other people were killed as a massive car bomb blast left a twenty-foot-wide, ten-foot-deep crater in the road, pouring debris on the streets for blocks.

The explosion reverberated far beyond the chic waterfront district where it hit. Within days, Beirut became a campsite for protesters. On March 14, Martyrs' Square hosted approximately 800,000 people—the largest demonstration in Lebanon's history. More than one in five people living in the country came out not simply to grieve their former prime minister's death;

they left their homes, slept in tents and waved their Lebanese flags to send a message: Syria out! Syria out!

I had been captivated by the coverage of this event. I had sat in my driveway, unable to exit my VW Bug until a reporter finished her analysis of the situation. I had blown off friends so as not to miss the evening news. The world and I were getting to watch a country be reshaped, a revolution happen without violence. After living in Israel for a year and seeing the complications and losses on both sides to the violent game of tag, I longed to see nonviolent indigenous moves toward peace in the Middle East. And right here Muslims, Christians and Druze came together in crossconfessional unity to ignite the Cedar Revolution, a revolution that caused the international community to finally respond to injustice.

Hariri's assassination had spotlighted Lebanon's love-hate relationship with its eastern neighbor, Syria. From 1975 to 1990 Lebanon was embroiled in a civil war. It erupted like a bar brawl, with Syria, Israel and the Palestine Liberation Organization (PLO) jumping into the fray. Beirut became the stage for a modern Wild West scene, with kidnappings and bank robberies but also car bombings and hijackings. Then the Iranian-financed Islamist group Hezbollah ("Party of God") started up in southern Lebanon. The United States stepped in as well to help with negotiations. Alliances shifted so often and so fast, at times it seemed hard to tell who was fighting whom.

The brawl slowed down in 1989 with the signing of the Taif Agreement, but by then the country's economy was overturned and its capital in shambles. When the civil war officially ended in 1990, not everyone went home. Syria's presence and influence only grew. With thousands of troops and hundreds of spies scattered throughout the country, Syria became slightly intrusive to some, including Prime Minister Hariri.

Hariri had been in good with Damascus at times, but his patience with Syria shut down in October 2004 when Lebanon's president, Émile Lahoud, a man Hariri regarded as a pro-Syrian puppet, had his term extended by Parliament for another three years. Hariri resigned in protest and stirred up attention by demanding an end to Syria's military and political roles in Lebanon. Hariri's death galvanized his supporters and some of his dissenters, and finally beckoned the international community to act.

I am eager to speak with Hussain about the revolution. I have longed to hear people's firsthand accounts of the rallies, to have my hope revived in the potential of change and in the potency of peace. I am like an addict needing a fix; "Share some hope," my exhausted soul ekes out.

Hussain seems just the guy. He is affable and quite a thinker. He's already engaged us in a conversation about the Bay of Pigs and reflected on Bill Clinton's leadership style only a mile or two into our excursion. Yet when I ask Hussain about the Cedar Revolution, he seems less than enthusiastic. He thinks Syria didn't need to leave so quickly. I'm confused. Then I remember what I had forgotten. Hezbollah put on counterprotests, visually reminding the nation that life in Lebanon is more complicated than unprecedented shows of unity. I quickly pack up my enthusiasm, and conversation with Hussain slides into analysis of the Bush administration and U.S. ambitions. It lingers there until we arrive at Sidon's big tourist site: Crusader ruins.

While ancient stones stacked up along the sea make for a charming photo, I am utterly sick of Crusader ruins. I have no desire to give homage to a place where Christians fought their enemies in the name of God. I was looking for a site a little more scandalous—evidence of one of my favorite stories, a story that is said to have taken place in the region of Sidon. During the mid-800s B.C.E., King Ahab of Israel made an alliance with his northern neighbor by marrying Jezebel, daughter of the king of the Sidonians. With the political alliance came religious compromise. An Israelite prophet named Elijah enters the scene, but before he has a showdown with the prophets of Baal, the god of the Sidonians, the plot line takes a twist. In the midst of a severe drought and famine, Elijah is sent by God to enemy territory. He arrives at Zarephath, in the region of Sidon, and asks a starving widow to share her last meal with him. A miracle happens: her meager oil and flour do not run out for the entire time Elijah stays with her. A friendship forms, a mutual reliance develops.

As I think about it, this approach to interdependence—including with one's enemies—may be even more revolutionary than the Cedar Revolution.

I know ancient Zarephath is near Sidon. I assume there must be some church, some physical tribute to this remarkable story. But Hussain doesn't know of one. And when I ask the guards at the Crusader ruins, they too have no idea what I'm talking about. We make our way to the center of Sidon. Certainly someone in this ancient souk will know the great story and direct us properly. But it is Friday afternoon; the Muslims have taken their day off, and the Christians seem to have gone home as well. I finally spot a nun walking the deserted street. She has a lovely disposition, but she doesn't speak English.

The nun and I exchange *bonjours* and I wish her a *bonne journée*. I silently curse my lack of *Francais* skills, and we leave Sidon. Before we make it out of the city limits, Hussain tries to salvage the trip by taking us to the Grand Mosque, recently completed by Hariri for the people in his hometown. When we get there, the doors are shut. Everyone is going home. The trip south has been a bust. So I attempt to rescue it for myself. I ask Hussain to describe God.

Hussain says, "I can't describe Allah. If I describe Allah it shows I don't know him. If I want to follow God, I don't need to describe him. I think my brain is a part of God. If we don't even know how our brains work— which we don't—how can we describe Allah? My God drives the sun. No man can control the atmosphere, the sun and the stars. No one can explain one's spirit."

I'm intrigued by Hussain's perspective. He has a strong intellect and defined opinions. I am slightly surprised by his grip of mystery and his embrace of faith. But what if I went with Hussain's description? What if my brain was a part of God? Does that mean that God too is selfish and tired? Is he a little suspicious and greedy?

Finding out that God is as messed up as I am would certainly be the climax to my day. I don't even bother with the expletives I'm tempted to spew and suggest we get food. We decide to return to the hip district where our supposed hostel was located. No, none of us is bitter, really. We're just indecisive, which takes us to the lowest common denominator: an outdoor mall, an Italian franchise restaurant. As I gnaw on a bread stick, our pilgrimage— our purpose for being here and my sense of God—feels further from my grasp than when we started.

≳ ≴

Days and countries ago it seemed that each morning I was handed a ticket to a full twenty-four hours of adventure. The price of admission was merely the energy to get out of bed and pray a prayer for divine encounters. Recently the price of energy has broken the bank. So today I forgo my simple prayer and throw back on my long flowing sundress—partly because it is at the top of my backpack but mainly because it is the closest garment I have to sleepwear. In an attempt to rally a little pride in my appearance I don my sliver and turquoise necklace. It's the one I got in Aleppo for a third of the price with the kiss-discount.

I slip from the room as Eric and Krista linger in their beds. I'm off to a date, in the meeting/appointment sense of the word. I'm having breakfast with Ramez, a Lebanese businessman I had dinner with once months ago. He's a friend of a friend. My memory is blurry, but I recall him being brilliant and unassuming. I think he's a Maronite Christian by birth and an agnostic by choice. Maybe Ramez can help navigate my understanding around Lebanon's tricky political terrain.

Ramez greets me with a generous smile. I greet him with a barrage of questions about the country's mood and the response of the international community. All of a sudden, with magical Middle Eastern charm, he stops me and asks how I am enjoying Lebanon. I explain our hostel fiasco, our trek to Sidon and our need to leave tomorrow afternoon. He is horrified. In midsentence he pulls out his cell phone and postpones his next meeting. Ramez declares it a criminal offense to move through the land without stealing a glance at a few of Lebanon's national treasures. We collect Eric and Krista and are suddenly moving along the coast.

Knowing we're on a pilgrimage, Ramez acts as if our next stop is nonnegotiable. We leave the comforts of the coast for a climb to the sky, to a fifteen-ton statue of Mary overlooking the bay of Jounieh.

We pull up to Harrissa, a Maronite holy place. Once again I'm unprepared for the caravan of tour buses. "Our Lady of Lebanon," Ramez exclaims. "People come here from all over Lebanon and beyond to give homage to Mary. The statue was built in the early 1900s in celebration of the fiftieth anniversary of the pope's announcing Mary's Immaculate Conception. The Lebanese Maronite Catholics embraced his high view of Mary and built a statue as a show of gratitude."

I climb the twenty-meter-high stairwell spiraling around Our Lady's base. I reach the top of the stairs and crane my neck to gaze at her. The sun softens her white-over-bronze complexion. The wind swirls around her face and the sea falls at her feet. This Virgin Mary is . . . formidable. Few times would I have thought to describe Mary as formidable, but no other words right now feel as apropos.

The total number of thoughts I've had about Mary over my lifetime hasn't rivaled the number of times she's come to mind on this pilgrimage. I still can't ascend to believe in the Immaculate Conception—the belief that Mary moved through life unscathed by sin. It is a belief, however, clung to by many Catholics, Orthodox and Muslims. While the Bible doesn't mention it, the Qur'an does.

But this fifteen-ton statue of Mary makes me think about how she described God. The Gospel of Luke records a song, often referred to as the Magnificat, attributed to Mary. In it she gives gratitude to God's generosity toward her. She describes God as her Savior, mindful of her, holy, merciful and just. "He has filled the hungry with good things," she says, "but has sent the rich away empty."

Perhaps it was Mary's humility that gave her the strength of character to bear the Son of God. When the angel Gabriel approached Mary, she said, "I am the Lord's servant; may it be as you have said." Being an unwed mother in those days was a dangerous proposition. Her reputation, her future marriage to Joseph and potentially her life was on the line. And yet she accepted the gift with grace. Not only was she willing to receive this mind-numbing task from God, she was courageous and grateful.

"Oh, Mary, formidable Mary, I have so much to learn from you." My prayer floats down as I descend the spiral stairs.

Once grounded I meet Shant, a twenty-six-year-old guy with a confident gait and bold, brown eyes. Shant tells me straightaway that his name means

"Thunderbolt." Although he lives in Lebanon, his heritage is Armenian. "I believe in God. I know him in my imagination. I can't do anything without God. I'm always in contact with him. If I want to do something I ask—if it is right or not, I always take the answer to my inner God. I listen to his voice to find out if it is right to do it or not.

"I go to church every Sunday, but I don't read the Bible. I don't like reading." Shant's gaze turns momentarily to the sea, then he adds, "In my difficult situations God has been there for me."

I stop in silence for a moment. This hip, twenty-six-year-old Thunderbolt articulates such a confidence in God and reliance on the Divine. I ask Shant if others his age think about God.

"Not so much. But I have a character of my own and must make my own decisions about God."

I thank Shant. He rejoins his friends and I introduce myself to a young woman sitting alone. "My name is Reine. Here, I'll write it down for you." Reine has blondish brown hair that streams down her back. She doesn't wear makeup yet looks sophisticated. Reine writes her name, then her age— "seventeen years old"—and that she is Maronite. When I ask her to describe God, she asks if she can write her response as well. She begins in English, "God is Dad of all people." Then she switches her writing to French.

Though I am at a loss conversing in French, fortunately I can get by reading it. From what I make out, Reine writes, "God protects us from all dangers, but he desires us to ask him for help. All the time he is considerate, like a father. We are his children."

"*C'est vrai! Merci*, Reine. *Au revoir.*"

Sometimes I wish we could write out all of our conversations. We could put our words on the page and decide whether we want to commit to them or not. We could access a thesaurus and edit our relationships en route. Perhaps our dates, our loved ones, our new friends would sound a little more like the people in the movies—those characters whose dialogues are scrutinized by a whole team of scriptwriters. But I suspect there is beauty in the candid, bumbling nakedness of words rolling off the tongue. I imagine in heaven, we will have no need of a team of scriptwriters, editors and thick thesauri.

As we leave, busloads of Shia Muslim women dressed in their traditional black hijabs descend on Harissa. Ramez tells me, "These women have traveled from Iran. Many Muslims from Iran come here. They love Mary."

Ramez decides to drive us northwest, through the Mount Lebanon range. As we pass little villages placed in the nooks and crannies of the mountains, Ramez points out that the last of the Syrian troops were just leaving these areas. We are both curious if the Syrians will stay out.

As we round another mountain Ramez gets a phone call. After a quick conversation with a business partner, he pronounces that he has canceled the rest of his meetings for the day. We're off to Byblos. Soon enough we are once again facing the sea; this time we climb out of the car into the epicenter of ancient Phoenician territory.

The Phoenician sea-faring people were known in antiquity as adventuresome merchants and skilled mariners. They were also slightly heady. Their concept of an alphabet—twenty-two symbols, all consonants and each one representing its own sound—laid the foundation for our modern-day Roman alphabet.

Ramez engages a woman with short brown hair and khaki shorts in an animated conversation. He hands her a wad of Lebanese money. The woman becomes our personal guide, leading us through the ancient Phoenician city–turned-Roman-turned-Crusader ruins.

Byblos is considered one of the oldest continuously inhabited settlements, dating back seven millennia, edging out Damascus's claim by about a thousand years. The Bible gets its name from Byblos. Apparently Byblos traded cedars with Egypt in exchange for papyrus. They then turned the papyrus into scrolls and exported them throughout the Mediterranean, including Israel. Our word for book, *biblia*, and the Book, the Bible, are tributes to an ancient city of language-loving mariners.

As we traverse through ruins of a Roman theater and a Crusader castle, our personal guide shares other fascinating information about Byblos, which I promptly forget. Afterward Ramez drives us to a paradisiacal restaurant that feels like it has its origins in the Garden of Eden. Purple and pink bougainvillea adorn the lush grounds, fountains create a surround-sound concert, and the scent of food fills the air. Here the world seems nothing but good.

When the waiter comes, no menus are distributed. Ramez just rattles off a long string of Arabic words. One gorgeous course after another follows. Hummus and bread, salads upon salads, meats grilled and fried, more salads and then a fruit parade across our plates. Superlatives don't give the dining experience justice.

Then the bill arrives. Suddenly the ease of the Garden of Eden devolves. I pull out my wallet. This will certainly be a credit card transaction. Ramez gives me a look like, *Don't insult me. You're in the Middle East.* Oh my gosh! I can't even calculate how much Ramez has spent on us today, and he's canceled a full day of work for random strangers.

Ramez says he has one last place he'd like to take us. "We will go back to my house and have coffee and dessert, and I will try to arrange an interview for you."

His house clings to one of the hills above Beirut. His mother lives with him. She gives us a tour of the house and then serves us coffee in bone china flowered cups. During our tour Ramez had found someone I could ask to describe God. He introduces us to a man who looks to be an on-call handyman. "This is George." Ramez offers to translate.

We sit on Ramez's patio sipping coffee and eating sweet pastries, as George tells us about his spiritual journey. "I was a Sunni Muslim, but now I am a Maronite Christian."

"Why did you convert?" I ask.

"I had this feeling, like someone was calling me. Most of my friends were Christians and there was such a loving environment around them. At no time did I feel hatred toward Muslims. The only difference was that Muslims couldn't take Communion.

"When I was a Muslim child, I attended an Irish Catholic school. Once a week I took religious courses and I had a special feeling. During the civil war my parents went to Syria, where they were from. I stayed in Lebanon and lived in the Christian community."

"What was that like to be Sunni living in a Christian community?"

"Our Lady Miriam"—Mary—"and Jesus show up in the Qur'an. Muslims consider Mary to be the greatest woman. So I was familiar with major characters of Christianity. Now I see that Islam is a deviation of Christianity. I think Muhammad was misinformed by the Apocrypha. What caused me to convert to Christianity was the comfort and love I felt."

"George, how would you describe God now?"

"He's the ultimate Creator of the universe. God is love. In these days it is difficult to find this between people. Love is what life is about. You have to love people, even if they are your competition. God can prevent anger; anger doesn't bring love."

The sun slips quietly in the sea. The arrival of evening cues George to return home to his family—a wife who is a Christian, their three daughters and son. We recall that Ramez has spent an entire day lavishing us with Lebanese hospitality, and we take our leave. Ramez orders a cab and insists on paying the driver.

I'm stripped of words to even properly thank Ramez. His generosity has been incalculable, and in some curious sense it's been incapacitating. I haven't been able to fight it.

The taxi driver takes us to Beirut's elegant Centre Ville. We stroll down the arcade of stone arches lined with boutiques and cafés. Live music and melodic conversations float through the air. Krista, Eric and I decide to split up for a while and then rendezvous for an evening appetizer.

In the midst of the boutiques and cafés I spot a Bible Society bookstore. The place is empty except for the lone worker, who seems delighted to have me join him. I introduce myself and launch right into a conversation about my pilgrimage and my question.

Charles tells me, "In 1984 I accepted a life with Christ after I read the story of the lost son in the Gospel of Luke. Since then my life has been full of grace and happiness and peace. I have four daughters, and they are now believers. One of my daughters has leukemia. She happens to be in the hospital right now. She's only six years old, but she already loves Jesus.

"I see God as a loving Father and Jesus as a Good Shepherd. My faith is in God and his Word. We don't know Christ without his Word. We have a new movement in the East. More Muslims want to know who is God, and who is Jesus. It's our responsibility to tell them. It's difficult if we feel that the Muslims are our enemy. If we are to preach to them, we need to love them. The Muslims need love. Love exists in Christianity. God is love."

I realize I have to meet Krista and Eric, so I thank Charles and ask if I can pray for his daughter. I then dash to our rendezvous point in hopes of having another leisurely meal. As I savor an array of Mediterranean salads and watch the fashionable Lebanese enjoy an evening out, my thoughts swing back and forth—forward with free-spirited gratitude for Ramez's generosity, back with a feeling of urgency: How can I repay Ramez's kindness? What can I send him from the States? What would he need? I can't forget to send him something straightaway.

My thoughts swing back and forth all the way to bed.

No alarm clock intrudes my sleep; no overambitious sun disturbs my slumber. I simply wake up—expectant, and not that "I-must-search-for-a-constipation-cure expectant" or that "Virgin-birth expectant." I've recovered that feeling of holy expectation from the beginning of our pilgrimage. Something amazing might happen today; I just need to be on the lookout.

We have the whole morning before we leave for Jordan, back through Syria. I pull out a map of the city, and it dawns on me that it's Sunday again. I count up churches in the vicinity; I need to get going! I promise to meet Eric and Krista back at the room by noon.

The first church I locate is Maronite. The service has just started. I don't know how long Maronite liturgy lasts, but people look settled into their pews. The liturgy sung in Arabic captivates me for a moment, but I'm overtaken with the sense that something awaits me and it's not here. I slip out and speed-walk to the historic St. George's Cathedral.

I gingerly open the large wooden door of this Greek Orthodox church.

While I do not understand the Arabic liturgy, the scent of the incense and the cadence of the chants feel familiar, like a friend's favorite perfume or song.

I join the people standing in the back, those like me who can't quite commit to sitting in a pew. My eyes are drawn to a priest with dark curly locks and a face that seems, well, illuminated. He looks immensely happy, but not that fake, plastic, scary happy.

I watch him join the other priests participating in the Eucharist to see if his expression of joy fades. I get tired standing and the priest hasn't dismissed his smile, so I guess I can leave. I don't want to miss out on whatever it is that awaits me today.

I see a bakery by the church and recognize some guys who were standing in the back of St. George's earlier. I ask if I can interview them. They invite me to sit at the table with them and offer me a pastry. As I eat their food, Saed, a twenty-two-year-old management student from Jordan, tells me, "Every night in my dreams I see God and I see beautiful things."

"You have visions of God?" I inquire.

"Yes," Saed responds. "God improves my life because I learn a new way to live. God is very important to me. I integrate God into the way I develop as a person and think about my future. God guides my life. I speak with God a lot." I'm astounded by Saed's description. If I were more open, more expectant, would God visit me in my dreams?

I notice people streaming out of St. George's, so I thank Saed and his friends and return to the cathedral. Perhaps I can interview the priest with the illuminating face. Maybe he has visions of God as well!

The priest is in a focused conversation with a young woman; others have gathered to speak with him next. I seek out another man wearing a black robe—George, who is studying to be a priest. When I ask him to describe God he responds, "We can't know what is really God because we are smaller than God. However God is like love and forgiveness." As George wraps up, I glance at the priest. He is still conversing with others, so I approach a woman who must be in her early twenties. Her name is Luana. We sit down on a pew and she asks me, "Do you want me to describe God in philosophical terms or say it very simply?"

"However you would like," I respond.

"When I was young I thought God was like they tell you in Christianity, that he was the Trinity, three in one. But as I have grown up and made my own research and become more scientific, I've realized that God is an energy, a light. He is a part of the universe, and we are a part of the universe, so we are a part of him too. God is love. God only wants us to love. He is not even judgmental. When we die, there's no such thing as hell. But if I die and I am a very bad person, I don't get to see God soon. If I'm a good person, I get to see God quickly. You get to be nurtured by that positive energy."

I ask Luana what that positive energy is like. "It's something I can't really explain. It is love. Your heart is overwhelmed by love." She tells me that she senses a peace when she comes to church; she can relax here. "I am proud to be a Christian, but I'm not a fanatic," she tells me.

As Luana and I finish chatting, the church has cleared out. The priest I longed to interview is nowhere in sight. Oh well. This morning has been a gift. I was so struck by Saed's experience with God, seeing the Divine in his dreams. And even though I didn't get to speak with that priest, I've gotten to soak in the beauty of an Orthodox service in a historic setting, and I got to meet George and Luana.

I turn to leave and notice an older priest tidying up in the front. Perhaps I can get one more description of God. When I ask if I can interview him he tells me that he and the other priests need to leave for a funeral. One priest is staying back. "I can ask him to come out," he offers.

Within a minute the priest with the illuminated face greets me. He would be delighted to speak with me. We sit on a pew close to the altar.

As I write down Father Nektarios's name, I ask him why he chose it for his ordination. I've never heard of St. Nektarios.

"He's a new saint. Nektarios was born in the mid-nineteenth century. He went to Aegina, a very small, very poor island off the coast of Athens. He founded a monastery with a tiny community of women who desired to be nuns. The poor people of the island saw how gifted Father Nektarios was. They saw his holiness. The people responded, growing in their faith more and more. And now they just built one of the largest Orthodox cathedrals in Greece.

"St. Nektarios had blessed me and my family more than once. The saint gave to me when I had nothing to give to him. This to me is a mark of the people of God. They are very generous."

"That generosity is very countercultural," I insert. "It leaves you empty-handed." I, however, am no longer talking about a saint but my own virulent struggle to receive generosity during this pilgrimage.

"Absolutely," Nektarios continues. "It is beautiful. So when I was ordained as a priest, I asked my bishop if I could take the name of St. Nektarios. He gave his blessing."

"How long have you been a priest?" I ask.

"Eight years."

"How do you describe God?"

Father Nektarios situates himself in the pew and proceeds. "You're asking a very big question, a heavy question. What I've been discovering in my personal experience is that an encounter with God is total stupefaction. I was . . ." He pauses for quite some time. "When you fall in love, it's like you're hit by something. It was something like that when I encountered God. It was an encounter with true life. I've come to realize that without God, there is no life. It's all organic functions running into death. God is life. Life for a human is so much bigger, greater, more important than organic functions. Aren't we more than a machine? I think so."

He speaks like a man smitten by love. I ask how he encountered Christ. I'm curious if he had a dramatic meeting like the apostle Paul, or saw God in a vision like Saed.

"It's a long story. I wasn't an atheist. I inherited my Orthodox beliefs from my family. In our society religion is still given by family. You know, the family bonds are still there. I was born an Orthodox into an Orthodox family. I experienced the Orthodox Church as much as one who has a social religion—no less, no more.

"In my teenage years and a bit more I started having my own way of looking at things as a young man. And the way I saw life around me wasn't meeting my expectations and my ambitions. Because of my misunderstanding and nobody presenting this real picture of Christ to me, I had a little deception of things. I thought Jesus to be the kindest man who ever lived. But I believed I couldn't meet with Christ here. He was too good for this world. He was too good even for his own institution, the church.

"All my idols began to fall, one after the other. When you see your gods—your perspectives of how life is supposed to work—get killed, there is a feeling. When you are expecting so much from these beliefs, these idols, and then you find out they've been good for nothing, it is painful. I went into a deep—not technically depression, in medical terms, but—a personal depression. Life began degrading. It's very hard to manage."

"Everything you thought would work was collapsing," I interject.

"Yes. Yes. Huge idols became little puffs of nothing. Imagine, you trust a friend or love someone and then the person deceives you, what would you feel?"

"Betrayed."

"Yes. And what if everything surrounding you decided to deceive you at the same moment?" Father Nektarios laughs. "It was too much! So I was put in the face of the harsh reality that everything is a lie, there is no truth in it. So where is the truth?

"Until came the moment I met a person by pure accident. A woman was leaving her family and her country to embrace the monastic life, to become a nun. She was very young, cultured, eloquent, very good looking and a very nice person—and she was very happy. *That* got my attention. When I saw this, I said, 'This is what I'm looking for. Where can I get this happiness?'

"I had the occasion to talk with this woman very casually. Then she went off to be a nun. I think that was the moment when our beloved Christ started nudging me. Questions. Questions. Questions. I started to find answers, only coming from God. I thought at that time 'Now I've met the truth.' That is how it started. I will tell you, God knows us better than we know ourselves. God knows how to get to us. So here I am. I'm married with two daughters: ten years and eight-and-a-half years old. I love my family. We have a happy life. My daughters are growing close to God; this is very important."

"What a powerful story!" I respond.

"Actually when I think about my story and my view of God, a story recorded in the Gospels comes to mind. There was a man who was completely out of sorts, deranged, demon-possessed. It says he no longer lived in a house but rather slept among the tombs. He used to hit himself and was so destructive that he had to be tied with chains. It even says the man was naked.

"One day Jesus encountered him. The man cried out, 'What do you want with me, Jesus, Son of the Most High God? I beg you don't torture me!'

"Jesus frees the man of his demons, and the next thing you read is that the man is sitting at Jesus' feet, dressed and in his right mind. Can you imagine what a change!

"For me this summarizes the life with Christ. Before his encounter with Christ this man was naked, a person who no one would even approach. He was captured by evil. He had lost his mind, his spirit and his dignity. He lost everything that made him human. Yet with Christ he got back everything that made him human."

"So we can't be human without God," I interject.

"When I think of my story I see that Christ came and clothed me with peace of mind and a sense of purpose. He made me human, truly human, more human than I knew to hope for."

I thank Father Nektarios. "Your love for Christ is contagious. It's obvious on your face and in your demeanor." I close my notebook and turn off my iPod and ready myself to leave. But then Father Nektarios turns to me—like a mentor or a big brother—and says, "God is taking care of you, even if you don't want him. He knows that he is the only Savior. We look for other saviors. Jesus was crucified for those who don't want him, not only those who want him."

"Father Nektarios," I confess, "I'm challenged to receive Christ's generosity, to accept grace. I want to pay God back."

"Our relationship with God is not a peer relationship; God is our Father. It's a relationship where you have to learn to take. We learn to love others without expectations when we learn to receive God's love. The most precious gift we can give God is to accept—only accept. When a daughter is tired, she becomes selfish. What does a father want? He wants his daughter to only accept his love."

I must leave to go to Jordan. I thank Father Nektarios and give him a hug. I take off running, the words "only accept, only accept" as my mantra with each step.

23

AMMAN, JORDAN

My mantra has turned into a list of arguments. "Only accept" just doesn't come easy to me. So from Beirut through Damascus to Amman, I have it out with God.

Like the naked man in Father Nektarios's story, I am exposed. So it takes a trek east to undress me? What do you want from me, Jesus, Son of the Most High God? I thought this pilgrimage was about *you*. Wasn't I supposed to learn more about who *you* are? It was my vision of you, God, not me, that was at risk. You were the one up for grabs, remember? But here I am caught in a trap by my own skin. I beg you don't torture me!

More than once on this journey Eric has nonchalantly remarked, "You're your own foil, you know." Perhaps—OK, I'm often my own foil. But this pilgrimage has also felt like a set-up. You knew, God, that the generosity of people—Father Bernardo, Tony, Salaam, Eldad and Mustaffah—would dismantle my defenses. You knew I don't like to be indebted, I don't want to impose on others. And you knew I desire to have things equal, and if I can have the upper hand in kindness, all the better.

If those hundred strangers before Beirut had not proved the point, you had to stick Ramez into the story. You knew a full day of one extravagant gesture after another would destroy my ability to keep track of gives and takes. You knew there was no way my pride could survive such generosity.

So, of course you knew my sacred encounters in the East would undo my great Western assumptions: "What's mine is mine, what's yours is yours. Work hard and make sure you get what you deserve." Then there was the whole money issue on the trip. Eric and I have yet to sort out who owes what. You knew how that would keep me on edge.

Then, on the off chance I would miss the plot line, you amassed a collection of taxi drivers to reveal my fury over getting gypped. What was the deal with those taxi drivers anyway? Was it about my dignity being disregarded, or perhaps spotlighting my belief that if I don't protect myself no one else will?

So what happens now? I give up. All my attempts to do better, to try harder, just have me walking around in circles in the desert.

I have had hours for my words to fly out of the window of a van that has carried us through the crisp green countryside of Lebanon and then into Syria. As the day and the distance have progressed, the sun has shone like a searchlight, washing out the rocky hills, the stone houses, the dusty ground of Syria. The afternoon has turned to eve, and the blinding white world outside the van window has become beige, then brown, then finally black as we arrive in Amman, Jordan.

Our driver drops us off a short walk from the Farah Hotel. For six dollars each we get a warm welcome, a bed and the promise of breakfast in a historic corner of Amman. We shake off our packs onto our bunks and locate the restaurant our hotel host just recommended.

We are greeted with exuberant "Ahlan wa-Sahlan!" The maitre d' insists we have *Mansaf*, the national Bedouin dish served on special occasions. I find Bedouin hospitality irresistible, so we accept the stewed lamb with a dried yogurt sauce, sprinkled with pine nuts, served on a bed of rice and accompanied by fabulous flatbread—all to be eaten with our hands.

Bedouins regard hospitality as sacred. Allah has specially brought each person they encounter to them. Any guest is the guest of God—*Day'fAllah*. When they honor their guests, they honor God, and in return God shows them generosity.

As Eric, Krista and I leisurely share our *Mansaf*, my mind gallops on to Jerusalem. It was there, volunteering with a group called Rabbis for Human Rights, that I first experienced Bedouin hospitality. A rabbi and I would visit a Bedouin family who had been forced to give up their nomadic ways to live on a small patch of land outside the city. The Israeli government had poured a concrete foundation for the family, but for some reason construction on the house had stalled, so they were living in a tent on a slab of stone. Not only had they lost their tradition of nomadic life, they had also lost their "health-care system"—herbs harvested from the land to heal ailments. Their health had subsequently declined. Though their resources were limited, they always offered me more than one cup of tea, and sweets along with it. I was supposed to be helping the girls in the family to learn English, but the time felt like I was simply going over to a favorite relative's house to be spoiled.

Oh, I can't wait to get to Jerusalem.

Our meal satisfies every last thought of hunger, though my yearning for Jerusalem grows stronger as the night wears on. One doesn't dare rush into Holy Land, I remind myself as I go to sleep.

I awake early. My bus conversation with God is hardly finished. I gather my Bible and my journal and descend the stairs to the Farah Hotel's serene back garden.

I listen. I hear "Come. Sit at my feet, dear love. I desire you to receive, to receive my grace. And let me remind you of who you are in the light of my love." In the sleepy song of the birds and in the gentle breeze of the morning, I let God describe me. I, like the possessed man, become clothed in human dignity. I become dressed in God's stunning love. "Only accept." I relax in my wrought-iron chair, draped in silence and gratitude.

Krista and Eric eventually join me in the garden. We consume our gratis breakfast, and then we mount one of Amman's ancient hills. To reach the citadel we take metal steps stuck like a ladder against a mountain; we then take a path pasted to the side of a cliff.

We come across no tourists on our makeshift trail. Perhaps there was another way to the top? Nonetheless, we now stand on sturdy ground atop the new city. The remains from the citadel date back to the Middle Bronze Age (second millennium B.C.E.) and the Iron Age (eighth century B.C.E.). Apparently the Roman officials and soldiers, when they came through in the second century, loved the view as well. Ancient Amman was a city of seven hills, and so it reminded them of their dear Rome. They even built an impressive Roman theater here. The city eventually became a part of the Decapolis, one of ten cities that served as the eastern frontier of the Roman Empire.

The Romans also built a temple in the second century C.E., similar to the Temple of Artemis in Ephesus. Rome and Ephesus now feel like worlds away. I look out past Amman to the dusty white land beyond: Jerusalem is only about fifty miles from here. Today I will be in the Holy Land. Today, *inshallah*.

Krista interrupts my thoughts of Jerusalem as she takes a photo of the ancient columns of a sixth-century Byzantine basilica. In our line of sight are the columns from an eighth-century Ummayd mosque eloquently postured on higher ground. I suddenly let the beauty of this place soak into me, and am reminded that this country itself is sacred; it too is a holy land.

Jordan is adorned with holy sites. Among them is Mount Nebo, the mountain Moses ascended to see the land of Canaan before dying. Jordan was as close to the Promised Land as he got. Bethany, on the east bank of the Jordan River, boasts of being the crossing point for Joshua, Elijah and Elisha. It's where John the Baptist preached and baptized countless people, including Jesus. If that's so, then Jesus actually started his public ministry in modern-day Jordan. And in the far north of Jordan is located one of the possible sites for Gadara, the place where Jesus restored the dignity of a demon-possessed man, the story Father Nektarios shared with me just yesterday.

Unfortunately we don't have time to visit Gadara or any of the other sacred sites. In fact, right now we must scamper down our makeshift trail in order to meet a friend back at our hotel.

We are met at the hotel's garden patio by a gathering of women dressed in traditional *hijabs*. They are chatting and laughing and playing with their small children. I wish I could understand Arabic and join in their revelry. Soon my friend Sarah and her young daughter Maymunah join us in the garden. Sarah and her husband, Steve, moved to Jordan from America a couple of years ago to contribute their medical and computer skills to those living in a village outside of Amman. They left the comforts of country and family to live out their love for Jesus among Muslims.

Maymunah plays with the other kids as Sarah dives into conversation with the women across from us. Sarah speaks gorgeous Arabic. Even her laugh sounds Middle Eastern. In between dialogue with the women, Sarah tells us that these ladies are from Iraq. They left their country for a three-month vacation in Jordan, Syria and Egypt.

I'm so curious what they think of America's involvement in Iraq, but they have come here to get away from it all, to escape. The moment is too pleasant to interrupt them with all my questions. So I refrain from inquiring about their husbands, and I don't ask how their Arab neighbors are receiving them. I realize that beyond my questions I want to say something to them.

I'm sorry you grew up in a country with a cruel dictator. I'm sorry my country invaded yours, especially without a thoroughgoing strategy for peace. I'm sorry for all your fellow countrymen and women and children who have been killed in the name of democracy. I'm sorry your Muslim brothers have become your enemies.

I know I don't control any of that, so my sorry must sound awkward. I'm just sorry you are suffering. I grieve with you. I cry when I hear the news from your country. I get angry and frustrated. I pray to God for your peace, for your protection. I pray that God will heal your land. I imagine my prayer sounds audacious, but I am learning that God loves to heal people. He is healing me—healing me through other people's generosity and his divine kindness. So I pray with hope for you too.

A sense of delight breaks out among the women. Sarah tells us, "I've visited their hometown. Last year Steve was working in Iraq, and so I got to go there."

Sarah and her daughter Maymunah have bright blue eyes and fair skin—they're all-American beauties. But Sarah seems absolutely in her element here. She has fallen in love with Arabs. She goes on to tell me how her own description of God has been enriched by the extravagant hospitality of the Jordanians.

We chat a little longer, but Jerusalem is calling. Krista, Eric and I collect our bags and board a shared taxi to the border. Soon, soon, soon we will be in the Holy City, *inshallah*.

I don't like waiting. I'm also not a fan of scrutiny; I don't like to have my motives manhandled, my intentions investigated, my character questioned. For the past three hours, that has been my life.

Eric, Krista and I have been shuffled from line to line to line at the Jordanian-Israeli border. We hold out our passports. We recite details about our pilgrimage. "Yes, we went to Bosnia. That's right, Syria too." We finally enter a massive holding room. Little girls languidly lean on their moms; dads try to keep their sons entertained. Everyone looks wearied, tired of waiting, fatigued by questions.

And then I realize I didn't ask one Jordanian to describe God. Oh no! I've been so fixated on crossing into Jerusalem that I've missed Jordan. And now it's too late. I'm almost through. As I impatiently wait to talk with one last border police I remember something—a description of God I had when I was young.

My love for borders is actually a love for what lies beyond them. And when I was young, God was the border police. This life was the border you crossed to get into the next life; this earth was simply Jordan. The Border Police God would let you know whether you got to go to the Promised Land or not.

My description of God has changed a great deal since then. Today I see God more as a peace activist, Jesus as the supreme peacemaker. Perhaps my vision of God has prompted my passion for expressions of peace—and my search to see if peace with each other is possible in this life. But as I stand in this line situated between Jordan and Israel, I'm reminded how arduous and complex peacemaking is.

Israel and Jordan are at peace with each other, but they have had a difficult history. They share a common people; the Palestinians make up approximately 20 percent of Israel's population—one million Palestinian citizens—and around half of Jordan's population. Jordan's Palestinians fled (or their parents fled) across the border during the 1948 Israeli War of Independence—also known as the Arab-Israeli War—and the Six-Day War in 1967.

Jordanian Palestinians share relatives across the border. They also share a holy site: the Dome of the Rock. Though Jerusalem isn't mentioned in the Qur'an, most Muslims believe Muhammad made a night journey there or had a vision that took him to Jerusalem. At that point, heaven lowered a ladder to carry Muhammad to the seventh heaven, where he was met by Abraham, Isaac, Joseph, Moses and Jesus and received their blessing to become the last prophet of God. So Muslims hold Jerusalem to be sacred. Jerusalem calls to them as well.

Israel has cause for concern. Though Jordan and Israel have become amicable, Jordan is surrounded by nations who believe Israel should be wiped off the map. An intifada has been going on for the past five years. The border guards must be convinced that we have no designs of destruction before they let us pass into Israel. So we, like hundreds of others, wait.

I finally get my passport stamped and am invited to cross the border. Though I no longer describe God as Border Police, I am thankful that there *is* a crossing to be had from earth to heaven. One day there will be peace without borders. I wonder how my description will change when I see God face to face.

For now, I simply can't wait to get to Jerusalem.

24

JERUSALEM, ISRAEL

Dateline: 326 c.e. Empress Helena and her entourage saunter into Jerusalem exhausted. Fourteen hundred miles of travel has led them to this decaying and desolate city. Rome, with its lavish parties and royal ease, seems worlds away. Yet Helena relishes the very feel of foreignness. Every tiny village and cosmopolitan center en route has held intrigue for her. She has met so many fascinating people and prayed in so many houses of worship, her journey would be worth all the exertion simply for the friendships made and experiences had. And while it would have been tempting to linger on in such notable cities as Antioch or Aleppo, a vision has commanded her forward.

Here in Jerusalem Helena will sip tea with locals and speak with the archbishop and see if she can find any physical evidence for the sacred faith she has embraced. She has come to the Holy City to discover the world of God, the places where Jesus called home. The very thought exhilarates her.

Dateline: 1483 c.e. The salty sea air slaps Felix Fabri's face as he squints to see the Holy Land. At first faint gaze, he and the others on board burst out in song. He belts out "Te Deum" in German as the Franks, Italians, Bohemians, Spaniards and Irishmen sing with equal zest in their own languages. The captain has certified that the coastline in the distance is indeed the land where Jesus walked this earth.

Before Felix's feet hit the sacred soil, he knows exactly where they'll take him. He will journey from Jaffa to Jerusalem, straight to the Holy Sepulchre. To do so he must get his final badge of a pilgrim: a Saracen (Arab) driver and an ass. He will have his Arab and his ass stop at every holy place so he can leave a cross there, having determined that each site he marks with a cross will earn him seven years' worth of indulgences. He will make it official and keep track of this ever-growing stockpile. If everything goes as planned he'll make his valiant speech in the Holy Sepulchre in less than three days. This should give him just enough time to put the final touches on it.

Dateline: 522 years later. I'm sweaty. The windows are half down. Arab music vies for the cracks between conversations. At least eleven of us are crammed into this white van heading west through the Judean desert. We each try to avoid touching one another, but I lose focus.

The guy I am sitting beside is pleasant enough. He's a Palestinian who has been working in the States for several years and is coming home for vacation. As we mount the final Judean hill before Jerusalem, I am ambushed with anticipation. I am coming home. I'm exhausted but so excited. Before I can sing my own version of "Te Deum" a discussion breaks out about paying for the ride. We have no shekels on us, and everyone seems confused about the exchange rate for dollars. I fight my natural urge to assume that the taxi driver is a cheat. Finally everyone arrives at a consensus rate, which happens to total all the dollars we own.

The reality of our money situation doesn't hit us until we are at the taxi station. Everyone is dispersing—either being greeted by family or hiring another taxi to take them to their final destination. And here we are once again without a plan for further movement and now without funds to set a plan in motion.

Our taxi driver offers to take us where we need to go, gratis. We have no other options; we have arrived in our beloved Jerusalem empty-handed. I am forced to feast on all my rotten thoughts about taxi drivers. I oblige; at last I'm learning to receive.

Still sweaty and wrapped in luggage, we open an iron gate and walk into a Fourth of July fete in motion. Familiar faces greet us with kisses and offers of hamburgers and beer. This little patch of grass in the German Colony in Jerusalem is filled with expats from America, Africa and Europe, as well as native-born Israelis. Independence Day has never felt so celebratory.

As we make our way to the apartment where we will crash for the next couple of nights, we detour at a friend's place to do a little salsa dancing. While I can't deny my combative relationship with rhythm, I give my rebellious motor skills a little grace. After all, I'm in Jerusalem. Tomorrow I will be a pilgrim in the Holy Land, but tonight I shall simply dance with friends.

All pilgrimages have a destination; all pilgrims move toward some sacred space. For millions of people through the millennia Jerusalem has been their destination. Once entering the city, a Jew's pilgrimage leads to the Kotel (Western Wall) in the Jewish Quarter, a Muslim's haj ends at the Dome of the Rock in the Muslim Quarter, and a Christian's sojourn takes her to the Holy Sepulchre in the Christian Quarter. That is how all proper pilgrimages to Jerusalem play out. Yet today I'm just not prepared to join the rest of Jerusalem's pilgrims. On this journey to discover the sacred in strangers, to encounter the holy in others, there are friends to see and sacred benches to sit on first.

Krista and Eric graciously allow me to introduce to them the people and spaces that shaped my vision of Jerusalem. So we are off to the Armenian Quarter in the Old City, my home while I lived in Jerusalem. Here I was tutored in the complexities of cultures and in new questions of my faith.

Before we set off, we make one stop to collect Ishmael, a friend of Eric's. "My son! My son! You are here!" Ishmael's dark eyes wet, his wrinkly smile stretches, and his tan arms circle Eric. I don't know if Eric told Ishmael he was coming or not, but Ishmael only shows signs of utter surprise. He begins to string together superlatives. "Eric, my son, look at you! You are the most handsome guy ever. Look at you, traveling with two beautiful women! Ladies, do you know Eric is the best man I know? I love him as a son."

Ishmael is just as I recall him: white hair, sparkling eyes, effusive speech, unbridled adoration for Eric. I take a little too much joy in seeing Eric awash in Ishmael's gush of emotion. Ishmael takes a little too much joy in simply seeing Krista.

"Krista, what a beautiful name! Where are you from? Welcome. Did Eric tell you I am Jerusalem's ambassador of peace? Please sit, I will make you some tea." We drink Lipton tea with fresh mint in Ishmael's little office, hear a poem Eric and Ishmael composed together, and establish the fact that Krista is indeed single. Finally we are off.

We begin on the far edge of the quarter, wandering down the tiny alley grandly named Maronite Patriarch Road. We pass a modest minaret and prayer courtyard tucked away to the right; it is so small and so hidden that it seems someone set it there when no one was looking. Every afternoon the call to prayer forces its way through the aged speakers; its muffled sound reminds me of one of those favorite mix tapes from the eighties that you'd play until you could barely make out the songs.

The speakers' less-than-stellar sound doesn't bother the faithful. Ishmael has come here for prayers every afternoon for more than a decade. He points out the courtyard with great pride. On this pilgrimage I've been deeply moved by Muslims' devotion to Allah. What a stunning practice, orienting one's schedule around adoration to God! I wonder what my description of God would be if afternoon after afternoon, year after year, decade after decade, I stopped my activity, left my office and knelt down on a mat in a small stone courtyard.

Before I have time to linger on the question, the serpentine alley pushes us left. On one side of the stone wall is the Maronite's Jerusalem Patriarchate; to the right is the entrance to my little neighborhood. "My Jerusalem" starts right here. But I sense a hesitancy to go further. Beyond this threshold I began to learn how individualistic I can be.

These Palestinian neighbors have a distinct understanding of community. They often leave their front doors wide open, indicating that they're game for a coffee and a chat. My next-door neighbors became like extended family to me. Their daughter, Ghadir, is around my age and instantly became a sister. On long evening walks I learned from her about the joys and challenges of being a single woman in the East. Ghadir's family often invited me over for dinners of chicken, vegetables, rice and yo-gurt. Sometimes I was too busy to stay for long or would simply decline; I was convinced I had too much to do to simply sit around and eat a scrump-tious meal with kind neighbors.

Eventually I learned that sitting around chatting and eating was one of the most important things I could do. This came to the fore when a twenty-six-year-old guy in my neighborhood died. For seven days all the neighbors and other friends gathered to stay with the family. They just sat together, sipped coffee and ate; many of them slept there. I tried to do things to help the family, offering to make coffee or serve coffee or buy coffee. It was so hard to just sit, to be there, hour after hour with nothing perceptible to contribute but my presence.

By the time the World Cup rolled around I had learned to relax a little more. All the neighbors gathered for the final game between Germany and Brazil. Men draped themselves in Brazilian flags while women fumbled with their prayers beads. My neighbors were all Palestinian Catholics, and Brazil is a Catholic nation, so there was a sense that not only the World Cup title was at stake, God's reputation must be fought for as well. During time-outs, the women would pray. At a critical point in the second half the man of the house grabbed the icon of Mary off the wall, kissed it and pleaded, "Mother of God, have mercy."

Brazil won.

It was such a gift to be a part of this community, but even as I knock on my neighbor's door, I look at my watch. "We won't be able to stay long. We have lots we must do," I rehearse.

My neighbors aren't home. At least I'll get to see Ghadir. We plan to spend our final day with her in Tel Aviv where she now lives. I'll try to re-turn here tomorrow. Maybe. I wonder if they'll remember me anyway.

We exit the neighborhood and see Sami the Tailor's 10' x 10' shop. Reams of material and intricately sewn cassocks are displayed on one wall of his shop; pictures of his family adorn the other. There is no sign, just an open door; anyone who needs to know about his business already does.

As I step in I hear "Tamara!" pronounced with Arabic flare. I am simultaneously relieved and overjoyed. My memories are real; "my Jerusalem" isn't just a sentimental construct in my mind, made up of people who have long forgotten my face and my name.

Before I can introduce my entourage Sami kisses my cheeks three times. This is his standard greeting for me, but he reminds me nonetheless that each kiss represents the Trinity: Father, Son and Spirit. I tell Sami what I'm doing here and ask him to describe God. He responds by telling me his full name for the first time: Sami Barsoum.

Sami has always been Sami the Tailor to me, but in his community he has held the title of Syrian *Muktar* (mayor) for twenty-five years. "God is the Creator of all. He has made everything." He abruptly shifts gears and tells me, "Early as children we learn that Jesus teaches us to love our enemies, to turn our cheeks in the face of hate. This is what separates Jesus' teachings from the teachings of Jews or Muslims. I don't want to speak badly of others, but this is a difference. Christianity comes by belief, not force. Yes, it's by belief, not force."

Sami's words aren't simple extractions from Sunday school lessons. His father escaped from Turkey during the 1915 genocide. At that time 500,000 Syrian Orthodox were murdered; among the dead were both of Sami's grandparents, killed by the Turks. His uncles were dispersed throughout the Middle East, and his dad was left as a youth to make his own way in life. Sami grew up with the stories of a family ripped apart by persecution. He heard about the horror of hate and learned about the way of love. His heritage and his faith taught him that though your mother and father may be murdered, though your home may be destroyed, though your brothers may be lost to you, you are to love your enemies. This is the way of Jesus.

Sami can trace his Syrian Orthodox heritage back a thousand years. I wonder if a thousand years would be enough time for me to understand this love-your-enemies kind of faith in Jesus. I work so hard not to have enemies. I avoid conflict. I fence off my world with friends. And on the rare occasions I sense that someone doesn't like me, I attempt to convert him or her to my side as soon as possible. Will I ever know what it means to love my enemy? Will I ever grasp the most defining teaching of Jesus?

We take our pictures and say our goodbyes. Within two minutes Krista, Eric, Ishmael and I are standing in front of St. Mark's Syrian Orthodox Church. This is where Sami learned the teachings of Jesus. It is also a possible site of the upper room, the home of St. Mark's mother, where Jesus hosted his last supper and where his followers gathered to pray after his death. As we walk into the courtyard I see a familiar face: Yosephina, a vivacious nun with an unusually high-pitched voice.

Yosephina shares with us the history of Mark's mother's house, describes the art that surrounds the altar and tells us about the church's prized icons. St. Mark's boasts of having its own painting of Mary by Luke the Gospel writer. I have heard Yosephina describe the icon many times, each time accompanied by stories of miracles. Will she have new stories? She launches into a story about a Bulgarian woman who recently journeyed here. "When the woman arrived in the Holy Land she had a tumor; after being prayed for and anointed with oil from this icon of the Mother Mary painted by St. Luke, she was healed. The doctors certified it."

Yosephina takes us downstairs to the place where she and others believe the first-century upper room once stood. There she sings the Lord's Prayer in Aramaic. Her high-pitched voice suddenly becomes a low wail, beautiful, dark and powerful. I stand in the middle of the small room with the words of our Lord crashing against the stone walls, washing over me like fierce waves.

After the last echo has dried up, I ask Yosephina to describe God. She says, in her startling speaking voice, "Our God is love. He is my Savior, my Lord." I wait for her to continue and she simply says, "What more?"

We set out for the epicenter of the Armenian Quarter. As we get closer and closer we encounter those weatherworn posters that introduced me to the horrifying plight of Armenians. "Don't forget!" "One and a half million Armenians murdered." "The Armenian Genocide: 1914-1917." Some of the posters only scream words; others show emaciated, dead bodies piled on each other. The blue and black posters cling to the walls with a sense of desperation, but the ancient stones seem unmoved by any story that climbs upon them.

Day appears to plummet into night when we walk through a narrow tunnel on Armenian Orthodox Patriarchate Road. Tucked away a few steps beyond the tunnel is a completely new world to Eric, Krista and Ishmael.

Vespers at St. James was the first Orthodox service I ever attended. Admittedly, I had no idea what was happening. But within minutes I became drunk with the mystery of it all, and sobered by the holiness I intuited. I wonder if I will feel that way again. What will Krista, Eric and Ishmael experience? Will they sense something more than an old, fragrant building?

We arrive just in time for 3 p.m. Vespers. A shaft of light follows us as we enter the darkness. Most people are standing along the far walls, but we are offered folding chairs. I sit and look up. St. James is like a black canvas illuminated by hundreds of little lights, most of them lamps brought by pilgrims from around the world. Each lamp is suspended by chains from the ceiling; each hangs there with its own story of pilgrimage. Each has found its home and its purpose.

The service has already begun. The priests and seminarians don black robes and triangular hoods shaped like a dome of an Armenian church. Each priest, symbolically, is a walking church in this world. They pace back and forth, crisscrossing, moving toward us and back again. They start their choreography from the center of the room, as a way of acknowledging that they come to God as one of us. They chant their ancient prayers as a way of presenting an offering for the people. They march slowly, deliberately. They swing their incense and chant. "Profound mystery. Profound mystery."

I shut my eyes and cringe. Images accost me of the march of the Armenians in 1915. I wonder if the priests chanted then as they walked step after step toward death. I wonder if liturgy was on their lips when they fell down from exhaustion, when they collapsed from starvation, when they saw their daughters violated by Turkish soldiers, when they saw their mothers struck by guns. Did the Armenian priests chant?

Did they find God when they repeated their liturgy's mantra? Did they know that one day their churches would be destroyed, that all they would have left would be their words to their God?

The Armenians' story is one of betrayal. They were told that the Young

Turks would protect them from the random and racist massacres they had experienced under the sultans. They had come to trust the Young Turks and their vision for equality. They had come to believe that the Christian West would protect them if the Young Turks didn't. They were betrayed with a kiss. Young girls were picked up by burly soldiers and dashed to the ground, dashed to their death. Physicians were hung upside down. Villages were evacuated, everyone over the age of five was taken and killed.

Where was God as the Armenian people were betrayed, beaten, led to their slaughter? Was God trapped in their churches when they were being burned? Was God left in their empty villages as a silent witness? Or was God—the profound mystery, as the Armenians describe him—with them?

My eyes locate the Armenian cross, known as the *khatchkar*. The Armenians depict the cross as being made from the tree of life. Jesus hangs on the tree from the Garden of Eden, the tree that was created to give eternal life. A people who revere holy places, Armenians have had to do what their liturgy instructs them to do all through the centuries: find the presence of Christ in his Word and through the Eucharist.

In the midst of hard questions and horrifying images of genocide, I'm reminded of the profound mystery of the Christian faith: God is intimately acquainted with affliction and infinitely capable of hope. Or, as Nancy said, God is both the Savior who suffered on the cross and the Savior who rose from the dead.

As we exit St. James, I ask Ishmael to describe God. He begins his description with the first of the ninety-nine names of Allah. "Allah is first patient." In hushed tones he tells me, "God rescued my life. When I was twelve, I was out playing in a cave. It began storming and God told me I must leave right away. I ran out, and right then the cave collapsed. My coat—my red, blood-red colored coat—got caught, but I'm fine. God saved my life. I believe God has some great purpose for my life. I knew then that I believed in God."

We say *alla ysalmak* to Ishmael and wind our way into the Christian Quarter. We eat homemade pizza at one of Eric's old haunts: *Abu Shanab* ("Father Mustache"). Over dinner Eric tells us that he used to wash dishes at this restaurant and barely made enough money to survive.

"In those lean days, I met Ishmael," Eric reveals. "On numerous occasions Ishmael bought me lunch. He treated me like a son. It was surprising that a Muslim was more generous to me than the Christians I knew, the ones I worked for at the time. Through Ishmael's grace, I found the kindness of Jesus. And Ishmael showed it to me without any hint of hesitation."

After dinner we exit the Old City through Jaffa Gate. I turn back and see the lines of the citadel and ancient walls; it's my favorite view of the city. *Good night, my Jerusalem.*

The Talmud says, "Ten measures of beauty descended to the world, nine were taken by Jerusalem." Jerusalem seems quite aware of her monopoly on beauty this morning. The sun subtly flirts with the city through the clouds. A gentle breeze strolls through the streets. I've already taken a brisk walk in the elegant, tree-lined German Colony, obtained coffee from the Café Hillel and called a few friends in the city.

I'm still not ready to make the rounds as a pilgrim in Jerusalem. So Eric heads off to hang out with Ishmael and Krista joins me for the day. Our first destination takes us through the pristine alleys of Yemin Moshe, a neighborhood made up of artists and wealthy people who like to surround themselves with successful bohemians. Today the white stone of the houses is bright as an empty canvas, and the purple and pink bougainvillea spill over the stone walls as if their colors are compelled to climb into a masterpiece.

As we descend the stone stairs, the seductive breeze splashes us with fragrance. Yemin Moshe drops off into the Hinnom Valley (or Gehenna), a valley often associated with hell. Its sordid past includes child sacrifice. As we walk, I'm reminded that every square foot of this city is marked by beauty and blood.

From the valley we take a narrow path up Mount Zion. Little stones mark the Psalms of Ascent, psalms sung by Jewish pilgrims for millennia as they climbed this mountain. When I lived here I joined a Jewish family on the Shavuot holiday coinciding with Pentecost. In the predawn dark hundreds of us streamed up this hill with psalms on our lips, proceeding to the Western Wall to pray before light drenched our day. On my lips during that trek was King David's prayer for unity in Psalm 133.

> How good and pleasant it is
>   when brothers live together in unity!
>
> It is like precious oil poured on the head,
>   running down on the beard,
>   running down on Aaron's beard,
>   down upon the collar of his robes.
>
> It is as if the dew of Hermon
>   were falling on Mount Zion.
>   For there the LORD bestows his blessing,
>   even life forevermore.

The path ends right where Eric and I studied. Jerusalem University College provided a feast of learning for me. What most marked my time at JUC was its fascinating professors—two in particular. Today I hope to see both. I ring the bell at the gate, and within minutes Dr. Petra Heldt appears. She looks unaffected by time.

Dr. Heldt is a German, ordained Lutheran pastor who has dedicated over twenty years to work for peace with the Orthodox Christians, Jews and Muslims in Jerusalem. She is one of the most learned and graceful souls I know. I hug her as she tells me to call her Petra, and she escorts Krista and me through the halls of my old school. The air feels sedentary, like it's been sitting on the couch since I left. Yet when I enter Petra's office the stagnant air becomes energized by the scent of musty books and new ideas.

Our conversation flows into Petra's work with the Orthodox community and her reflections on pilgrimage in the East. She has a deep passion for bringing the faith community together in ways that enrich the city. While I was studying under her in the height of the intifada, she helped organize the

Alexander Agreement, which brought together top leaders of the Jewish, Muslim and Christian communities to condemn killing in the name of God.

Her hopes for peace could have been easily shattered a decade or so ago. While shopping in the crowded market in the Jewish *shouk*, she got caught in the chaos of a suicide bomber's successful attack. Her arm was badly burned. I ask her the question I've asked throughout our pilgrimage: "How would you describe God?"

Petra's laugh captures the audacity of my question. "Describe God? I don't know, God is just indescribable. He is just amazing. I think how I see God is that Christ sends people my way who help guide my life beautifully, leading me to experiences and ideas and paths so different from where I would go on my own. But God knows what is best. So I follow his leading as much I can.

"What amazes me is God's abundant love and faithfulness. You might be disappointed by people, but never by Christ—never, never. And whatever happens, God is always there, especially when you are in pain, when something is wrong. He's there and guides you gently onto a path that is healthy and good.

"The signs of true life aren't necessarily great positions or money. What is most healthy and good is eternal life. You know, the wealth of this world is very little. If you want one word, one sentence or something to describe God—which is impossible anyway—I would say, 'Grace, grace, grace.' It's a gift."

I nod my head. *Yes! Yes! Yes!* I tell Petra it was a gift to see her.

Right now I feel generous-spirited and humble, ecumenical and courageous. Gratitude sloshes around in my soul and spills out in my step. Speaking with Petra makes me sense that God is working his glorious magic in our midst. So much good can happen. I just need to be wide-eyed to search it out in others and look for Christ in my midst.

Krista and I make our way to Jaffa Gate, walking along my favorite piece of wall. There are stones from Herod's day and stones from the reign of

Saladin the Magnificent, stones that change day after day with the mood
of the sun. We walk briskly and talk effusively about learning from a wise
woman.

We arrive at what now feels like home base in Jerusalem: Ishmael's tiny
office. A guy wearing a cowboy hat is engaged in animated conversation
with Ishmael. Krista and I introduce ourselves; his name is Couy. He's from
New Mexico. With long, drawn-out syllables Couy tells us he has come to
Jerusalem with a dream to ride horseback through the Middle East, proclaiming Jesus.

My exuberant generosity toward the world begins to leak. I am slightly
amused and somewhat skeptical about his approach. He asks us why we're
here and we tell him about the pilgrimage, and the people we've spoken
with along the way, and the wild hope of putting people's responses in a
book. He says I can interview him, but instead of asking him to describe
God, I'd like to hear more about why he's in Jerusalem.

"That's about the hardest question for me to answer, you know," Couy
starts out. "I don't know really why. I feel like the Lord's used me here. And
that's really all I want to do, to be of service to the Lord. I've had a chance to
meet a lot of people around here—a lot more of the Arab community than
the Jewish community.

"The relationship between the Arab community and the American community needs all the help it can get right now, you know. I feel like my
personal, individual politics can help. I think I have a pretty good handle on
the Bush administration. So maybe in a way I can kind of smooth over some
of the rough edges."

I want to laugh. *Oh no. Don't laugh,* I tell myself. Couy is a gentle, God-
loving man. Still, I envision Couy on a horse passing out American flags
and Bibles to Arabs, declaring victory in the war on terror. I'm a very bad
person. But I do refrain from laughing.

Couy continues over my inner monologue. "A lot of the Arabs that you
talk to over here think that American soldiers are in Iraq killing innocent
Iraqi children, and that's not the case. They don't see that we're there to try
to help the people. There are all kinds of different opinions on it, of course,

from oil to everything else, but I want to think that America's there solely to help the people who live in that place. I get the chance to sit around here and visit with the Arabs in Jerusalem, and I enjoy it."

Sweet Couy. He has such good intentions. He wants to believe in God and country. And he desires to be a relational representative. A part of me wants to tell Couy that life isn't so simple, but another part doesn't want to ruin it for him. So, I just ask him to tell me more.

"I go to big events in Tel Aviv—music festivals, whatever—and hand out literature on the Lord and on faith and on Jesus. Israel, the Jews, faithfully pray every day for their Messiah to come; they just haven't realized yet that the Messiah has come and gone. I feel like this is a very closed community over here as far as how faith goes. They want to try to keep the truth about the Lord out as much as they can.

"These outreaches are a way that we can get New Testaments to them. I truly do feel like the Lord is the only way to peace around this place. In Christ, he makes everybody one. There's not any Jew or Gentile, Arab or whatever. We're all one. I think that the outreaches have been very good."

Wow. It sounds like he has a longing to see unity. But I wonder how effective passing out literature is here. Couy goes on, "I've also noticed that a lot of the Jews shut down as soon as they hear Christianity. There's been so much—the word I like to use is *brainwashing*—over the years from generation to generation about Christianity. As soon as these young people hear of Christianity they think of Hitler, Nazis or the Crusaders. They just have all this negativity about Christ, about Christians. It's a shame; it's sad. It's what the devil wants."

Ishmael jumps in. "You know, before just a few days ago I discovered this description in the Qur'an about Jesus, that he's coming again."

Couy doesn't let Ishmael finish his thought. "Yah. He will come. I truly believe that he's the only answer for those people. The Muslims will go on and on about Jesus but they don't accept him as the Son of God." Does Couy notice Ishmael sitting right there?

"You know, it really makes me happy to know that Jesus is coming," Ishmael says in his gentle voice.

"Yah, yah," Couy responds.

"Don't forget that all of the prophets are in our Qur'an."

Couy launches back in. "But see, just to remind the reader here"—he looks at me and my little iPod—"Jesus will return to become a leader in the Muslim nation as he has been revealed in the Qur'an. So yah, see, that's what's funny. Muslims believe that Jesus is going to come back as a Muslim, as an Arab. But Jesus isn't going to come back as a certain race or ethnicity. He's going to come back as the King of Kings of all people, because we are all one in Christ."

That's interesting. I hadn't thought of whether Jesus was coming back as a certain race or ethnicity. But did Couy just say, "To remind the reader"? I did mention to him I was hoping to write a book, but we're having a conversation here, aren't we?

"Couy, we too think about Jesus. Listen, what Jesus does we must follow," says Ishmael.

"I'm no prophecy buff, but I believe Jesus is coming back. He's coming back to judge," Couy says as he looks at me. Ishmael pipes in, "Jesus says you must leave your women and your children to follow him. You are to submit to God; you are to give God everything."

Couy tries to interrupt. "In the Islam faith—"

"You give God your body, your health, your energy," Ishmael keeps on talking.

Couy finally addresses Ishmael. "In the Islam faith, don't you believe that Jesus was born of a virgin?"

"Yes, of course, from Mary," says Ishmael.

"So if Jesus was born of a virgin, then who would be Jesus' father?" Couy asks.

"Jesus has no father," responds Ishmael.

"Everyone has a father," presses Couy. "Even Adam. Adam's father was God."

"Listen, Couy, we have two Adams: the first Adam God created—"

Before Ishmael can complete his thought, Couy interrupts again. "But wouldn't God be considered Adam's father? Wouldn't he be created . . ."

I become so frustrated I turn my iPod off. I can't take it any longer. I just want to leave. Couy's accent sounds just like George Bush. Ishmael and Couy sound like political pundits.

At first Couy was an amusement to me: a cowboy riding across the Middle East for Jesus, helping seam up relations between Arabs and Americans and helping bring the message of Jesus to the Muslims. But a great prejudice has begun to brew inside me. Maybe I am frustrated with Couy because I see in him things that annoy me about much of American Christianity—that desire to be right, that inability to engage others, that attempt to win people to Jesus without hearing their story, understanding their context, sitting on a sacred bench with them.

Yet I'm a complete hypocrite at the moment. I didn't listen to Couy's story to get to know him. I didn't turn on my iPod just now for a divine encounter, a sacred exchange between strangers. For what I think is the first time on this trip, I stereotyped the person sitting across from me and heard only the "blah, blah, blah, blah, blah" of my assumptions. Why is it sometimes so hard to love Christians?

I excuse myself from the conversation. I need to meet my other favorite professor for lunch anyway. Krista decides to stay and chat with Ishmael, to his obvious delight. I pound my feet to a café in West Jerusalem.

After an hour of engaging banter with my Modern Middle East Politics professor, I scurry back to retrieve Krista, and we head into the Jewish Quarter. I am amazed that the empty cobblestone streets of the quarter I knew in 2001 and 2002 are now crammed with people—people packing the sidewalk cafés, people descending the stairs to the Kotel, people walking up to the gallery shops.

We turn the corner and there it is: Shoroshim. This little bookstore/ Judaic jewelry/art boutique is so unassuming, yet when tourism seemed extinct, its spirit was still strong. The owners, Moshe and Dov—Orthodox Jewish brothers from Canada—came to Jerusalem to be in the land but also to stimulate a dialogue between Jews and Christians. Increased understanding and exchange are passions of theirs.

Moshe directs us to a loud little café twenty steps across from their store.

Moshe is jovial but always ready to dive into the depths of conversation.

"Two words which describe the totality of God are 'our Father' and 'our King,'" Moshe begins. "It's the struggle, the dichotomy, between those two aspects that really make up our understanding of God. He's our King in the sense that God is ruler of the universe, but he's also the ruler of our future and our destiny. As a result of our being connected to God, we are obedient. That is the most natural thing in this universe. He is the source of all life, all creation. We want to be connected to his will. We cannot connect to his will in order to get some type of reward—in heaven or eternity. It's simply because on one level, relating to his will is relating to the most natural thing in the universe. That *is* the will of the universe."

There is a whole industry dedicated to helping people sort out the will of God; books on the subject take up entire rows in bookstores, and conferences on it fill arenas. But with a steady confidence Moshe is saying that knowing God's will is the most natural thing. Curious. But what does he mean? What is he saying God's will is?

"Doing God's will is critical, because his will is to fix the world. The world is in a state of disrepair; it's not the way God intended it. In the midst of the chaos we build barriers between us and God; we create Towers of Babel where we can become god instead of God. And yet in the midst of all that disrepair comes a yearning to set the world aright. And setting it right is being obedient to the ultimate will of God. That's number one."

I'm intrigued by Moshe's description of God as king, a benevolent ruler whose decrees turn the globe and keep our feet firmly planted on earth. This image of a king bent on righting the world seems to clash against the powerful characters who make headlines and lead nations.

"He's also our Father," Moshe continues. "God knows all of our mistakes and our desires to make the world right. We're in a relationship with such a beloved, and so the fulfillment of his will is simply a gift to pursue. If I know my wife desires something, I want to give her it as a gift. If God says, 'This is what I want from you,' forever—as long as the sun and the moon and the stars are in the heaven—fulfilling that will becomes a very simple act of love."

As Moshe has shared, I've caught glimpses of fathers with their children here in this packed café. The image of God as father is such a strong, hopeful description for me. My dad has such integrity and compassion. He's brilliant and unassuming. When he asks me to do things—a rare occurrence these days—it's a delight. But when many of my friends think of God as father, a gut-level ache comes back to them. All they know through that image is recurring disappointment, pressure to fulfill expectations, anger or silence, fear or distance. Obedience to a father has in some way been an act of self-hatred, capitulation, resignation. It was never simple or lovely.

I'm so grateful to get to learn from Moshe; it's a gift. There are such striking similarities in how we see God. Yet I get this impression that he believes he's the one in the know. Ugh! Is that where I've been coming from with my own faith in Jesus? The sense that each of us believes we have the corner on truth feels so divisive.

From East Jerusalem we scoot back to the West side. We consume a feast of Ethiopian food and teeter home. Tomorrow we leave. I told Ghadir I'd spend my last day with her in Tel Aviv—after all, she's like family. But I haven't even been a proper pilgrim yet. I don't know what I even think about going to the holy sites any more. After longing for unity and yet being reminded of the divides of religion, do I really want to go?

Once again I wonder: can't we all just love God and love others? If we do that well, does it matter if God is described as YHWH, or Jesus, or Allah?

25

JERUSALEM, ISRAEL

"So, you'll come with me?" Empress Helena asks Macarius, the archbishop of Jerusalem. Together with a team of workmen, they set out to locate the blessed cross of Jesus. They pray. They fast. They plead for divine guidance. Soon a vision comes to the archbishop. "The cross lies underneath the temple of Aphrodite."

The search for the old wooden cross will require tearing down an entire stone edifice. The proposition is ridiculous, an impossible scenario—impossible, that is, for anyone without royal blood and a divine vision.

"Tear down the temple!" Helena declares in her strong, dignified manner. The workmen dig and dig and dig until they break through the temple foundation. A cross is found, then another, and another. As Helena muses about how to tell which one is actually the blessed cross of her Lord, the archbishop gets an idea. "We will take the crosses to a woman I know who is unconscious and at death's door. Jesus' cross that once brought death should have the power to bring life."

Helena sits beside the dying woman as the crosses are brought forward. With the touch of one particular cross it's as if new blood and breath are infused into the woman. She regains lucidity and leaps up in joy. Helena enthusiastically promises, "We will build a church where the cross was found." Helena finds herself at the fulfillment of her vision: fourteen hundred miles from Rome she stands beside Jerusalem's archbishop beholding Jesus' blessed cross.

"I need you to take me to the Holy Sepulchre today. It's very important that I get there. Do you understand?" Felix Fabri makes sure that his Arab guide agrees.

Since arriving in the Holy Land Felix has relied on the Arab and the ass to bring him to one holy site after another. While the visits to Jesus' nativity and to the Mount of Olives were special, Felix's time at the Holy Sepulchre is sure to be the most memorable experience of his pilgrimage.

The pilgrimage has been successful, albeit just a little lonely. Felix has worshiped God in many places and received a surplus of indulgences, but he's been on his own a great deal. He has tried hard to avoid Jews and Eastern Christians, since he has heard that they are dodgy and renowned tricksters. His Arab guide has been accommodating—actually quite hospitable—but Felix reminds himself not to let his guard down around the infidel.

When Felix arrives at the Holy Sepulchre he bows down, kisses the ground and articulates an elaborate prayer of thanksgiving. Once inside the church, he goes straight to the holiest of sites. He crosses himself, bows his head and lights a candle in the cave of the sepulcher. He prays again, a prayer of praise and a request for divine favor.

Then the climactic moment arrives. Felix will give the most important speech of his life. He rallies other pilgrims, knights and anyone else who will oblige him.

He begins with a passionate plea for piety, calling his fellow sojourners and soldiers to seek God's will. "Let your hearts, pray you, be kindled like fires with zeal for those things which are of God, more especially to succor the necessities of the Lord's sepulchre and of this Holy Land. . . . Let every one of you gird his mighty sword upon his thigh to avenge the wrongs offered to God. . . .

"A Christian rightfully glories in the death of a pagan, because Christ is glorified therein. Wherefore rouse yourselves, most valiant knights, and rise up to avenge the insults offered to our God and the shame of the people of Christendom, even as did those most doughty Maccabees of old, and make it your aim to slay or put to flight the infidels, and bring back the heritage of the Lord into Christendom."

After Felix delivers his fiery call, he mounts the ass and follows his Arab guide to the port at Jaffa. Felix's boat back to Italy leaves shortly.

"Ghadir?. . . *Merhaban,* my sister. I'm so sorry I can't come to Tel Aviv right now. . . . No, everything is fine. It's just that I'm behind schedule. I need to spend some more time in Jerusalem. We should see you this afternoon. I'll call before we leave. *Le' hitra'ot."* I clunk down the phone and turn to Krista. "I've got to get to the Holy Sepulchre."

I jog down the sidewalk through the Hinnom Valley and over to Jaffa Gate. I slow down to a respectable pace as I enter the Old City.

"*Merhaban.* I'm sorry I can't come in your shop right now. Maybe later. *Ma'a Salama."* As I make my way through the serpentine alleys I repeat my greeting and apology to one shopkeeper after another until I turn that familiar corner in the heart of the Christian Quarter. There before me, sequestered between other stone buildings of the same camel color, stands the most sacred of Christian pilgrimage sites.

Since this church—or more accurately, complex of churches—is plunked down in the midst of shops and homes, it is visually unassuming and integrated. Once I step foot inside the oversized doors, however, I remember why this is *the* pilgrimage site for Christians the world over. I enter a sea of darkness with streams of light flowing from the open door, from a few high windows and from one candle being lit after another. Directly in front of me is the Stone of Anointing. This marbled rock is said to mark the spot where Jesus' body was prepared for burial. A woman in front of me kneels and kisses the stone.

I turn right and mount a narrow stairwell. At the top is believed to be Golgotha, the site where Jesus' cross was flanked by two criminals. It is now adorned with icons, candles, and Latin and Greek crosses. I stand in line to kiss the rock that marks where the cross of Christ stood two millennia ago. I murmur, "Jesus, Son of David, have mercy on me," as I rise from the rock.

I descend the stairs and pass by where Adam's skull is said to be buried. Once I am halfway around this cobbled-together church I descend more stairs and enter the St. Helena Chapel. It feels like a serene subterranean world. The walls of this expansive underground Armenian chapel are covered with crosses etched by medieval pilgrims. I trace over a couple of the crosses; the stone is cool and smooth. Suddenly the reality of the moment seeps in. I am a pilgrim. I join the collection of Christian pilgrims who have traveled to Jerusalem since the fourth century—many of them risking their lives—to witness the holy sites of Jesus.

I offer up a prayer. After lingering in unhurried gratitude, I go down the thirteen narrow steps to the Roman Catholic Chapel of the Invention of the Holy Cross. This is the place where St. Helena, the archbishop and their team is said to have discovered the blessed cross.

I climb back up dozens of steps and make my way to an alcove near the sepulcher. There is a stone bench close to a trough of lit candles. I read and prayed here in this tucked-away place many times during my year in Jerusalem.

I pull out my Bible and journal from my pack and read Jesus' Sermon on the Mount again. I only make it a few verses in when I am halted by the words of Matthew 5:3: "Blessed are the poor in spirit, / for theirs is the kingdom of heaven."

So that's it. Fortunate are the empty-handed, those who are ready to receive from others, poised to experience the Divine, desperate for grace. The kingdom of God, with its powerful love, belongs not to those rich in pride and self-sufficiency. It belongs to those who are willing to receive—those who *must* receive.

Jesus, I whisper. *Help me receive from you and others today. Once more, please provide divine encounters.*

I slowly stand and progress to the sepulcher. Before I catch a glimpse of the tomb believed to be where Jesus was buried and rose again, I hear the voices of pilgrims singing in Italian. The ancient liturgy washes me pure like baptismal water. As I duck my head to enter the holy cave a priest blesses me. I then light a candle for the brothers and proceed further in the tomb.

I kneel for a moment and whisper a prayer: *I receive*. A feeling of home engulfs me. My body relaxes and my breath slows. I've made it. Home.

A realization settles in me. I love Jesus—more deeply, more thoroughly than ever. I had feared this pilgrimage might be my undoing with Jesus. Despite all my questions, my love for Jesus has only solidified. No matter how my journey to describe God turns out, I am grateful my relationship with Jesus has survived. What a grace!

I exit the sepulcher and walk straight into the Greek Orthodox chapel. In the midst of the ornate, spacious chapel is a gold omphalos. I stand on the gold circle, and upon doing so I am said to stand in the center of the Holy Sepulchre, the center of Jerusalem, and ultimately the center of the world. I linger in the center of it all, profoundly grateful.

After walking out the door of the Holy Sepulchre I turn right and step through what looks like a maintenance worker's entrance. I am suddenly in the middle of the Ethiopian Orthodox lower chapel. My eyes go directly to the black Madonna icon on the wall. As I walk past an Ethiopian priest I'm reminded how stately Ethiopians appear. I climb a narrow staircase to the next chapel. An Ethiopian woman in a colorful robe greets me. I realize I have gone this whole morning without asking anyone to describe God.

I introduce myself to Tenat. She seems delighted to respond. "God is our Father, our everything, our praise. He's my father and my mother. I love him and I know God is not just for me, but for all." Tenat's description of God seems to come from a heart enlarged by joy.

I climb up one last set of stairs, step out on the roof and stand in the midst of the simple but saintly monastery of my Ethiopian brothers and sisters. Sun showers me as I survey the city.

I clamor down the stairs and decide I need to interview a few more people in this city of pilgrims.

I'm so looking forward to seeing Ghadir, but I call her again apologetically, postponing my arrival for a couple of hours. I locate Krista and strike out for the Jews' most holy site, the Kotel (Western Wall).

At the terrace that overlooks the wall, I notice a group of pilgrims sporting orange ball caps with Crusader crosses. With them is a priest. Father José tells me he and his group are from Toledo, Spain.

When I ask Father José to describe God he shares, "God is our Father and the Savior of the world." He then starts talking about his pilgrimage. "Pilgrimages are important to our faith so we can know the Holy Land and walk in the steps of Jesus. As I make this pilgrimage, I desire to walk in peace, to be a help to both Jews and Palestinians. I desire to care for them well."

As I descend the stairs to the entrance of the Western Wall, a hope builds. I glance back at Father José and his fellow pilgrims with their orange Crusader-cross hats. I think of Felix Fabri and his skullcap with the Crusader cross and his desire to walk in the steps of Jesus. For Felix, being a faithful pilgrim also meant taking up the sword; wearing the cross called for the slaying of infidels. Oh, I hope that in this age those of us who bear the cross will walk in peace.

I open my daypack for the guard to inspect. The security checkpoint at the entrance of the Kotel serves as a conspicuous reminder that the Jews' most holy of sites is continually under threat.

The first temple of the Jews, built by King Solomon in 957 B.C.E., was destroyed by the Babylonians in 586 B.C.E. The Roman general Pompey the Great desecrated the second temple in 63 B.C.E., massacring priests as he entered the sanctuary. Then the Roman general Titus ransacked the temple in 70 C.E. This sacred space of worship became the setting for heinous violations. As Titus and his guards stormed out of Jerusalem, the holy of holies, where God's *Shekhinah* presence was said to reside, lay in shambles. Only the retaining walls remained.

I approach the Kotel. My walk, typically hurried and at times clumsy, transforms to a slow, deliberate march. For Jewish pilgrims this swath of the retaining wall is now the most tangible connection to God's *Shekhinah*. I too sense an indescribable gravitas.

I advance as close as I can to the multiton stones. A young girl stands beside me with her prayer book open. She whispers her prayers in Hebrew, softly, passionately. I open my Bible and mouth a psalm as well. I then take my notebook, rip out a piece of paper, scribble a word and fold it. I stuff it into a crack that for centuries has been filled with folded-up prayers. I then make my march backward in reverence, so as not to turn my back on the stones that are said to be the gateway to heaven.

Once I am at the end of the women's section, I'm able to turn around. I notice that the courtyard wall is lined with people. It's one long sacred bench!

Gitty, a Jew from Russia, tells me, "God is the only one. He is everything and anything. You start speaking and it's him. That's what I think. It's simple; it's not complicated."

Mike from Arizona muses that "God is an answer to explain things that aren't explainable." His wife, Jennifer, says, "God is all positive energy, whether the Divine is an entity or not."

Sandy, a Jew from New York who moved to Jerusalem nine years ago, describes God as "all-encompassing. He knows what he is doing in the world."

Yael, a thirty-five-year-old Israeli, says, "Ha-Shem is the King of the world. We are waiting for the Messiah, then all the world will change. Everything that is bad will end, and all the world will be pure, without fighting. Everything will be simple. There will be a guiding light, and all will learn from it. Not everyone will be Jewish, but all will be good and one with each other."

"God is Father," says Guenter from Austria. "He is right here with us as we speak about him. Jesus is the way to God; without him there is no way to God. And just think, the main event of Jesus' return will happen in Jerusalem."

I'm breathless going from one interview to another. I look at my watch and realize I must go.

I scurry over to the entrance of the Dome of the Rock. During the time I lived in Israel, it was forbidden for non-Muslims to enter this area—a response to violence that took place here in September 2000. I used to stare up at that gorgeous gold dome and wonder what it was like inside. In the midst of checkpoints and blockades in Israel, the Dome stood as the most pronounced place I couldn't enter.

Once I get in line, I discover that the holy site isn't open for non-Muslims at this time. I need to come back a different day. But I don't have a different day.

I return to the shopkeepers in the Christian Quarter, the ones I had earlier greeted and denied. I end up at a familiar shop that sells colorful handmade ceramics. Eli, the owner, is an active member of his Syrian Orthodox church. As he bubble-wraps my new dishes, I ask him to describe God.

"God's everything. Every minute in my life, I always mention God because he is my helper. I am living only from God, and God gives me very good business because I am a good believer and my prices are low and I have good quality. God gives me a small profit, and we have lots of business."

Eli starts loading up my bags and then adds, "God is my road in life."

What a great image. That makes Eli a pilgrim for life. I thank Eli and ask if I can leave my bags at his shop while I interview one last person.

I wind my way to the Greek Patriarchate Road and enter a doorway so small that it forces me to bow my head. The Greek archbishop of Jerusalem, Aristarchos, is gracious enough to speak with me. His schedule is packed with pressing issues from his own community, yet he enthusiastically welcomes me into his office.

Nothing seems pretentious about this spiritual leader of Jerusalem. His black robe and cap are plain, his face solemn, his beard full, his desk small. Nothing is assuming except that tradition requires me to address him as "Your Grace." I thank him for agreeing to meet with me. "The one question that I've been asking people on my pilgrimage from Rome to Jerusalem is how they describe God. So, that's my question for you."

"That's a difficult question, a significant question. It's a question of life for us. For our life depends upon our description of God. And the description of God depends upon our understanding of God. According to our own understanding we approach God, yes? And approaching God we communicate with God, we commune with God. And in this communion, we have life."

Time seems to pause around me as thoughts speed through my mind. Of course I knew our description of God was important. I've spent the past forty days and fourteen hundred miles exploring it, paying homage to it. I've spent the past several hours collecting as many descriptions as I could.

OK, in the midst of all my asking I admit I have often questioned its importance. Now Archbishop Aristarchos tells me it's a matter of *life*. He's given me back my question, and graced it with deeper meaning.

"Without communion to God, we don't have life," the archbishop continues. "We might have biological life but not spiritual life. Not a life of quality. Now, to the word *description*. Is God describable or indescribable? This is a big question, a great question. At first you could say we cannot describe God. We cannot understand him. The fathers of the church say that in the end we can't understand God. However, this doesn't mean that we lack knowledge. We have a certain knowledge of God due to the fact that he revealed himself to the world through the prophets in the Old Testament, and through his Son in the New Testament.

"How can we describe God? Ultimately through the fact—the event—that he sent his Son. His Son, who is Christ, took our body and our nature. And this is remarkable. He describes himself in a body. He became for us describable.

"So our approach to God, our understanding of God, is through his Son who took flesh and became like one of us—though without sin—in order to unify us with the Father. This description of God also has to do with the icons, for the icons describe the nature of God—not the Father, because the Father we didn't see, but the Son because we saw him. If Christ were here today we could photograph him, which means we could paint him. This is why the church insisted very much—actually fought for during the eighth and ninth centuries—to have the icons. Without the icons, it's as if Christ didn't appear. If we refuse the description of Christ in icon, it's as if we refuse his incarnation, his appearance in the world. It's as if Christianity becomes a religion like Judaism and Islam. Icons are forbidden for Judaism and Islam, but in Christianity it is not forbidden. Why? Because we saw the icon of the Father, who is the Christ.

"Now again to your question. I would describe God the Father, the Son and the Holy Spirit as love. We should understand him—experience God—as love, humility and sympathy to humanity. And we should try our best to be like him, for we are created in his image, according to his image. We come to his imitation and are made to be like God according to grace."

I thank Archbishop Aristarchos for the gift he's given me. "I hope this will be a drop in the ocean of what you will write," he offers on my way out.

I barrel out of the archbishop's office through the serpentine streets to the Holy Sepulchre. Though we should be leaving Jerusalem now, I must return to the holy church and offer up a prayer. As I dash to the epicenter of Christian pilgrimage I think of how Archbishop Macarius helped Helena unearth the presumed cross of Jesus. And now Archbishop Aristarchos has helped me to dig up my question, a question I had begun to bury. I return to the familiar alcove where I prayed for divine encounters only hours ago. I light a candle and sit on the stone bench. I stare at my question, my question that has been illuminated anew.

Who is this God I commune with, this Divine One who is my life? Face after face appears in my mind. I imagine each of the sacred strangers along my pilgrim path, offering me their descriptions of God like little ancient stones. Their descriptions bring color and add distinction to my own mosaic. Maria. Jorge. Archbishop Aristarchos. God is . . .

The Mystery beyond description.

The Spirit who cannot be contained.

The Divine who disrobes his otherworldliness and dresses in a body so to be seen, known, painted and described.

Father Alexander. Salaam. Theodora. Beldad. God is . . .

The Holy One, without a hidden agenda.

The Powerful One, with no intention to harm.

The Divine who enters a world of second-guessing, and steps into the dust of accusations and betrayals in order to live out peace, mercy and fraternity.

Carla. Sead. Bill. Joseph. God is . . .

The Good Soul, free of folly.

The Merciful Judge, untainted by selfish ambition.

The Divine who shares a meal with prostitutes and priests, reaches out to the poor and poor in spirit, so to invite all to confess their over-reaching egos.

Erin. Nancy. Sister of Sednaya. Ishmael. God is . . .

The Suffering One who knows pain without bitterness.

The Victorious King who conquers without pride.

The Divine who rescues a young boy from a cave and dives in to save a woman from the hungry sea so skeptics would know a world of miracles.

Francis of Assisi. Eldad. Father Bosko. Paul. God is . . .

The Artist of the sky who savors beauty.

The Architect of the earth who revels in wonder.

The Divine who ventures into a war zone and sallies into a city under siege to paint a mural of hope and create an escape route of freedom.

Tony. Marianna. John. Yael. Moshe. God is . . .

The Self-Sufficient One, who lacked nothing.

The Community of Three, whose love was complete.

The Divine who sets out to explore greater love and becomes Father, Mother, Sister, Brother and Son to extend an invitation to an extravagant, eternal feast.

Father Bernardo. Barbara and Kevin. Lisa. Ramez. Father Nektarios. Petra. All the others along the way gather in front of me chanting: God is . . .

The Generous One, who lives without a ledger.

The God of Grace, who is above all.

The Divine who entices me with one question and collects a hundred or so strangers to tell me a story of ten thousand graces.

I consider this mosaic made up of the little colored stones from my divine encounters, and I see one face. It is Jesus—"the Icon of God," as the archbishop expressed.

How curious. While my description—ultimately, my experience—of God has been challenged and enlarged by this pilgrimage, I am led back to Jesus. That haunting sense of home returns; my relationship with God and my description of the Divine have come together in this place. As I stand up, one more descriptive comes to me. God is . . .

My soul's True Home.

I locate Krista and Eric, and we head to the stone slab by the entrance of the Ethiopian chapel outside of the Holy Sepulchre. We have someone take a picture of us on our last sacred bench. As we leave, I take one final gaze at this holy site that has been the destination of Christian pilgrimages for centuries upon centuries.

Goodbye, Holy Sepulchre. It's amazing you're still here. Since Helena and Archbishop Macarius found a crop of crosses and had you built, you've been scarred by fires, cracked open by earthquakes, rebuilt and refurbished. You've suffered from infighting among your Christian caretakers, so much so that a Muslim family has to keep your keys. But century after century you open your doors to pilgrims. With all you've seen, Holy Sepulchre, how would you describe God?

My conversation with the ancient stones is interrupted by screams. "Is that woman slapping her son?" I finally eke out.

"Yes," Krista confirms. A blond-haired boy about five years old stands bawling near the entrance. A woman with short auburn hair also has a river of tears flowing from her face; her tears flow as she screams and slaps. She keeps slapping the boy; he just quivers in place.

Shopkeepers gather. "I'll get the police," one passerby offers. The woman goes back inside as the boy stands alone, cheeks bloody red, head hanging down. Then the woman marches back out of the ancient church. She screams and slaps some more. The horrifying scene has paralyzed us.

Krista exclaims, "I've got to get out of here. This is literally making me sick." Me too. I've become nauseated with anger, dizzy from the injustice and heartbroken over our capacity to hurt each other. Yet this can't be our last image of the Holy Sepulchre. This can't be the finale of our pilgrimage.

The woman stomps back in the church. The boy sits on the little stone slab by the Ethiopian chapel; once again he's alone. I go to him. More tears dribble down his battered cheeks. I want to scoop him up and buy him an ice cream cone and take him far, far away. Instead I sit down beside him on this sacred bench.

I pull out a piece of paper from my notebook and make an airplane. We take turns flying it. Our little paper plane takes flight and then crashes and flies again only to land hard on the ancient stones. This journey of grace is so fragile at times.

The woman returns, presumably from praying. Before I get up, I tear out another piece of paper for the boy to make his own plane. I will interview one more person. The first person who comes through the door will be my final sacred encounter. A woman meanders out the huge open doors. She has sparkling eyes and a young boy by her side. I introduce myself and tell the woman a little about our pilgrimage and that I'd be honored if she would share her description of God with me.

Nava, a native of Jerusalem, replies, "I am Jewish; would you still like for me to describe?"

"Of course," I respond.

For a moment she looks at her son. She turns her gentle gaze back to me as she says, "It's difficult for me to describe God; I can't see God." Nava looks down at her son again. "If he can see Jesus, he can understand the Christian faith. But I'm still trying to figure out how to describe my God."

I express my appreciation to Nava and walk away. I turn around momentarily and see Nava tenderly take the hand of her son. I whisper, *Jesus, Icon of God, surely it doesn't matter how we describe you if we fail to love one another? Please help us to love.*

An hour later my journey finally faces west, yet I can't help but crane my neck east. I gaze back at Jerusalem until every last glimpse of the Holy City has faded from view. *Thank you,* I whisper. *Thank you for the graces along the way—the ten thousand graces that help me to love.*

BEYOND THE HOLY CITY

326 C.E. Helena kisses Archbishop Macarius on the cheek three times as she says goodbye. She will miss her new friend and her dear Jerusalem. She had arrived in a city that was decaying and forgotten. She leaves with important holy sites identified, a plethora of churches planned to be built and a friendship forged with the city's archbishop.

Perhaps ties between Rome and Jerusalem will grow stronger and richer. Perhaps these Roman roads she traveled will be traversed by other pilgrims. Maybe it will become a corridor of exchange, where ideas about the world flow, relationships between peoples form, cultural understandings grow and people's views of God expand.

Maybe.

1483 C.E. Felix Fabri thanks his Arab driver and pays him the precise fee. The Arab's service has been worth every coin; Felix's pilgrimage has been a great success. Indulgences have been collected, knowledge of the Holy Land has been acquired, and a rousing speech has been delivered.

Perhaps Jerusalem will be recaptured, protected and cherished for the sake of Christ. Perhaps more people will get to be pilgrims, walking where Jesus walked, experiencing the holy sites and relics. And perhaps the world will be set aright.

Perhaps.

SURPLUS OF GRACE

When I finally made it to Tel Aviv I gave Ghadir a huge hug, met her gorgeous baby boy and consumed the scrumptious meal she had spent the day preparing for us. Then I promptly fell asleep. All my body, mind and spirit could do was accept—only accept.

On the flight back to America, I began the fiercely beautiful journey of uncovering the meaning of the past forty days. Krista, Eric and I mused about it as much as our weary souls could while suspended over the Atlantic.

Eric's discovery of "encountering the other" was significant. He was struck with the importance of exchanging ideas about God with those whose questions and assumptions were different from his own.

Krista was humbled by the realization that people all around the world are on a quest for truth, a search for God.

I was grateful that this pilgrimage had expanded the borders of my description of God and my understanding of others. The trip also invited me to see that my description of God is limited by my love—my love for God and others. If I pray to God but slap my child in anger, my description comes into question. If I call the Divine "God of Grace" yet strive to make things equal with him and keep things on par with others, so much truth is lost. Since my description of God is ultimately a signifier of my relationship with God and others, it must be lived.

I wish I could tell you that I arrived back to the States as a paragon of grace, receiving generosity with great ease and distributing kindnesses to strangers, friends and family with effortless grandeur.

I wish I could tell you that my mosaic of God has remained perfectly intact, my love for Jesus and others is without question, and my "Only Accept" mantra continues to be fully embraced.

I also wish I could tell you that I've incorporated all I've gained from the East and from the remarkable strangers along the way, that my understanding of religion and politics in the Balkans and Middle East is incisive and instructive, that I am championing clear paths to peace in both regions.

I wish I could. But only a few months after returning from my pilgrimage from Rome to Jerusalem, I began another journey, my own Trail of Tears. For a thousand different reasons, in the year that followed my pilgrimage I spilled more tears than the rest of my life collected. I cried in the bathtub and bawled on the way to work.

In those tears my description of God continued to take shape.

Although I came back to a loving community, I ultimately had more to receive. I still had strongly held assumptions about God, assumptions that didn't line up with that stunning mosaic of the Divine I had experienced in the East. This journey of aligning the god of my gut with Jesus, the Icon of God, is a long one for me; I suspect it will be a lifelong pilgrimage.

However, through the age-old spiritual practices of prayer, Scripture reading and community, my gut and Icon are gradually being reconciled. And as I've returned to the sacred strangers on my pilgrimage through writing their stories, I've discovered more of my own story. I've seen that my story can only properly be told as a tale of ten thousand graces.

With such a surplus of grace I feel freer to trust that God has a stockpile of grace for others. I'm still learning how to live this out; currently it involves leading a writing club with a collection of ten-year-old girls who live in a marginalized neighborhood near me, and exploring more about peace and reconciliation issues. I'm considering a move to Africa. But the grittiest learning right now entails forgiveness. I'm continuing to learn about extending forgiveness to friends and receiving forgiveness when I screw up. I still sometimes forget that life isn't about the equal ledger but about that surplus of grace.

I just recently realized perhaps the most gorgeous gift of this journey: I thought I was on this grand search for God, but all along God was pursuing me. In the most extravagant of ways, God rallied the language of my soul—travel and people—to tell me the story of who he is.

So here's my parting hope for you. Continue to explore your description of God. Let others challenge it, speak into it and help expand it. Be open to sacred encounters with God, with those beyond your borders and with your neighbors across the street. Know that as you search for God, the Divine One is pursuing you with desperate love, longing to tell you who he is through your soul's own language.

And as you explore and receive, may your story only be properly told as a tale of ten thousand graces.

ANOTHER SACRED BENCH

I sit alone on a bench in Freedom Park, accompanied by a crowd of *thank-yous*. For a moment I'm taken aback as I survey the many who carried and at times inveigled *Sacred Encounters* along. But I really shouldn't be surprised; my desperate need for community remains undeniable.

I join the chanting *thank yous* expressing gratitude for Krista and Eric, whose depth of friendship and capacity to dream audacious dreams with me is stunning; for the collection of people who entrusted me, a stranger, with their description of God—for those I captured in story and the others I simply treasure in memory; for my writing partner and *anam cara* Tabitha, who I can't envision writing without; for my Pinklings (Marie, Joy and Danielle), who make writing a weekly fete; for my small group (Deb, Dennis, Laurie, Steve, Tami, Jenn, Anthony, Melissa, Chad, Simon, Tim, Eric and Tabs), who for the sake of the journey threw a yard sale, tiled a bathroom and schooled me in grace before I even packed my bags; for the Warehouse 242 staff (Bruce, Marc, Steve, Kelly, Shannon, Priscilla and Nicole), who continue to generously support my wanderlust and buoy my spirit.

"Thank you. Thank you. Thank you," the refrain carries on, for my spiritual director Jean and mentor Elizabeth, who remind me who I long to become; for my spiritual formation group (Amy, Lisa, Yvonne, Roxanne, Rachelle and Emily), whose gracious listening and wise insights honor my laughter and tears; for my dear allies and sojourners (Heather F., Tosha, Tricia, Kelly, Marla, Danielle L., Greg, Heather H., Carmita and Reuben, Deborah, Amy, Aunt Linda, Deb S., Mark, Rachel, Marion, Jenny, Nann, the Graves, Teagues, Martins, Boyces, Landrys, Grays and my sister Ghadir), who make life a feast.

Appreciation stretches on to Catherine Sanders, Tony Jones and Melanie Dobson for being guides in the foreign terrain of publishing, and for the Parks, Icards, Coles, Evans and Newtons for providing winsome spaces to write.

Todah to Dr. Tim Laniak, who gave me Jerusalem, and to Ken Garfield, who invited me to write about it; *merci* to Dr. Gwenfair Adams, who introduced me to Helena, Felix and so many other fascinating figures; and *danke schoen* to Dr. Petra Heldt, who showed me faith beyond Protestantism.

Gratitude's song swells for my editor Dave Zimmerman, whose wit, wisdom, encouragement and belief in this story has made my foray into writing feel like a dance party; and for Lisa Rieck and the others at IVP, who spoil me with gorgeous hospitality; and for my mom and dad, who love with extravagance and approach the day with holy expectation.

There, of course, would be no sacred bench, no divine encounters, no story worth sharing without God, the one whose kindness I can never repay. Thank you.

NOTES

Chapter 1: Charlotte, North Carolina (U.S.A.)

p. 16   "Felix Fabri": Aubrey Stewart, trans., *Felix Fabri,* accessed June 30, 2008, at <http://chass.colostate-pueblo.edu/history/seminar/fabri/fabri1.htm>.

p. 22   "Constantine became": "Why Did Christianity Succeed?" *From Jesus to Christ: The First Christians, Frontline,* accessed May 2, 2008, at <www.pbs.org/wgbh/pages/frontline/shows/religion/why/legitimization.html>.

Chapter 2: Rome, Italy

p. 28   "Felix didn't trust": Tony Jones, *The Sacred Way* (Grand Rapids: Zondervan, 2005), p. 153.

Chapter 3: Florence, Italy

p. 35   "Savonarola reentered Florence": "The Medieval Synthesis Under Attack: Savonarola and the Protestant Reformation," *The History Guide: Lectures on Modern European Intellectual History,* accessed May 2, 2008, at <www.historyguide.org/intellect/lecture5a.html>.

p. 36   "We Italians are irreligious": Niccolò Machiavelli, quoted in Jacob Burckhardt, "The Civilization of the Renaissance in Italy," trans. S. G. C. Middlemore, 1878 <www.boisestate.edu/courses/hy309/docs/burckhardt/6-2.html>.

Chapter 4: Assisi, Italy

p. 46   "The sultan didn't convert": Recorded in Jacques de Vitry, bishop of Acre's book *Historia occidentalis: De Ordine et praedicatione Fratrum Minorum* (1221). From St. Francis lecture <www.london.anglican.org/SermonShow_5071>.

p. 48   "As Krista and Eric Banter": Francis of Assisi, "Canticle of the Sun," trans. Benen Fahy, O.F.M., from *St. Francis of Assisi: Writings and Early Biographies,* ed. Marion A. Habig (Chicago: Franciscan Herald Press, 1973).

Chapter 9: Belgrade, Serbia

p. 106   "At first we were confused": Letter from St. Sava to Irenaeus, quoted in "Balkan Mediations," accessed May 6, 2008, at <www.pomgrenade.org/BM/pages/balkanism.html>.

Chapter 12: Meteora and Delphi, Greece

p. 145   "biblical scholar Walter Brueggemann's description": Walter Brueggemann, quoted by John Eldredge in Douglas LeBlanc, "Wildheart," *Christianity Today,* accessed June 30, 2008, at <www.christianitytoday.com/ct/2004/august/14.30.html>.

Chapter 13: Athens, Greece

p. 152   "One legend says": "Athena," Encyclopedia Mythica Online, accessed September 18, 2007, at <www.pantheon.org/articles/a/athena.html>.

p. 153   "My hometown's god": "Charlotte: Leading Financial Center," Charlotte Chamber, accessed May 7, 2008, at <www.charlottechamber.com/clientuploads/Economic_pdfs/FactSheets/Financial_Center.pdf>.

p. 158   "As a scholar once put it": Paul Veyne, *A History of Private Life,* vol. 1, *From Pagan Rome to Byzantium,* ed. Phillippe Aries and Georges Duby (Boston: Harvard University Press, 1987), p. 207.

Chapter 14: Patmos, Greece

p. 174   "Among the lampstands": Revelation 1:13-16.

p. 178   "The text itself hints": Revelation 10:10.

p. 179   "The Spirit and the bride": Revelation 22:17.

Chapter 15: Ephesus, Turkey

p. 194   "I know your deeds": Revelation 2:2, 4.

Chapter 16: Izmir/Smyrna, Turkey

p. 195   "Nancy, a forty-something acquaintance of Eric's": For security purposes, the woman's name has been changed to "Nancy."

p. 196   "Polycarp, a disciple": "Polycarp," accessed May 7, 2008, at <www.allaboutreligion.org>.

p. 199   "These are the words": Revelation 2:8-10.

Chapter 17: Istanbul, Turkey

p. 205   "In 532 c.e.": With the construction of the Hagia Sophia, Justinian "surpassed" Solomon, whose temple construction in Israel is described in great length in 2 Chronicles 2—7. Solomon's temple took seven years to build and was completed in 957 b.c.e.

p. 210   "Jesus suggested": The healing of the blind man and ensuing interchange are recorded in John 9.

p. 215   "raise Turkey to the level": Andrew Davison, *Secularism and Revivalism in Turkey* (New Haven, Conn.: Yale University Press, 1998), p. 147.

Chapter 19: Antioch, Turkey
p. 239   "Joseph begins translating": For security purposes, the pastor's name has been changed to "Ibrahim."

Chapter 20: Aleppo, Syria
p. 244   "rogue state": John Bolton, "Beyond the Axis of Evil," address to the Heritage Foundation, May 6, 2002, accessed May 8, 2008, at <www.state.gov/t/us/rm/9962.htm>.

Chapter 21: Damascus, Syria
p. 256   "Yet such places as Straight Street": Recorded in Acts 9:11-19.

Chapter 22: Beirut, Lebanon
p. 275   "The Gospel of Luke records a song": Recorded in Luke 1.
p. 285   "There was a man who was completely out of sorts": Recorded in Luke 8:26-39.

Chapter 23: Amman, Jordan
p. 291   "Soon my friend Sarah": All the names in this story have been changed for security purposes.

Chapter 24: Jerusalem, Israel
p. 303   "The Talmud says": Talmud: Kiddushin 49b. The Talmud contains rabbinic discussions on Jewish law, history and customs. It includes the Mishnah (c. 200 C.E.), the first written compilation of Jewish oral law, and the Gemara (c. 500 C.E.).

Photos
p. 164   clockwise from top: Maria, Rome; Fr. Bernardo, Florence; Tony, Split; St. Peter's Basilica, Vatican City (background)
p. 165   from top to bottom: Salaam, Mostar; Kenan and Eldad, Sarajevo; Diana (left) and Tamara, Elbasan, Albania; prayer beads, Mostar (background)
p. 166   from top to bottom: Tamara (left), Kat and Eric, Tirana; Christopher, Ohrid; Gabriel, Samos, Greece; St. John at Kaneo, Ohrid (background)
p. 167   inlay: Domitian's temple, Ephesus; background: students on Mars Hill, Athens
p. 168   from top to bottom: Chimney Fairies, Cappodocia; Mehmet, Istanbul; Krista in front of ancient library, Ephesus (background)
p. 169   from left: Father Ignace and Tamara, Aleppo
p. 170   inlay: Convent of Our Lady, Greek Orthodox Church, Sednaya, Syria; background: ancient ruins, Amman
p. 171   from top: Krista (left), Eric and Tamara, outside of Holy Sepulchre, Jerusalem; Archbishop Aristarchos, Jerusalem; Wailing Wall, Jerusalem (background)

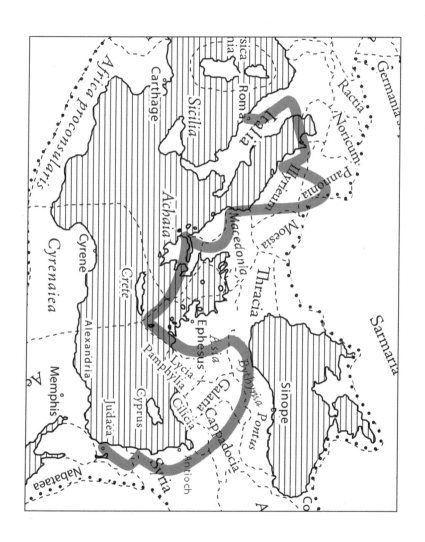

LIKEWISE. *Go and do.*

A man comes across an ancient enemy, beaten and left for dead. He lifts the wounded man onto the back of a donkey and takes him to an inn to tend to the man's recovery. Jesus tells this story and instructs those who are listening to "go and do likewise."

Likewise books explore a compassionate, active faith lived out in real time. When we're skeptical about the status quo, Likewise books challenge us to create culture responsibly. When we're confused about who we are and what we're supposed to be doing, Likewise books help us listen for God's voice. When we're discouraged by the troubled world we've inherited, Likewise books encourage us to hold onto hope.

In this life we will face challenges that demand our response. Likewise books face those challenges with us so we can act on faith.

likewisebooks.com